Microsoft® WORD 97
Step by Step

Other titles in the *Step by Step* series:

*Microsoft Access 97 Step by Step
Microsoft Excel 97 Step by Step
*Microsoft Excel 97 Step by Step, Advanced Topics
*Microsoft FrontPage 97 Step by Step
Microsoft Internet Explorer 3.0 Step by Step
Microsoft Office 97 Integration Step by Step
*Microsoft Outlook 97 Step by Step
*Microsoft PowerPoint 97 Step by Step
Microsoft Team Manager 97 Step by Step
Microsoft Windows 95 Step by Step
Microsoft Windows NT Workstation version 4.0 Step by Step
*Microsoft Word 97 Step by Step, Advanced Topics

Step by Step books are also available for the Microsoft
Office 95 programs.

* These books are approved courseware for Certified Microsoft
Office User (CMOU) exams. For more details about the CMOU
program, see page xvii.

Microsoft®
WORD 97

Step by Step

Microsoft Press

PUBLISHED BY
Microsoft Press
A Division of Microsoft Corporation
One Microsoft Way
Redmond, Washington 98052-6399

Library of Congress Cataloging-in-Publication Data
Microsoft Word 97 step by step / Catapult, Inc.
     p.   cm.
    Includes index.
    ISBN 1-57231-313-7
    1. Microsoft Word for Windows.   2. Word processing.   I. Catapult,
Inc.
Z52.5.M523   IN PROCESS
652.5'5369--dc21   96-44021
                                          CIP

Printed and bound in the United States of America.

5 6 7 8 9 WCWC 2 1 0 9 8

Distributed to the book trade in Canada by Macmillan of Canada, a division of Canada Publishing Corporation.

A CIP catalogue record for this book is available from the British Library.

Microsoft Press books are available through booksellers and distributors worldwide. For further information about international editions, contact your local Microsoft Corporation office. Or contact Microsoft Press International directly at fax (206) 936-7329.

ActiveX, FrontPage, MSN, and Outlook are trademarks and Microsoft, Microsoft Press, MS, PowerPoint, Visual Basic, Windows, and Windows NT are registered trademarks of Microsoft Corporation.

Other product and company names mentioned herein may be the trademarks of their respective owners.

Companies, names, and/or data used in screens and sample output are fictitious unless otherwise noted.

For Catapult, Inc.
Managing Editor: Diana Stiles
Writer: Marie L. Swanson
Project Editor: Annette Hall
Technical Editors: Vincent Abella, Alan Spring
Production/Layout: Jeanne K. Hunt, Editor;
   Anne Kim
Indexer: Julie Kawabata

For Microsoft Press
Acquisitions Editor: Casey D. Doyle
Project Editor: Maureen Williams
Zimmerman

Catapult, Inc. & Microsoft Press

Microsoft Word 97 Step by Step has been created by the professional trainers and writers at Catapult, Inc., to the exacting standards you've come to expect from Microsoft Press. Together, we are pleased to present this self-paced training guide, which you can use individually or as part of a class.

Catapult, Inc., is a software training company with years of experience in PC and Macintosh instruction. Catapult's exclusive Performance-Based Training system is available in Catapult training centers across North America and at customer sites. Based on the principles of adult learning, Performance-Based Training ensures that students leave the classroom with confidence and the ability to apply skills to real-world scenarios. *Microsoft Word 97 Step by Step* incorporates Catapult's training expertise to ensure that you'll receive the maximum return on your training time. You'll focus on the skills that can increase your productivity the most while working at your own pace and convenience.

Microsoft Press is the book publishing division of Microsoft Corporation. The leading publisher of information about Microsoft products and services, Microsoft Press is dedicated to providing the highest quality computer books and multimedia training and reference tools that make using Microsoft software easier, more enjoyable, and more productive.

Table of Contents

Table of Contents

Table of Contents

*Quick*Look Guide

Creating form letters and merging fields, see Lesson 11, page 198

Aligning text, see Lesson 3, page 52

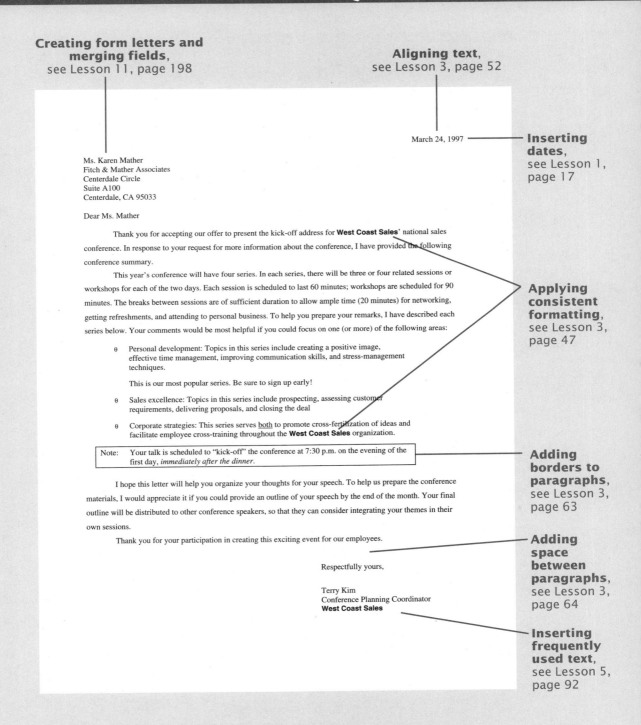

March 24, 1997

Ms. Karen Mather
Fitch & Mather Associates
Centerdale Circle
Suite A100
Centerdale, CA 95033

Dear Ms. Mather

Thank you for accepting our offer to present the kick-off address for **West Coast Sales**' national sales conference. In response to your request for more information about the conference, I have provided the following conference summary.

This year's conference will have four series. In each series, there will be three or four related sessions or workshops for each of the two days. Each session is scheduled to last 60 minutes; workshops are scheduled for 90 minutes. The breaks between sessions are of sufficient duration to allow ample time (20 minutes) for networking, getting refreshments, and attending to personal business. To help you prepare your remarks, I have described each series below. Your comments would be most helpful if you could focus on one (or more) of the following areas:

θ   Personal development: Topics in this series include creating a positive image, effective time management, improving communication skills, and stress-management techniques.

This is our most popular series. Be sure to sign up early!

θ   Sales excellence: Topics in this series include prospecting, assessing customer requirements, delivering proposals, and closing the deal

θ   Corporate strategies: This series serves <u>both</u> to promote cross-fertilization of ideas and facilitate employee cross-training throughout the **West Coast Sales** organization.

Note: Your talk is scheduled to "kick-off" the conference at 7:30 p.m. on the evening of the first day, *immediately after the dinner.*

I hope this letter will help you organize your thoughts for your speech. To help us prepare the conference materials, I would appreciate it if you could provide an outline of your speech by the end of the month. Your final outline will be distributed to other conference speakers, so that they can consider integrating your themes in their own sessions.

Thank you for your participation in creating this exciting event for our employees.

Respectfully yours,

Terry Kim
Conference Planning Coordinator
West Coast Sales

Inserting dates, see Lesson 1, page 17

Applying consistent formatting, see Lesson 3, page 47

Adding borders to paragraphs, see Lesson 3, page 63

Adding space between paragraphs, see Lesson 3, page 64

Inserting frequently used text, see Lesson 5, page 92

xi

*Quick*Look Guide

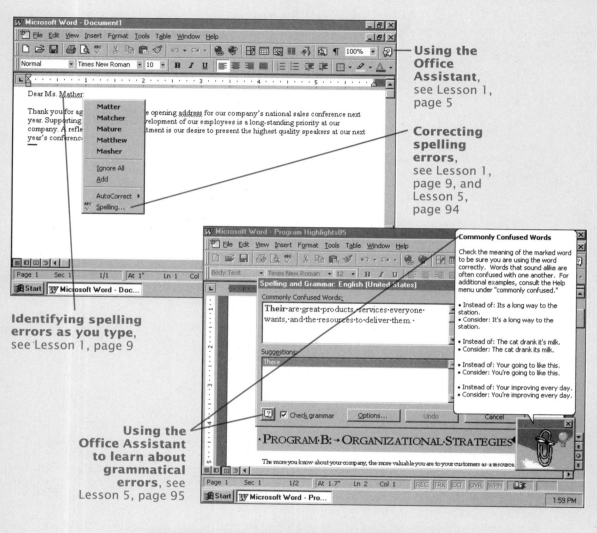

Using the Office Assistant, see Lesson 1, page 5

Correcting spelling errors, see Lesson 1, page 9, and Lesson 5, page 94

Identifying spelling errors as you type, see Lesson 1, page 9

Using the Office Assistant to learn about grammatical errors, see Lesson 5, page 95

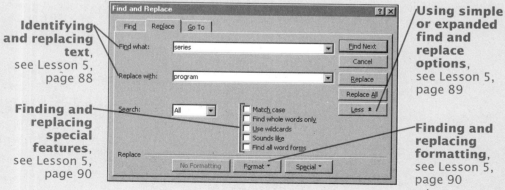

Identifying and replacing text, see Lesson 5, page 88

Using simple or expanded find and replace options, see Lesson 5, page 89

Finding and replacing special features, see Lesson 5, page 90

Finding and replacing formatting, see Lesson 5, page 90

Using the ruler, see Lesson 3, page 57

Moving and copying text, see Lesson 2, pages 34–40

Formatting text, see Lesson 3, page 44

Creating bulleted and numbered lists, see Lesson 3, page 54

Selecting text, see Lesson 2, page 34

Searching for specific objects, see Lesson 5, page 96

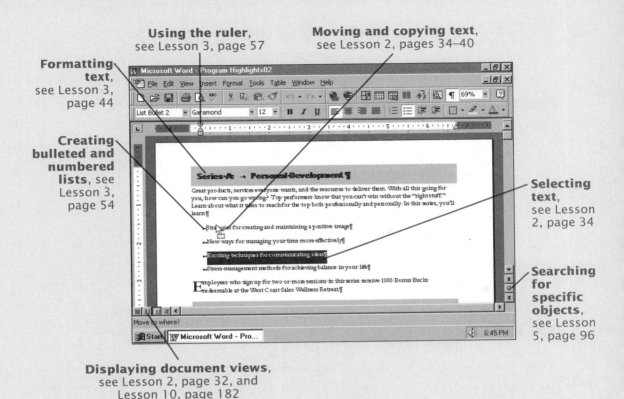

Displaying document views, see Lesson 2, page 32, and Lesson 10, page 182

Previewing a document, see Lesson 4, page 70

Adding headers and footers, see Lesson 6, page 106

Inserting section breaks, see Lesson 6, page 111, and Lesson 12, page 218

Changing page orientation, see Lesson 6, page 103

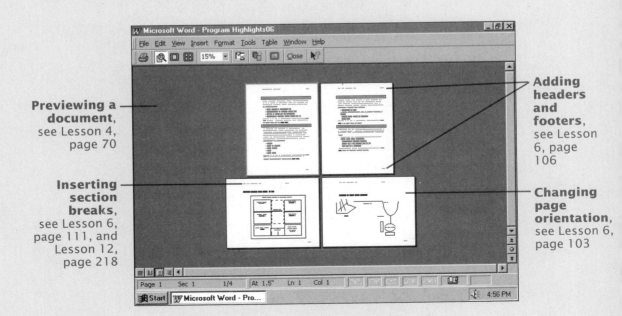

Applying styles,
see Lesson 7, page 125

Formatting text in columns,
see Lesson 12, page 216

Inserting AutoShapes,
see Lesson 12, page 231

Program 1:

PERSONAL EFFECTIVENESS

Great products, services everyone wants, and the resources to deliver them. With all this going for you, how can you go wrong? Top performers know that you can't win without the "right stuff." Learn what it takes to reach for the top both professionally and personally. In this series, you'll learn:

- Dynamic strategies for creating and maintaining a positive image
- New ways for managing your time more effectively
- Exciting techniques for communicating ideas
- Stress-management methods for achieving balance in your life

Program 1: Day One - Aspen Room

9:00 - 10:10
Image Strategies   Dr. Timothy Davis
No one strategy works for everyone. An industry leader in visualization and guided imagery techniques, Dr. Davis provides a survey of techniques you can use to develop and then project a positive self-image to colleagues and clients alike.

10:30 - 11:40
Time & More   Dr. Rita Lopez
There are only 24 hours in a day, and no matter what we do, we can't make more time. What we can do, however, is look at our day in new ways. Developer of the RealTime System™, Dr. Lopez will help you bring order and effectiveness to your day. Free RealTime Time-Finders™ are provided to attendees of this session.

"My sales increased 25% over the previous year after attending WCS '96. I owe it all to WCS!"

*Dale Moon
Sales Leader '96*

1:00 - 2:10
Communication Styles   James Carlson
Why do some memos get read while others are destined for the circular file? What makes some presentations dynamic and others dull? Why are some meetings motivational while others seem to waste your time? Mr. Carlson explores why the standard ways we communicate so often go awry and provides techniques for ensuring successful communication.

2:30 - 4:50
Stress Awareness   Kim Lee
After a day of attending seminars and networking away from the daily grind, it is easy to manage stress. But what about after you return to the job? In this workshop session, you will spend the afternoon learning Ms. Lee's proven techniques for focusing your energies, directing your thoughts, and preparing for new learning.

Arranging text in text boxes,
see Lesson 12, page 224

Drawing and formatting lines,
see Lesson 12, page 230

Personal Effectiveness Hospitality Room
Aspen Room Annex

Throughout the day, each of the speakers in this series will be available for one-on-one meetings to discuss the ideas presented in their sessions.

Creating drop caps,
see Lesson 12, page 228

Finding Your Best Starting Point

Microsoft Word is a powerful word processing program that you can use to efficiently create and modify many kinds of documents. With *Microsoft Word Step by Step*, you'll quickly and easily learn how to use Microsoft Word to get your work done.

 IMPORTANT   This book is designed for use with Microsoft Word 97 for the Windows 95 and Windows NT version 4.0 operating systems. To find out what software you're running, you can check the product package or you can start the software, click the Help menu at the top of the screen, and click About Microsoft Word. If your software is not compatible with this book, a Step by Step book for your software is probably available. Many of the Step by Step titles are listed on the second page of this book. If the book you want isn't listed, please visit our World Wide Web site at http://www.microsoft.com/mspress/ or call 1-800-MSPRESS for more information.

Finding Your Best Starting Point in This Book

This book is designed for readers learning Microsoft Word for the first time and for more experienced readers who want to learn and use the new features in Microsoft Word. Use the following table to find your best starting point in this book.

If you are	Follow these steps
New... to computers to graphical (as opposed to text-only) computer programs to Windows 95 or Windows NT	**1** Install the practice files as described in "Installing and Using the Practice Files." **2** Become acquainted with the Windows 95 or Windows NT operating system and how to use the online Help system by working through Appendix A, "If You Are New to Windows 95, Windows NT, or Microsoft Word 97." **3** Learn basic skills for using Microsoft Word by working sequentially through Lessons 1 through 4. Then, you can work through Lessons 5 through 12 in any order.
Switching... from WordPerfect	**1** Install the practice files as described in "Installing and Using the Practice Files." **2** Learn basic skills for using Microsoft Word name by working sequentially through Lessons 1 through 4. Then, you can work through Lessons 5 through 12 in any order.
Upgrading... from Word 95 or Word 6	**1** Learn about the new features in this version of the program that are covered in this book by reading through the following section, "New Features in Microsoft Word." **2** Install the practice files as described in "Installing and Using the Practice Files." **3** Complete the lessons that cover the topics you need. You can use the table of contents and the QuickLook Guide to locate information about general topics. You can use the index to find information about a specific topic or a feature from previous version of Word.
Referencing... this book after working through the lessons	**1** Use the index to locate information about specific topics, and use the table of contents and the QuickLook Guide to locate information about general topics. **2** Read the Lesson Summary at the end of each lesson for a brief review of the major tasks in the lesson. The Lesson Summary topics are listed in the same order as they are presented in the lesson.

Certified Microsoft Office User Program

The Certified Microsoft Office User (CMOU) program is designed for business professionals and students who use Microsoft Office 97 products in their daily work. The program enables participants to showcase their skill level to potential employers. It benefits accountants, administrators, executive assistants, program managers, sales representatives, students, and many others. To receive certified user credentials for a software program, candidates must pass a hands-on exam in which they use the program to complete real-world tasks.

The CMOU program offers two levels of certification: Proficient and Expert. The following table indicates the levels available for each Microsoft Office 97 program.

Software	Proficient level	Expert level
Microsoft Word 97	✔	✔
Microsoft Excel 97	✔	✔
Microsoft Access 97		✔
Microsoft PowerPoint 97		✔
Microsoft Outlook 97		✔
Microsoft FrontPage 97		✔

Microsoft Press offers the following books in the *Step by Step* series as approved courseware for the CMOU exams:

Proficient level:
Microsoft Word 97 Step by Step, by Catapult, Inc. ISBN: 1-57231-313-7
Microsoft Excel 97 Step by Step, by Catapult, Inc. ISBN: 1-57231-314-5

Expert level:
Microsoft Word 97 Step by Step, Advanced Topics by Catapult, Inc.
   ISBN: 1-57231-563-6
Microsoft Excel 97 Step by Step, Advanced Topics by Catapult, Inc.
   ISBN: 1-57231-564-4
Microsoft Access 97 Step by Step, by Catapult, Inc. ISBN: 1-57231-316-1
Microsoft PowerPoint 97 Step by Step, by Perspection, Inc. ISBN: 1-57231-315-3
Microsoft Outlook 97 Step by Step, by Catapult, Inc. ISBN: 1-57231-382-X
Microsoft FrontPage 97 Step by Step, by Catapult, Inc. ISBN: 1-57231-336-6

Candidates may take exams at any participating Sylvan Test Center, participating corporations, or participating employment agencies. Exams have a suggested retail price of $50 each.

To become a candidate for certification, or for more information about the certification process, please call 1-800-933-4493 in the United States or visit the CMOU program World Wide Web site at http:/www.microsoft.com/office/train_cert/

New Features in Microsoft Word 97

The following table lists the major new features in Microsoft Word that are covered in this book. The table shows the lesson in which you can learn how to use each feature. You can also use the index to find specific information about a feature or a task you want to do.

To learn how to	See
Find answers to your questions about Microsoft Word with the Office Assistant.	Lesson 1
Insert AutoText entries provided by Microsoft Word	Lesson 1
View document headings along side document text using the Document Map	Lesson 2
Highlight important ideas in a document using AutoSummarize	Lesson 2
Use new font formatting options	Lesson 3
Identify and correct grammatical errors as you work	Lesson 5
Use new options on the Headers and Footers toolbar	Lesson 6
Create custom tables using the Draw Table toolbar	Lesson 8
Use new graphics effects using the Drawing toolbar	Lesson 12
Apply exciting text effects with new WordArt features	Lesson 12

Corrections, Comments, and Help

Every effort has been made to ensure the accuracy of this book and the contents of the practice files disk. Microsoft Press provides corrections and additional content for its books through the World Wide Web at

http://www.microsoft.com/mspress/support/

If you have comments, questions, or ideas regarding this book or the practice files disk, please send them to us.

Send e-mail to

mspinput@microsoft.com

Or send postal mail to

Microsoft Press

Attn: Step by Step Series Editor

One Microsoft Way

Redmond, WA 98052-6399

Please note that support for the Word software product itself is not offered through the above addresses. For help using Word, you can call Microsoft Word AnswerPoint at (206)-462-9673 on weekdays between 6 a.m. and 6 p.m. Pacific time.

Visit Our World Wide Web Site

We invite you to visit the Microsoft Press World Wide Web site. You can visit us at the following location:

http://www.microsoft.com/mspress/

You'll find descriptions for all of our books, information about ordering titles, notice of special features and events, additional content for Microsoft Press books, and much more.

You can also find out the latest in software developments and news from Microsoft Corporation by visiting the following World Wide Web site:

http://www.microsoft.com/

We look forward to your visit on the Web!

Installing and Using the Practice Files

The disk inside the back cover of this book contains practice files that you'll use as you perform the exercises in the book. For example, when you're learning how to check the spelling in a document, you'll open one of the practice files—a partially completed letter—and then use the Spelling feature. By using the practice files, you won't waste time creating the samples used in the lessons—instead, you can concentrate on learning how to use Word. With the files and the step-by-step instructions in the lessons, you'll also learn by doing, which is an easy and effective way to acquire and remember new skills.

 IMPORTANT Before you break the seal on the practice disk package, be sure that this book matches your version of the software. This book is designed for use with Microsoft Word 97 for the Windows 95 and Windows NT version 4.0 operating systems. To find out what software you're running, you can check the product package or you can start the software, and then on the Help menu at the top of the screen, click About Microsoft Word. If your program is not compatible with this book, a Step by Step book matching your software is probably available. Many of the Step by Step titles are listed on the second page of this book. If the book you want isn't listed, please visit our World Wide Web site at http://www.microsoft.com/mspress/ or call 1-800-MSPRESS for more information.

Install the practice files on your computer

Follow these steps to install the practice files on your computer's hard disk so that you can use them with the exercises in this book.

 NOTE If you are new to Windows 95 or Windows NT, you might want to work through Appendix A, "If You Are New to Windows 95, Windows NT, or Microsoft Word 97," before installing the practice files.

In Windows 95, you will also be prompted for a username and password when starting Windows 95 if your computer is configured for user profiles.

Close

1 If your computer isn't on, turn it on now.

2 If you're using Windows NT, press CTRL+ALT+DEL to display a dialog box asking for your username and password. If you are using Windows 95, you will see this dialog box if your computer is connected to a network. If you don't know your username or password, contact your system administrator for assistance.

3 Type your username and password in the appropriate boxes, and then click OK. If you see the Welcome dialog box, click the Close button.

4 Remove the disk from the package inside the back cover of this book.

5 Insert the disk in drive A or drive B of your computer.

6 On the taskbar at the bottom of your screen, click the Start button.

The Start menu opens.

Click Start...

...and then click Run.

7 On the Start menu, click Run.

The Run dialog box appears.

8 In the Open box, type **a:setup** (or **b:setup** if the disk is in drive B). Don't add spaces as you type.

9 Click OK, and then follow the directions on the screen.

The Setup program window opens with recommended options preselected for you. For best results in using the practice files with this book, accept these preselected settings.

10 When the files have been installed, remove the disk from your drive and replace in the package inside the back cover of the book.

A folder called Winword SBS Practice has been created on your hard disk, and the practice files have been put in that folder.

Microsoft
Press
Welcome

Camcorder
Files On The
Internet

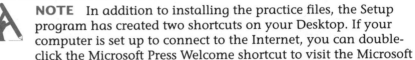 **NOTE** In addition to installing the practice files, the Setup program has created two shortcuts on your Desktop. If your computer is set up to connect to the Internet, you can double-click the Microsoft Press Welcome shortcut to visit the Microsoft Press Web site. You can also connect to this Web site directly at http://www.microsoft.com/mspress/

You can double-click the Camcorder Files On The Internet shortcut to connect to the *Microsoft Word 97 Step by Step* Camcorder files Web page. This page contains audiovisual demonstrations of how to do a number of tasks in Word, which you can copy to your computer for viewing. You can connect to this Web site directly at http://www.microsoft.com/mspress/products/374/

Using the Practice Files

Each lesson in this book explains when and how to use any practice files for that lesson. When it's time to use a practice file, the book will list instructions for how to open the file. The lessons are built around scenarios that simulate a real work environment, so you can easily apply the skills you learn to your own work. For the scenarios in this book, imagine that you're responsible for a variety of corporate communications at a large West Coast distribution company. West Coast Sales specializes in outdoor recreational equipment and leisure products and has recently acquired The Terra Firm, an innovative lawn care and garden supply company. As a vice president in this company, you will use Microsoft Word to create and enhance effective documents concerning West Coast Sales products, services, and the organization's events, including an upcoming sales conference.

The screen illustrations in this book might look different from what you see on your computer, depending on how your computer has been set up. To help make your screen match the illustrations in this book, please follow the instructions in Appendix B, "Matching the Exercises."

For those of you who like to know all the details, here's a list of the files included on the practice disk:

Filename	Description
Lesson 1	*No practice files*
Lesson 2	
02Lesson	Draft of conference program highlights document

Filename	Description
Lesson 3	
03Lesson	Partially completed letter to keynote speaker
Lesson 4	
04Lesson	Multiple-page letter to keynote speaker
Review & Practice 1	
P1Review	
Lesson 5	
05Lesson	Draft of conference program highlights document
Lesson 6	
06Lesson	Draft of conference program highlights document
Lesson 7	
07Lesson	Draft of conference program highlights document
Lesson 8	*No practice files*
Review & Practice 2	*No practice files*
Lesson 9	
09Lesson	Draft of conference program highlights document containing changes from reviewers
09Original	Original conference program highlights document before changes from reviewers
Lesson 10	
10Lesson	Draft of conference program highlights document before reordering
10Subdoc	Additional text to include in program highlights document
Lesson 11	
11Data	Data source document containing names and addresses
Lesson 12	
12Lesson	Draft of conference program highlights document suitable for a newsletter
Review & Practice 3	
P3Original	
P3Review	
RP3 Data	

Need Help with the Practice Files?

Every effort has been made to ensure the accuracy of this book and the contents of the practice files disk. If you do run into a problem, Microsoft Press provides corrections for its books through the World Wide Web at

> http://www.microsoft.com/mspress/support/

We also invite you to visit our main Web page at

> http://www.microsoft.com/mspress/

You'll find descriptions for all of our books, information about ordering titles, notices of special features and events, additional content for Microsoft Press books, and much more.

Deleting the Practice Files

Use the following steps to delete the shortcuts added to your Desktop and the practice files added to your hard drive by the Step by Step Setup program.

1   Click Start, point to Programs, and then click Windows Explorer.

   If you are using Windows NT, click Windows NT Explorer.

2   In the All Folders area, scroll up and click Desktop.

   The contents of your Desktop appear.

3   Click the Microsoft Press Welcome shortcut icon, hold down CTRL, and click the Camcorder Files On The Internet shortcut icon. Press DELETE.

   If you are prompted to confirm the deletion, click Yes. The Desktop shortcut icons are removed from your computer.

4   In the All Folders area, click Drive C.

   The contents of your hard drive appear. If you installed your practice files on another drive, view the contents of that drive.

5   Click the Winword SBS Practice folder, and then press DELETE.

   If you are prompted to confirm the deletion, click Yes. The practice files are removed from your computer.

6   In the Contents area, double-click the Windows folder, and then double-click the Favorites folder.

7   Click the Winword SBS Practice shortcut icon, and then press DELETE.

   If you are prompted to confirm the deletion, click Yes. All practice files installed on your computer are now deleted.

Conventions and Features in This Book

You can save time when you use this book by understanding, before you start the lessons, how instructions, keys to press, and so on are shown in the book. Please take a moment to read the following list, which also points out helpful features of the book that you might want to use.

 NOTE If you are unfamiliar with Windows, Windows NT, or mouse terminology, see Appendix A, "If You Are New to Windows 95, Windows NT, or Microsoft Word 97."

Conventions

- Hands-on exercises for you to follow are given in numbered lists of steps (1, 2, and so on). An arrowhead bullet (➤) indicates an exercise that has only one step.
- Text that you are to type appears in **bold**
- A plus sign (+) between two key names means that you must press those keys at the same time. For example, "Press ALT+TAB" means that you hold down the ALT key while you press TAB.

The following icons identify the different types of supplementary material:

	Notes labeled	Alert you to
	Note	Additional information for a step.
	Tip	Suggested additional methods for a step or helpful hints.
	Important	Essential information that you should check before continuing with the lesson.
	Troubleshooting	Possible error messages or computer difficulties and their solutions.
	Demonstration	Skills that are demonstrated in audiovisual files available on the World Wide Web.

Other Features of This Book

- You can learn how to use other Microsoft products, such as Outlook and FrontPage, with Word by reading the shaded boxes throughout the lessons.
- You can learn about techniques that build on what you learned in a lesson by trying the optional One Step Further exercise at the end of the lesson.
- You can get a quick reminder of how to perform the tasks you learned by reading the Lesson Summary at the end of a lesson.
- You can quickly determine what online Help topics are available for additional information by referring to the Help topics listed at the end of each lesson. The Help system provides a complete online reference to Microsoft Word. To learn more about online Help, see Appendix A, "If You Are New to Windows 95, Windows NT, or Microsoft Word 97."
- You can practice the major skills presented in the lessons by working through the Review & Practice sections at the end of each part.
- If you have Web browser software and access to the World Wide Web, you can view audiovisual demonstrations of how to perform some of the more complicated tasks in Word by downloading supplementary files from the Web. Double-click the Camcorder Files On The Internet shortcut that was created on your Desktop when you installed the practice files for this book, or connect directly to http://www.microsoft.com/mspress/products/374/. The Web page that opens contains full instructions for copying and viewing the demonstration files.

Basic Skills

Creating and Saving Documents

Estimated time
45 min.

In this lesson you will learn how to:

- Start Microsoft Word.
- Use toolbars and other basic features in the document window.
- Type text in a new document window.
- Correct spelling errors using automatic spell checking.
- Insert, delete, and replace text.
- Name and save your document.

In Microsoft Word, it's easy to create documents and make them look the way you want. In this lesson, you will type a short letter that you'll use to help you become familiar with the AutoCorrect feature (which corrects your spelling as you type) and learn how to edit text by deleting, replacing, and inserting words and phrases. You will also save your work by storing the document on your computer hard disk.

Using Microsoft Word to Customize Your Documents

You use word processing software when you want to create a new document—such as a letter, memo, or report—or when you want to modify a document that you or someone else created. You can use Microsoft Word to type in text, edit existing text, and format text to add emphasis, clarify ideas, and arrange text attractively on the page. You can also use Microsoft Word to insert graphics, tables, and charts, as well as to check your document for spelling and grammatical mistakes. In addition, you can use Microsoft Word to create and modify Web pages that you can display on the Internet.

In addition to these features, Microsoft Word offers other capabilities that make creating documents a snap. Below is a summary of the features you will probably use most often.

- The AutoCorrect feature corrects your spelling of certain words as you type. In addition, you can use Microsoft Word to identify words not found in the Word dictionary; a wavy red underline indicates words that might be misspelled. This feature helps you quickly locate and correct errors. Similar features are available to correct grammatical errors as you type and to identify grammatical errors in your document.

- If you use hyphens as list bullets, fractions, ordinal arabic numbers (such as 3RD), and trademarks or other symbols in your documents, the AutoFormat feature automatically inserts the correct symbol as you type.

- If you need to arrange text in a grid of rows and columns, Word's table feature helps you format your text quickly and attractively. If your table contains numbers, you can use the table feature to format your numbers as in a spreadsheet, and you can use MS Graph to display the numbers in a chart.

- To store and insert frequently used text and graphics, you can use the AutoText feature. In addition, Word already provides many AutoText entries for common expressions and phrases.

- To store and apply formatting combinations easily, consistently, and accurately, you can create and apply styles.

- To create form letters, envelopes, and labels, you can use the Mail Merge feature.

- To create attractively formatted documents quickly, you can use the variety of document wizards and templates provided in Word. These templates and wizards give you a great head start in the formatting of your documents. Use a wizard to create a document based on your responses to a series of questions, or use a template to begin creating a document right away.

 TIP If you are already familiar with previous versions of Microsoft Word, be sure to review the "Conventions and Features in This Book" section earlier in this book for a list of the features that are new in this version of Microsoft Word.

An Introduction to the Office Assistant

While you are working with Microsoft Office 97, an animated character called the *Office Assistant* pops up on your screen to help you work productively. The Office Assistant offers helpful messages as you work. You can ask the Office Assistant questions by typing your question, then clicking Search. The Office Assistant then shows you the answer to your question.

You can close any Office Assistant tip or message by pressing ESC.

You will sometimes see a lightbulb next to the Office Assistant—clicking the lightbulb displays a tip about the action you are currently performing. You can view more tips by clicking Tips in the Office Assistant balloon when the Office Assistant appears. In addition, the Office Assistant is tailored to how you work—after you master a particular skill, the Office Assistant stops offering tips.

Clippit, an Office Assistant, in action

The Office Assistant appears in the following situations:

- When you click the Office Assistant button on the Standard toolbar.
- When you choose Microsoft Word Help on the Help menu or when you press F1.
- When you type certain phrases. For example, you might see the Office Assistant when you type the text **Dear Ms. Rasmussen:** and press ENTER.

Office Assistant

The Office Assistant is a shared application—any settings that you change will affect the Office Assistant in other Office 97 programs. You can customize the Office Assistant in two ways. You can:

Determine when you want to see the Office Assistant

Use the right mouse button to click the Office Assistant and click Options to open the Office Assistant dialog box. You can then define when you want the Office Assistant to appear, and what kind of help you want it to offer.

Change your Office Assistant character

Use the right mouse button to click the Office Assistant and click Options to open the Office Assistant dialog box. Click the Gallery tab.

Starting Microsoft Word

There are several ways to start Microsoft Word. If Word is installed as part of the Microsoft Office suite, you can use the Office Shortcut bar to open the program. Otherwise, the easiest way to start Microsoft Word is from the Programs menu, which is available when you click the Start button.

Start Microsoft Word from the Programs menu

1 On the taskbar, click Start.

2 On the Start menu, point to Programs, and then click Microsoft Word.

IMPORTANT If the Office Assistant appears, click the Start Using Microsoft Program option. If the User Name dialog box appears, fill in your name and initials, and then click OK. On the Office Assistant, click the Close button.

For the purposes of this book, the Office Assistant will not appear in the illustrations. If you want to match the illustrations, any time the Office Assistant appears, use the right mouse button to click the Office Assistant, and then click Hide Assistant. If you want to leave Office Assistant on top to help guide you, but it is in your way, simply drag it to another area on the screen.

Maximize

3 If the window is not already maximized, click the Maximize button. Your screen should look similar to the following illustration.

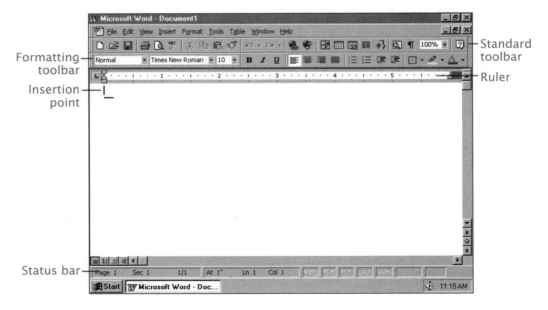

Exploring the Microsoft Word Document Window

When you start Microsoft Word, a new blank document appears in a *document window*. The document window is the Microsoft Word equivalent of a sheet of paper in a typewriter—it is where you type your text. The buttons and ruler you see at the top of the window offer easy ways to work on your documents.

Using Toolbars to Perform Basic Operations

The first row of buttons below the Microsoft Word menu bar is the Standard toolbar. This toolbar contains buttons for performing basic operations, such as opening, closing, and printing a document, in Microsoft Word. It is generally much faster to click a button on a toolbar than to select a command from a menu.

There are several toolbars in Microsoft Word; you can display or hide these toolbars depending on your needs. Each toolbar is composed of buttons that perform related tasks. For example, you use the Formatting toolbar (located below the Standard toolbar) to enhance the appearance of your document, including the style and size of the type.

When you click certain toolbar buttons—for example, the Print button—Microsoft Word carries out the corresponding command using the command default options. A *default* is a setting or option that is in effect if you do not specify another choice. Clicking other buttons turns features on and off. For example, the Show/Hide ¶ button displays or hides nonprinting characters, such as spaces between words and paragraph marks between paragraphs. Still other buttons, such as the Open button, perform in the same way as their corresponding commands. The instructions in this book emphasize using the toolbars whenever possible.

Take a quick tour of the Standard toolbar

Undo

Take a moment to familiarize yourself with the buttons on the Standard toolbar. If you accidentally click a button, you can click the Undo button on the Standard toolbar.

> Move the mouse pointer over a button, and wait.

After a moment, a ScreenTip, which is an on-screen description of a toolbar button, appears. If you do not see the button name, on the Tools menu, choose Customize, and then click the Options tab. Click Show ScreenTips On Toolbars.

ScreenTip

Typing Text

As the communications manager at West Coast Sales, your duties include developing a wide variety of documents. The key to your success has been your effectiveness at getting the message out to employees and customers by creating attractive and professional-looking documents. Using Microsoft Word will help you develop the documents you need both quickly and with a minimum of effort. One of your major projects this year is to coordinate a national sales conference for West Coast Sales employees. After an initial telephone call to a motivational speaker who has expressed interest in delivering the keynote address, you decide to follow up with a letter.

You can begin typing in the empty document window, just as you would begin typing on a clean sheet of paper. The blinking insertion point, which is already positioned for you at the top of the window, shows where the text you type will appear. For the next exercise, you'll start by typing the salutation. Later, you will insert the date and inside address. Whenever you see the name "Terry Kim," you can type your own name in the document.

Type text in a letter

1 Type **Dear Ms. Mather:** and press ENTER.

> **NOTE** If the Office Assistant asks you if you would like to use the Letter Wizard, click the option to create a letter without the Letter Wizard (the second option). Working without the Letter Wizard for now will help you focus on typing and simple editing. If you would like to try creating a letter with the help of the Letter Wizard, you can complete the One Step Further exercise at the end of this lesson.

Pressing ENTER places the insertion point at the start of a new blank line. If a red, wavy underline appears below a word you type, it means that the automatic spell checking feature is enabled and the word is identified as misspelled or unknown. You will learn more about this feature later in this lesson.

2   Press ENTER to create another blank line.

Type a paragraph of text

When you type sentences that are longer than one line, you do not need to press ENTER at the end of each line. Instead, you can just keep typing. When the insertion point approaches the right margin, it automatically moves to the beginning of the next line as you continue typing. This feature is known as *wordwrap*. You press ENTER when you want to begin a new paragraph or to create a blank line.

➤   Type the body paragraph below without pressing ENTER. If you make a typing mistake, either press the BACKSPACE key to delete the mistake and then type the correct text, or ignore the mistake and correct it later.

Thank you for agreeing to present the opening address for our company's national sales conference next year. Supporting the professional development of our employees is a long-standing priority at our company. A reflection of that commitment is our desire to present the highest quality speakers at our next year's conference.

Correcting Mistakes as You Type

If you tend to make certain kinds of spelling or typographical errors, you might notice that Microsoft Word automatically makes the necessary corrections as you type. This is the AutoCorrect feature. For example, some common spelling mistakes, such as typing "adn" instead of "and," are corrected as soon as you type the first space after the word. Similarly, with the exception of certain abbreviations, if you type two capitalized letters in a row, the program automatically changes the second character to lowercase as you continue typing. Word also changes a lowercase character immediately following a period to uppercase.

If you misspell a word that is not corrected right away, or you type a word that is not in the Word dictionary, the program underlines the word with a red, wavy line. Repeated words (such as "the the") are also identified by a red, wavy underline. This feature is known as Automatic Spell Checking. After you finish typing, you can place the mouse pointer on the underlined word, and click the right mouse button to open a shortcut menu of correction options. You can:

- Choose the correct spelling from the suggested words at the top of the list.

- Choose Ignore All to remove the underlining and ignore every occurrence of the word.

- Choose Add to add the word to the dictionary. This means that in the future, Microsoft Word will no longer identify the word as misspelled or unknown.

- Choose the Spelling command to display the Spelling dialog box in which you can specify additional spelling options.
- If no suggested spelling appears on the shortcut menu, click the word and edit it to correct the spelling.

Correct typing errors

1   Use the right mouse button to click the word "Mather."

   The Spelling shortcut menu opens. Your screen should look similar to the following illustration.

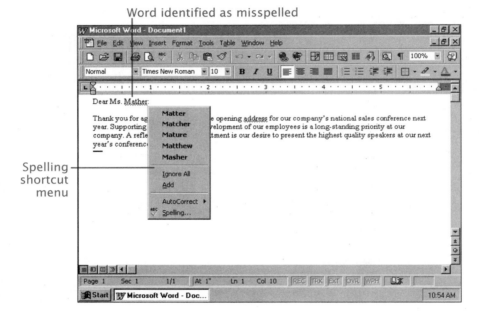

2   Click Ignore All to ignore all occurrences of this word in the document.

3   Use the right mouse button to click any other words underlined with a red, wavy line to display the Spelling shortcut menu. Then, click the correct spelling of the word, or click Ignore All. If you repeated a word, click Delete Repeated Word.

   For now, do not click Add or Spelling. You will learn how to use these options in Lesson 5, "Increasing Editing Productivity."

Deal with a potential grammatical error

Grammatical errors, or errors in punctuation or usage, are identified with green, wavy underlines. In the same way you can click the right mouse button on a possible spelling error to correct it, you can use the right mouse button to correct possible grammatical errors. If you do not see the green underlines, you can skip this exercise.

1 Use the right mouse button to click the word "address."

In this case, this usage of the word "address" is correct.

2 Click Ignore Sentence to ignore all possible errors in this sentence.

 NOTE The Automatic Spell Checking feature is enabled by default. If you wish to turn the feature off or hide the red, wavy underlines in your document, on the Tools menu, click Options. Click the Spelling & Grammar tab to bring it to the front. Under the Check As You Type section, click the Spelling check box to clear it. Automatic Spell Checking will be turned off until you select the feature again. You can also hide the red, wavy underlines by clearing the Hide Spelling Errors In Current Document check box. To hide any green, wavy underlines, click the Hide Grammar Errors In Current Document check box to clear it.

Displaying Special Characters

In Microsoft Word, any amount of text that ends with a paragraph mark is treated as a paragraph. Even a blank line is a paragraph. Microsoft Word also displays small dots that represent the spaces between words; these dots appear when you press the SPACEBAR, if nonprinting characters are being displayed. Paragraph marks and space dots do not appear in printed documents.

Display paragraph marks and special symbols

When you typed the salutation for the letter, Microsoft Word inserted a paragraph mark (¶) each time you pressed ENTER. You can display or hide paragraph marks and space dots by clicking the Show/Hide ¶ button. When nonprinting characters are displayed, you can see how many paragraph marks are between lines of text and the number of spaces between words. In this exercise, you display these nonprinting characters.

Show/Hide ¶

➤ On the Standard toolbar, click the Show/Hide ¶ button if your paragraph marks are not already displayed. Your screen should look similar to the following illustration.

Nonprinting characters

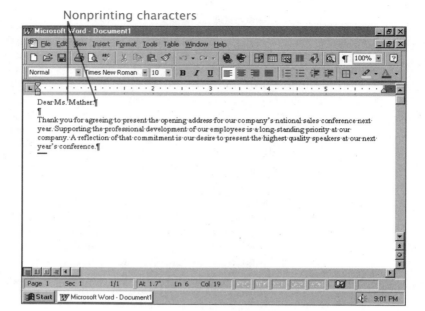

Type additional paragraphs of text

In this exercise, you will add text to the body of your letter. The AutoFormat feature makes ordinal numbers easier to read by changing them to superscripts as you type the dates.

1 Place the insertion point at the last paragraph mark, and then press ENTER twice to create another blank line.

2 Type:

We are still in the planning stages of this conference, so our schedule is still flexible at this point. So far, we have discussed your availability on two tentative dates: October 21st and 22nd. In addition to paying your travel expenses to the conference site (the Park View Center) and your accommodations, we are offering an honorarium of $1500.

3 Press ENTER twice to create another blank line.

4 Type:

If these terms are agreeable to you, please sign both copies of the attached contract and return them to me as soon as possible.

5 Press ENTER twice to create another blank line.

Type a nonbreaking space

When you type words that you want to appear together, you can insert a nonbreaking space between each word. By using a nonbreaking space between words, you prevent the wordwrap feature from separating words at the end of a line. In this exercise, you want to ensure that all the words in the company name appear together.

1 Type **I would like to extend my personal thanks for considering our offer. On behalf of the entire West**

2 Press CTRL+SHIFT+SPACEBAR, and then type **Coast**

3 Press CTRL+SHIFT+SPACEBAR, and then type **Sales organization, I look forward to your timely confirmation.**

4 Press ENTER twice to create another blank line.

5 Type **Terry Kim** and press ENTER.

6 Type **Conference Planning Coordinator** and press ENTER.

7 Type **West Coast Sales** and press ENTER.

Improving Document Creation by Using AutoText Entries

There are certain common words and phrases most people use in letters and documents. The Microsoft Word AutoText feature provides a fast way to insert such frequently used text. Using AutoText entries not only saves you time, but it also prevents typing mistakes. With the AutoText command, you can insert AutoText entries for many common words, phrases, and expressions.

Insert an AutoText entry

Instead of typing "Sincerely" at the closing of a letter, you can insert this word by choosing it from the AutoText menu.

1 Click to position the insertion point in front of the name in the signature block.

2 On the Insert menu, point to AutoText.

If a menu item has a right-pointing arrow after its name, this means it opens another menu—a *cascading menu*.

3 On the cascading menu, point to Closing, and then click Respectfully yours.

Word inserts the text in the document.

4 Press ENTER twice.

NOTE   Although Word provides AutoText entries for some of the more common words, phrases, and expressions, you can also create your own AutoText entries for your own frequently used text and graphics. You will learn how to create your AutoText entries in Lesson 5, "Increasing Editing Productivity."

Inserting and Deleting Text to Edit Your Document

Editing text simply means making changes by inserting new text, removing (*deleting*) existing text, or replacing text by removing old text and inserting new text in its place.

Insert text in a sentence

You can easily insert new text anywhere in a document.

1   Press CTRL+HOME to position the insertion point at the beginning of the document.

2   Position the pointer just before the word "professional" in the second sentence, and then click immediately to the right of the space character.

3   Type **training and** and then press the SPACEBAR to insert a space between the words.

Delete extra spacing between paragraphs

You can delete text one character at a time using either BACKSPACE or DELETE. Use BACKSPACE to remove characters to the left of the insertion point. Use DELETE to remove characters to the right of the insertion point.

1   Click before the first word ("I") of the last body paragraph to position the insertion point—the last paragraph in the main body of the document.

2   Press BACKSPACE twice to delete the paragraph marks.

3   Press the SPACEBAR to insert a space between the two sentences.

Edit text in a sentence

Pressing DELETE removes characters to the right of the insertion point. After removing text, you can insert new text in its place.

1   Click before the number 5 in $1500 to position the insertion point.

2   Press DELETE, and then type **7**

Select and delete a word

Of course, it would be cumbersome to backspace a letter at a time through an entire document. In this exercise, you can delete as much text as you want by selecting the text first.

1 In the second sentence of the second body paragraph, double-click the word "tentative" to select the word and the space that follows it.

Selected text is highlighted so that you can easily distinguish it from text that is not selected. Double-clicking to select words maintains the correct spacing after you delete a word.

2 Press DELETE to remove the word from the text.

The text in the document moves to fill the space left by the deleted word.

Select text and replace it

Double-clicking a word selects only that word, but you can select any amount of text by dragging across it with the mouse. When text is selected, the next text you type—regardless of its length—replaces the selected text. In this exercise, you select and replace text.

1 In the first body paragraph, place the insertion point in front of the first o in the text "our company's."

2 Drag the pointer across the next two words, so that both "our" and "company's" are highlighted.

3 Type **West Coast Sales**

4 Check the spacing before and after the new text you typed. If you need to add a space, click where you need to add the space to position the insertion point, and then press the SPACEBAR.

Undoing Your Changes

A useful feature in Microsoft Word is the Undo button, which you can use to reverse your changes. For example, in the next exercise, you use the Undo button to remove the new text and restore the original text to your document.

 NOTE You can undo most Microsoft Word commands; operations that cannot be undone include saving, printing, opening, and creating documents.

Undo the last change

Undo

You can also press CTRL+Z to undo the most recent change.

➤ On the Standard toolbar, click the Undo button to undo your last change.

If this action did not remove the new text and restore the original text, you might have pressed another key before you clicked the Undo button. Clicking Undo once reverses only the last change. Click the Undo button again until the original text is restored.

Undo more changes

You can also click the Undo down arrow to see a list of the actions you can reverse. For example, if you want to return the document to the way it looked before you made the last three changes, you would scroll to the last of the three changes listed in the Undo list and select it. This action would undo all three changes. In this exercise, you'll see how this works.

➤ On the Standard toolbar, click the Undo down arrow, and then select the third change in the list to undo your last three actions: deleting the word "tentative," typing a 7, and deleting the 5 in $1500.

All the changes you made are reversed. The changes in the Undo list appear so that your most recent change is at the top of the list, with each previous change appearing below it. Because several changes in sequence often depend on preceding changes, you cannot select an individual action on the list without undoing all the actions that appear above that action.

Change your mind again

The Redo button on the Standard toolbar allows you to reverse an undo action. You can reverse the results of the last change by clicking the Redo button. In this exercise, you redo your actions.

Redo

➤ On the Standard toolbar, click the Redo button to redo your last undo action.

The 5 is again deleted from $1500.

Redo all changes

➤ On the Standard toolbar, click the Redo down arrow, and then select all the changes in the list to redo all actions.

Your document should look like the following illustration.

Inserted text Replacement text

Deleted text No extra space

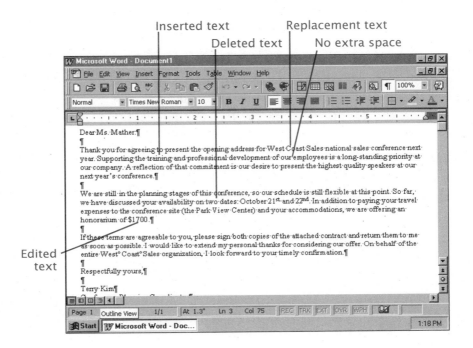

Edited text

Inserting Dates Quickly

The Microsoft Word Date And Time command provides a fast way to include today's date in a document. With the Date And Time command you can select from a variety of date and time formats. Using this command saves time and eliminates errors. In these exercises, you insert the date and an address.

Insert today's date

1 Press CTRL+HOME to place the insertion point at the top of the document.

2 On the Insert menu, click Date And Time.

The Date And Time dialog box appears.

3 In the Available Formats box, click the fourth date format from the top, and then click OK.

The current date is inserted at the insertion point. This date is based on your computer's date and time setting.

4 Press ENTER twice.

Insert the inside address

1 Type **Ms. Karen Mather** and press ENTER.

2 Type **Fitch & Mather** and press ENTER.

3 Type **1800 Centerdale Circle** and press ENTER.

4 Type **Centerdale, CA 95033** and press ENTER twice.

Saving Your Documents

To keep your work for future use, you must give the document a name and save it. After you save it, the document is available each time you want to use it.

It is best to name and save a document soon after you start working on it. After that, it's a good idea to save a document every 15 minutes or so to minimize the amount of work you could lose if power to your computer is interrupted. The Save button on the Standard toolbar makes this quick and easy to do.

 NOTE The first time you save a document, clicking either Save or Save As on the File menu will open the Save As dialog box, because the first time you save, you need to name the document.

Save the document

When you save a document, you must give it a name and specify where you want to store it. Although you can specify the drive and folder where you want to save your documents, for now save the letter in the same folder as the Step by Step practice files.

 TIP The AutoRecover feature saves the document periodically so that it can be automatically restored in the event of a loss of power. You can specify how often Word saves your document on the Save tab when you choose the Options command on the Tools menu. The AutoSave feature does not eliminate the need for saving the document yourself.

Save

1 On the Standard toolbar, click the Save button.

The Save As dialog box appears the first time you save a document. The dialog box should look like the following illustration.

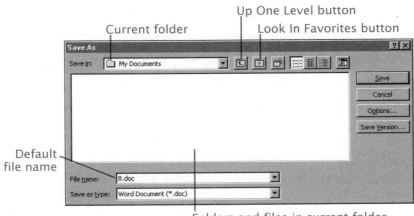

Current folder

Up One Level button

Look In Favorites button

Default file name

Folders and files in current folder

Look In Favorites

2 If the Winword SBS Practice folder is not currently displayed in the Save In box, click the Look In Favorites button, and then double-click Winword SBS Practice Folder.

3 Be sure the text in the File Name box is selected, and type **Mather Letter01**

You can enter a filename that is up to 255 characters long. You can also use spaces and other characters as part of the name. You can enter a name in lowercase or uppercase letters; however, text in mixed case (for example, a capital first letter, and lowercase for the following letters) is usually easier to read than text in all capital letters.

You can also press ENTER.

4 Click the Save button to close the dialog box and save the document as you've specified.

Your letter is saved with the name Mather Letter01 in the Winword SBS Practice folder.

5 On the File menu, click Close.

 NOTE If you'd like to build on the skills that you learned in this lesson, you can do the One Step Further. Otherwise, skip to "Finish the lesson."

One Step Further: Creating a Letter by Using the Letter Wizard

Wizards can be a big help when you want to create a new document. You simply choose the kind of document you want to create—such as a letter, brochure, report, or fax—and the document wizard prompts you to answer a series of questions. You can choose the style of document and select other options. Then

19

Microsoft Word creates a professionally designed document based on the selections you made, but without you having to do any of the formatting yourself. With the basics of the document established, you just type the text and edit the document as you wish.

Start the Letter Wizard

In your role as a conference planner you must arrange for the equipment needed by presenters at the conference. To follow up on an attractive bid from a contractor who provides this service, you decide to write a quick letter that summarizes your requirements. In this exercise, you use the Letter Wizard to get a head start on your letter.

New

1   On the Standard toolbar, click the New button.

    You must have a document open in order to select Letter Wizard from the Tools menu.

2   On the Tools menu, click Letter Wizard.

    The Letter Wizard dialog box and the Office Assistant appear. The Letter Wizard looks like the following illustration.

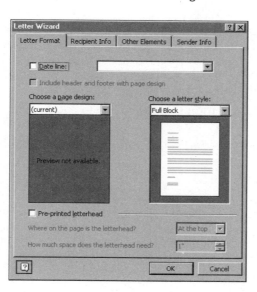

Format the letter

If you are using preprinted letterhead, click the Pre-Printed Letterhead check box and specify the location and size of the letterhead on the page.

On the Letter Format tab, you specify the overall appearance of the letter. The Preview area of the dialog box shows you what the document will look like as you make your selections.

1 On the Letter Format tab, click the Date Line check box.

2 Click the Date Line down arrow, and be sure that the third date format is selected.

3 Click the Choose A Page Design down arrow, and select Contemporary Letter.

4 Click the Choose A Letter Style arrow, and choose Modified Block.

Enter recipient information

On the Recipient Info tab, you can specify information about the individual to whom the letter is addressed.

1 Click the Recipient Info tab.

The Recipient Info tab looks like the following illustration.

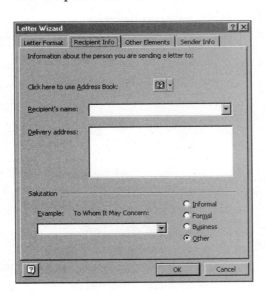

2 In the Recipient's Name box, type **Mr. Eric Bustos**

3 In the Delivery Address box, type the following information:

Bits, Bytes & Chips, Inc.
1001 Industrial Drive
Centerdale, CA 95033

Inserting Addresses from Your Address Book

Using the Insert Address button that is available in some dialog boxes (including the Recipient Info tab in the Letter Wizard), you can insert name and address information that is stored in your Microsoft Exchange Address Book, in your Schedule+ Contact List, or in Outlook. Simply click the Address Book button, and select the Address Book you want to use. Then double-click the name you want to insert.

4 In the Salutation area, click the Business option.

Enter subject information

On the Other Elements tab, you can specify subject, reference line, mailing instructions, and attention information.

1 Click the Other Elements tab.

The Other Elements tab looks like the following illustration.

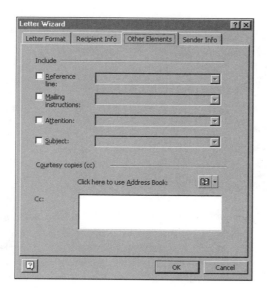

2 Click the Subject check box.

3 In the Subject box, type **West Coast Sales Conference Equipment Proposal**

Enter sender information

On the Sender Info tab, you can specify information about the sender, including the closing and how your name should appear in the signature block. In this exercise, you set up your closing.

1 Click the Sender Info tab.

The Sender Info tab looks like the following illustration.

If your letter includes enclosures, click the Enclosures check box and specify the number of enclosures that will accompany this letter.

2 Click the Sender's Name down arrow, and select your name.

3 Select the Omit check box so your address will not appear in the letter.

4 For a closing, click the Complementary Closing down arrow, and then select Yours truly.

5 Click the Job Title down arrow, and choose your title.

6 Click the Company down arrow, and choose your company's name.

7 Click the Writer's/Typist's Initials down arrow, and choose your initials.

8 Click OK.

The Letter Wizard creates a letter formatted according to your selections.

Type the text of the letter

With the basic formatting of the letter established, you are ready to type the text of the letter.

 Type:

As I mentioned on the phone this morning, my management is quite pleased with your proposal. We would like to accept your bid to provide the equipment needs for the West Coast Sales conference as specified in your proposal. We have processed your invoice that represents your retainer fee for the week of the conference. If there is anything else you require to begin the project, please let me know.

Save the letter

Save

Look In
Favorites

*You can also
press ENTER.*

1   On the Standard toolbar, click the Save button.

     The Save As dialog box appears.

2   Be sure that Winword SBS Practice is in the Save In box.

     If the folder is not in the Save As box, click the Look In Favorites button, and then double-click Winword SBS Practice.

3   If the text is not selected, drag to select all the text in the File Name box, and then type **Equipment Letter01**

4   Click Save in the dialog box to close the dialog box, and then save the file.

     Your file is saved with the name Equipment Letter01 in the Winword SBS Practice folder.

Finish the lesson

1   To continue to the next lesson, on the File menu, click Close for each document you have open.

2   If you are finished using Microsoft Word for now, on the File menu, click Exit.

Lesson Summary

To	Do this
Start Microsoft Word	On the taskbar, click Start, point at Programs, and then click Microsoft Word.
Create a new paragraph or a blank line	Press ENTER.

To	Do this	Button
Display or hide paragraph marks	Click the Show/Hide ¶ button.	¶
Insert frequently used text	Choose Insert, and then click AutoText and choose an entry.	
Insert text into existing text	Click to position the insertion point at the place where you want to insert the text, and start typing.	
Remove characters	Press BACKSPACE to remove characters to the left of the insertion point. Press DELETE to remove text to the right of the insertion point.	
Select a word	Double-click the word. *or* Drag across the word.	
Select any amount of text	Drag to highlight text.	
Replace text	Select and type over text.	
Undo the most recent action	Click the Undo button immediately after the action.	↰ ▾
Undo multiple actions	Click the Undo down arrow, and then select the appropriate number of changes.	
Reverse the most recent undo action	Click the Redo button.	↱ ▾
Reverse multiple undo actions	Click the Redo down arrow, and then select the appropriate number of changes.	
Save a new document	On the File menu, click Save or Save As.	

For online information about	On the Help menu, click Contents And Index, click the Index tab, and then type
Creating a simple document	**documents**
Saving documents	**documents**
Typing and editing text	**text, correcting**
Inserting text	**text, inserting**

Moving and Copying Text

Estimated time
45 min.

In this lesson you will learn how to:

- Open an existing document and save it with a new name.
- Display a document in Page Layout view.
- Move text to a new location in a document.
- Copy text to a new location in a document.
- Use the Clipboard to move and copy text.

In Microsoft Word, it's easy to edit your documents. If you want to edit a document but you want to keep the original document unchanged, you can open the document and save it with a new name. That is, you can keep the original document unchanged while you make changes in the new document. By moving and copying text, you can take advantage of work you've already done. For example, you can copy text, move it to a different location, and edit it. To get a better idea of how your document looks, and to edit it easily, you can work in Page Layout view. In this lesson, you'll move and copy text within a document—by dragging text and dropping it in new locations and by using the Clipboard.

Opening a Document

If you have not yet started Microsoft Word or set up the Word SBS practice files, refer to "Installing and Using the Practice Files," earlier in this book.

A new, blank document window opens when you start Microsoft Word. You can also open an existing document and modify that document in the same way you would a new document.

Start Word and open a practice file

In this exercise, you'll open the practice file called 02Lesson and then save the file with a different name, Program Highlights02. This process creates a duplicate of the file that you can work on and modify during the lesson. The original file, 02Lesson, is unchanged so that you can practice the lesson as many times as you wish. This procedure for using practice files is followed throughout this book.

1   On the taskbar, click the Start button.

2   Point to Programs, and then click Microsoft Word.

3   On the Standard toolbar, click the Open button.

Open

The Open dialog box appears. In the Open dialog box, you select the folder and document you want to open. The Look In box shows the folder that is currently selected.

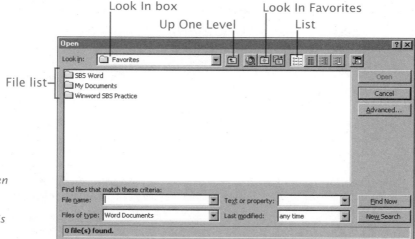

Depending on how your system is configured, your Open dialog box might look different from this illustration.

List

*Look In
Favorites*

Preview

4 On the toolbar of the Open dialog box, verify that the List button is selected.

The names of all folders and files within the selected folder appear in the file list.

5 Be sure that the Favorites folder is in the Look In box, as shown in the illustration in step 3.

If a folder name other than Favorites or Winword SBS Practice appears in the Look In box, click the Look In Favorites button on the toolbar.

6 In the file list, double-click the Winword SBS Practice folder.

7 On the toolbar of the Open dialog box, click the Preview button.

A small image of the document appears in the dialog box, so you can preview the document before you open it.

Preview of document

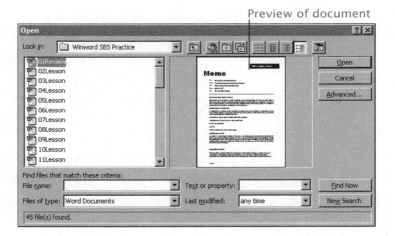

8 In the file list, double-click the 02Lesson file.

The Open dialog box closes, and the 02Lesson file opens in the document window.

 TIP When you click Start on the taskbar and point to the Documents menu, you can see the filenames of the last 15 documents you have opened. When you click a document on the Document menu, the correct program opens and displays the document. At the bottom of the Word File menu, you can see a filename list of your four most recently opened documents.

Searching for Documents by Using the Open Dialog Box

In the Open dialog box, you can search for a document even if you can't recall the entire document name. You can enter a partial filename in the File Name box, and Word will locate all the documents with filenames containing the characters you typed. You can also locate a document based on other factors, such as a word or phrase in the document or when the document was last modified.

1   On the Standard toolbar, click the Open button.

2   In the File Name box, type part of the filename.

- To locate files that begin with the text you type, type an asterisk (*) after the filename.

- To locate files that end with the text you type, type an asterisk (*) before the filename.

- To locate files based on a word or phrase stored in the document, type the text in the Text or Property box.

- To locate documents based on when the document was last modified, choose a time period in the Last Modified box.

3   Click Find Now.

The filenames that match the text you type (or any other specifications you entered) appear in the Name area of the Open dialog box.

4   Double-click the document you want to open.

Save the practice document with a new name

When you save a file, you give it a name and specify where you want to store it. The name you give a document can contain up to 255 characters, including spaces and numbers. For each file you use in this book, you'll usually save it in the SBS Word folder with a new name; therefore, the original practice file remains unchanged, and you can repeat the exercises as many times as you want. In this exercise, you will create the SBS Word folder and then save the document in that folder.

Look In Favorites

1   On the File menu, click Save As.

The Save As dialog box appears.

2   In the Save As dialog box, click the Look In Favorites button.

3   Click the Create New Folder button.

Create New Folder

4   In the New Folder dialog box, type **SBS Word**

5 Click OK to create a new folder.

The SBS Word folder is created within the current folder, Favorites.

6 Double-click SBS Word to make it the new current folder in the Save In box.

7 If the text is not selected, drag to select all text in the File Name box, and then type **Program Highlights02**

You can also press ENTER.

8 In the Save As dialog box, click Save to close the dialog box and save the file.

Your file is saved with the name Program Highlights02 in the SBS Word folder. When the dialog box closes, the original document is no longer open; the new document is open, and the new document name appears on the title bar.

Opening Documents Using Microsoft Outlook

If you have Microsoft Outlook, you can easily find and manage your documents directly from the Desktop. When Outlook is open, you can use it to open documents quickly. To open a document using Microsoft Outlook:

1 On the taskbar, click the Start button, point to Programs, and click Microsoft Outlook.

2 On the Outlook Bar, click the Other shortcut bar.

3 Double-click each folder you want to open.

4 Double-click the document you want to open.

Disabling Automatic Spell Checking and Automatic Grammar Checking

Whenever Automatic Spell Checking is enabled, the misspelled or unknown words in a document are underlined with red, wavy lines. When Automatic Grammar Checking is on, grammatical errors are underlined with green, wavy lines.

Turn off Automatic Spell Checking and Automatic Grammar Checking

The Program Highlight02 document is a draft of the program for next year's West Coast Sales national sales conference. As the conference coordinator, you are responsible for completing the program and preparing it for distribution.

In this exercise, to help you focus on moving around in the document (rather than on misspelled words, unknown words, or grammatical errors), you will disable Automatic Spell Checking and Automatic Grammar Checking.

1   On the Tools menu, click Options, and then click the Spelling & Grammar tab.

2   In the Spelling area, click the Hide Spelling Errors In This Document check box to select it.

There should be a check mark in the check box. Selecting the Hide Spelling Errors In This Document option hides the red, wavy underlines in the document.

3   In the Grammar area, click the Hide Grammatical Errors In This Document check box to select it.

Selecting the Hide Grammatical Errors In This Document option hides the green, wavy underlines in the document.

4   Click OK to close the dialog box and return to the practice document.

The misspelled or unknown words and grammatical errors are no longer underlined.

Display nonprinting characters

To make it easier to see exactly where to move text around in the document, you can display nonprinting characters.

Show/Hide ¶

➤   If paragraph marks are not already displayed, click the Show/Hide ¶ button on the Standard toolbar.

Selecting the Best View for Examining Your Document

In the document window, there are several display options, known as *views*, for examining your document. In each view, you can focus on different parts of the editing process. For example, you will probably most often use the default, Normal view. In Normal view, you can see basic text and paragraph formatting, which makes Normal view ideal for focusing on text and revising your document. On the other hand, Page Layout view is the best view to use when you want to see the arrangement of text and graphics on the page while you edit text. For example, in Page Layout view, you can see text formatted in columns, but in Normal view, you cannot. Outline view is great for organizing ideas and establishing a structure for your document, because you can easily see the structure and organization of the headings in the document. You will learn how to work in outline view in Lesson 10, "Organizing a Document by Using Outlining." You can switch between these three views quickly by using the View buttons located to the left of the horizontal scroll bar.

In addition, you can use the Online Layout view, which is ideal for reading documents on the Internet. Another view, called the Document Map, is a convenient way to move through a long document.

Switch to Page Layout view

To help you get a better idea of the formatting used in your Program Highlights document, you decide to display the document in Page Layout view.

*Page Layout
View*

1 Make sure you are in Page Layout view. If not, click the Page Layout View button.

2 Click the scroll down arrow at the bottom of the vertical scroll bar to view the contents of the first page.

You can now see the special formatting applied to the first character of some of the paragraphs.

Next Page

3 Click the Next Page scroll button at the bottom of the vertical scroll bar until the third page of the document is in the document window.

Using the scroll down arrow, you can now see that parts of the document are formatted in multiple columns. You also see where graphics appear in relation to text on the page. Your document should look similar to the following illustration.

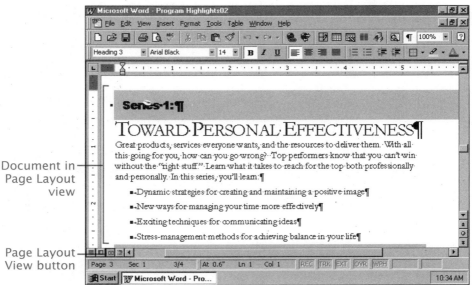

Document in Page Layout view

Page Layout View button

Remain in Page Layout view as you move and copy text in the next part of this lesson.

33

Adjust magnification

When you want to copy or move text, if you can see the place to which you want to move the material, dragging is the most efficient method of making your changes. Depending on the size and resolution of your monitor, you might not be able to see all the text on a line without scrolling to the right first. If so, you can change the magnification, which adjusts the size of the display so that all the text fits in the window.

Zoom

➤ On the Standard toolbar, click the Zoom down arrow, and then click Page Width.

Moving and Copying Text by Dragging

For a demonstration of how to drag and drop text, double-click the Camcorder Files On The Internet shortcut on your Desktop or connect to the Internet address listed on p. xxviii.

You can reuse and rearrange text in your documents by using the drag-and-drop feature in Microsoft Word. By dragging selected text, you can quickly copy or move text to a new location. When you can see the final destination for the text on the screen, dragging is the most efficient way to copy or move selected text.

Select a line of text

At the left of every paragraph, there's an invisible selection bar. By clicking in the selection bar, you can select an entire line. You can also drag the mouse pointer down the selection bar to select several lines at once. In this exercise, you will select a line in a list.

 TIP If you are selecting a large amount of text, it is easier to click where you want the selection to begin and then, while holding down the SHIFT key, click where you want the selection to end. Microsoft Word selects everything between the first place you clicked and the second place you clicked. This technique is especially useful when you want to select text that spans more than one screen.

1 Press CTRL+HOME to move to the beginning of the document. Position the mouse pointer to the left of the line that begins "Exciting techniques."

When the mouse pointer is in the selection bar, the pointer changes to a right-pointing arrow.

2 Click to select the line.

When the line is selected, the text changes to white text on a black background. Your screen should look similar to the following illustration.

Selection bar   Selected line

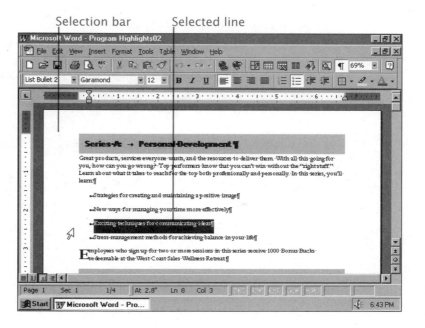

Drag to move text

Next, you'll move the selected line to the start of the list.

1 Position the mouse pointer over the selection until the pointer turns into a left-pointing arrow.

2 Hold down the left mouse button. A small, dotted box and a dotted insertion point appear. Drag up until the dotted insertion point is at the beginning of the line that starts with the word "Strategies," as shown in the following illustration. Then, release the mouse button.

Release mouse here.

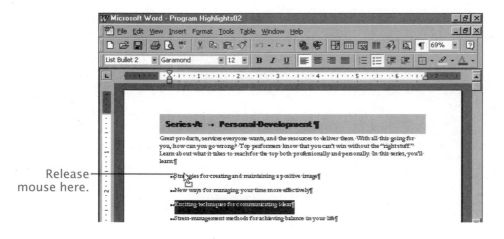

3 Click anywhere outside the selected text to clear the selection.

Your screen should look like the following illustration.

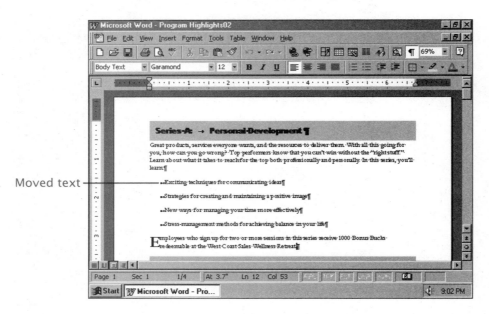

Moved text

Copy text using the mouse

Copying text by using the mouse is similar to moving text by using the mouse. If you have to repeat the same text many times in a document, copying not only saves you time and effort—it also helps you maintain consistency and guard against typographical errors. In this exercise, you will copy the words "your customers," and then insert them at another location in the sentence.

1 Scroll to the paragraph below the heading "Series B: Organizational Strategies."

2 Drag to select the words "your customers" in the second sentence.

3 Hold down the CTRL key on the keyboard, point to the selected text, and then hold down the mouse button.

4 Drag to position the dotted insertion point immediately after the word "prepare" in the next sentence. Release the mouse button, and then release CTRL.

A copy of the selected text is inserted; the original text is unchanged.

5 Click anywhere outside the selected text to clear the selection.

Copying and Moving Text Using Buttons

You can also select text, use the right mouse button to click the selected text, and click Copy or Cut.

You can use the Copy and Paste buttons to copy or move text that is not visible on the screen. When you copy (or cut) text, Microsoft Word stores the copy on the *Clipboard*—a temporary storage area that you can't see on the screen. The text remains on the Clipboard, so you can insert the same text multiple times. The contents of the Clipboard remain the same until you cut or copy other text, or until you shut down your computer.

The following illustration shows how you can use the Copy and Paste buttons on the Standard toolbar to insert text in a new location.

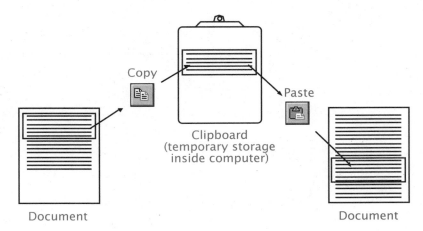

Copying Text Over a Long Distance

When you copy text using the Clipboard, the original text remains in its original location; you copy the Clipboard contents to new locations in the document. To quickly move to different parts of a document without scrolling, you can switch to Document Map view. In this view, you see the major headings of the document in the left side of the window, and the entire document in the right side of the window. By clicking a heading on the left side, you can quickly move the insertion point to that heading in the document on the right side of the window. By clicking on the plus or minus sign, you can expand or collapse the heading to display or hide its subheadings.

Switch to the Document Map

Document Map

➤ On the Standard toolbar, click the Document Map button.

Your screen looks like the following illustration.

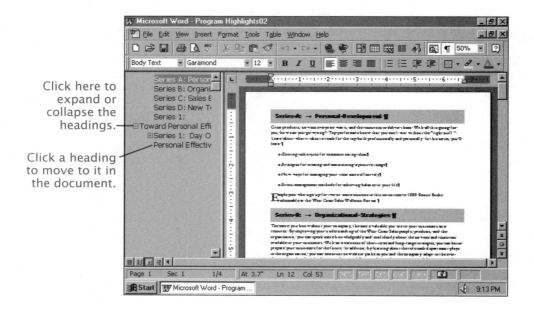

Click here to expand or collapse the headings.

Click a heading to move to it in the document.

Copy a heading

If you copy the heading "Series 1: Day One" and insert the text in a new location, you need to change only one word to create a new heading, "Series 1: Day Two." The formatting of the new heading is identical to that of the original heading.

1 In the left side of the window, click the heading "Series 1: Day One – Aspen Room."

The insertion point moves to this heading in the right side of the window.

2 Select the text in the heading and be sure to include the paragraph mark, but not the section break, in your selection.

3 On the Standard toolbar, click the Copy button.

You'll see no change in the document, but a copy of the selected text is placed on the Clipboard.

4 Scroll to the bottom of page 3, and place the insertion point in front of the line "Section Break (Continuous)."

5 On the Standard toolbar, click the Paste button.

A copy of the heading is inserted.

Copy

Paste

Edit the new heading

➤ Double-click "One" in the new heading, and then type **Two**
The word "Two" replaces the word "One."

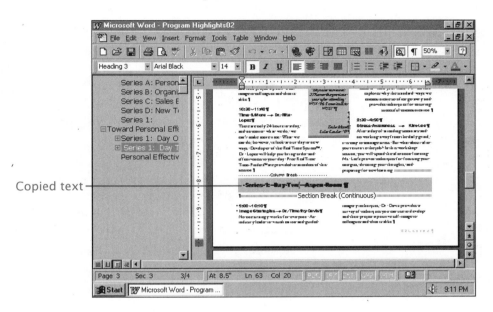

Copied text

 IMPORTANT If the word "Two" does not replace the word "One" but instead appears next to "One," be sure that the Typing Replaces Selection check box is selected on the Edit tab of the Options dialog box of the Tools menu. For more information, see the Edit Options section in Appendix B, "Matching the Exercises."

Moving Text Over a Long Distance

Moving text over a long distance within a document is similar to copying text over a long distance. The Standard toolbar makes moving text easy. The difference is that instead of copying the text, you *cut* the text from its original place in the document and store the text on the Clipboard. Then, you scroll to where you want to insert the text and paste it into the document.

Move text from the end of the document to the middle

You decide that people attending the first day of the conference might overlook the last three paragraphs after the schedule for Day Two. You decide to change the layout of the scheduling information. In this exercise, you'll move the last three paragraphs so that they appear at the end of the first day's schedule, on page 3.

1 In the left side of the window, click the heading "Personal Effectiveness Hospitality Room."

The insertion point moves to this heading in the right side of the window.

2 Select the two-line heading and the following paragraph. Do not select the last paragraph mark in the document.

Cut

3 On the Standard toolbar, click the Cut button.

The text is removed from the document and stored on the Clipboard.

Previous Page

4 Click the Previous Page scroll button at the bottom of the vertical scroll bar to move quickly to the previous page.

5 Scroll downward, if necessary, and place the insertion point at the start of the heading "Series 1: Day Two – Aspen Room."

Paste

6 On the Standard toolbar, click the Paste button to insert the text from the Clipboard.

Close the Document Map

Document Map

➤ On the Standard toolbar, click the Document Map button.

Save the document

➤ On the Standard toolbar, click the Save button.

Save

Microsoft Word saves the changes you made in this document.

 **NOTE** If you'd like to build on the skills that you learned in this lesson, you can do the One Step Further. Otherwise, skip to "Finish the lesson."

One Step Further: Summarizing a Document

To get an idea of the contents of a long document, you can have Word summarize the document for you. By using the AutoSummarize command on the Tools menu, you can identify the kind of summary you want and how you want to view the summarized information. If you choose to view a highlighted summary in the document window, you can adjust the amount of detail you want to see.

Summarize a document

Your colleagues at West Coast Sales contributed to this document, but it was assembled by an assistant, so you are not familiar with its contents. In this exercise, you use the AutoSummarize feature to learn more about the information in the document.

1 On the Tools menu, click AutoSummarize.

After summarizing the document, Word displays the AutoSummarize dialog box.

AutoSummarize options ─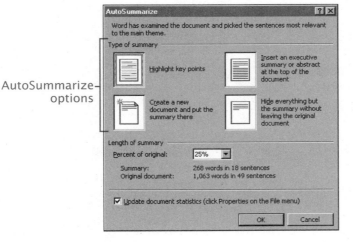

2 Click the first box to see a highlighted summary of the document.

3 Click OK.

You can also display only the summarized text, add summarized text to the start of the document, or create a new document that contains the summarized text.

The important ideas and text are highlighted in the document window. The AutoSummarize toolbar allows you to hide or display only the summarized text and to change the amount of detail highlighted.

4 Scroll through the document to review the highlights.

5 On the AutoSummarize toolbar, click the Close button.

Finish the lesson

1 To continue to the next lesson, on the File menu, click Close.

If you are prompted to save your changes, click Yes.

2 If you are finished using Microsoft Word for now, on the File menu, click Exit.

Lesson Summary

To	Do this	Button
Open an existing document	Click the Open button, and in the File Name list, double-click the document name. If you don't see the document name, check to make sure that the correct drive and folder are selected.	
Display the document headings	On the Standard toolbar, click Document Map button.	
Preview a document before opening it	In the Open dialog box, click the Preview button.	
Adjust the magnification of the screen	On the Standard toolbar, click the Zoom down arrow, and then select your magnification preference.	100%
Move or copy text to a location not currently visible	Select the text, and click the Cut or Copy button on the Standard toolbar. Scroll to the new location, and click. Click the Paste button to insert the selection.	
Display a document in different views	Click the appropriate view button located to the left of the horizontal scroll bar.	

For online information about	On the Help menu, click Contents And Index, click the Index tab, and then type
Opening and saving documents	**opening documents** **saving documents**
Moving and copying text	**text, editing**
Scrolling through a document	**scrolling**

Changing the Appearance of Text

In this lesson you will learn how to:

- Apply formatting.
- Change the magnification of the document window.
- Set paragraph indents.
- Create numbered and bulleted lists.
- Align text in columns with tabs.
- Add a border around a paragraph.
- Change the line spacing within and between paragraphs.

Estimated time
60 min.

Changing the appearance of your text allows you to enhance the look of your document. More than mere aesthetics, the appearance of your documents can make the material easier to read and can help your reader quickly locate important ideas. In this lesson, you'll learn about using the buttons on the Formatting toolbar to emphasize and align text. You will also indent paragraphs, add a border around a paragraph, and add bullets and numbers to lists. You'll increase the space between lines within a paragraph and between paragraphs. And you'll learn to adjust the magnification of the document window to see more of the page at one time.

Start the lesson

Follow the steps below to open the practice file called 03Lesson, and then save the file with the new name Speaker Letter03.

Open

*Look In
Favorites*

1 On the Standard toolbar, click the Open button.

2 Make sure the Winword SBS Practice folder is in the Look In box.

You can click the Look In Favorites button to display the Winword SBS Practice folder, and then double-click the Winword SBS Practice folder.

3 In the file list, double-click the 03Lesson file to open it.

This file is a draft of a letter that provides additional conference information to the motivational speaker hired to deliver the opening remarks.

4 On the File menu, click Save As.

The Save As dialog box appears.

5 Click the Look In Favorites button, and then double-click the SBS Word folder.

6 Be sure Word Document is in the Save As Type box. Select and delete any text in the File Name box, and then type **Speaker Letter03**

7 Click Save, or press ENTER.

If you share your computer, the screen display might have changed since your last lesson. If your screen does not look similar to the illustrations as you work through this lesson, see Appendix B, "Matching the Exercises."

Applying Character and Paragraph Formatting

When you change the appearance of text—by centering it or by making it bold or italic, for example—you are *formatting* the text. Character formatting and paragraph formatting are two examples of formatting you can use to change the appearance of text. Character formatting, such as bold, italic, underlining, and highlighting, affects only selected text. Paragraph formatting, such as center alignment or indentation, affects entire paragraphs. The Formatting toolbar gives you quick access to the formatting options you are likely to use most often. Additional character formatting options are available by using the Font command, and additional paragraph formatting options are available by using the Paragraph command.

TROUBLESHOOTING The AutoFormat feature might be affecting your formatting. To turn AutoFormatting off, on the Format menu, click AutoFormat , and then click Options. On the AutoFormat As You Type tab, clear the Define Styles Based On Your Formatting check box, and then click OK.

Changing Character Formatting

On the Formatting toolbar, you can click a button to apply bold, italic, underlining, and highlighting to selected text. For example, you select text and then click the Bold button to apply bold formatting. If you click the Bold button again, you remove the bold formatting from the selected text. The Formatting toolbar also contains Font and Font Size boxes for changing the type face and the type size of selected text. Additional character formatting options—such as small caps—are available in the Font dialog box.

NOTE   Your printer might not be able to print combinations of formatting applied to the same word. Check your printer documentation for any limitations.

Apply bold formatting

As the conference coordinator for the West Coast Sales national sales confer-ence, you want to add the finishing touches to a letter to the keynote speaker. In this exercise, you will apply bold and italic formatting to the company name in the signature block. You begin by selecting the text you want to format.

1   Press CTRL+END to move to the end of the document.

2   Position the mouse pointer in the invisible selection bar to the left of the company name "West Coast Sales."

When the mouse pointer is in the selection bar, the pointer changes to a right-pointing arrow.

3   Click to select the line.

4   On the Formatting toolbar, click the Bold and Italic buttons.

Click anywhere to deselect the text. The formatted text should look like the following illustration.

Bold

Italic

   TIP   To apply character formatting to a single word, you do not need to select the word. When no text is selected, Microsoft Word applies character formatting to the current word (the one containing the insertion point).

Change the design and size of text

Microsoft Word displays your text in the font and font size in which it will print. The *font* is the design of the text characters (letters, punctuation, and numbers), and the *font size*, which is measured in points, is how large the characters are. A point is a standard measurement in the publishing industry. There are 72 points in an inch. The larger the number of points, the larger the text. You can change the font and font size for selected text by selecting from the Font and Font Size lists on the Formatting toolbar.

1 Click in the selection bar next to the company name to select the line "West Coast Sales."

2 To display the list of fonts, click the Font down arrow.

The font names in your list might be different from those shown in this illustration.

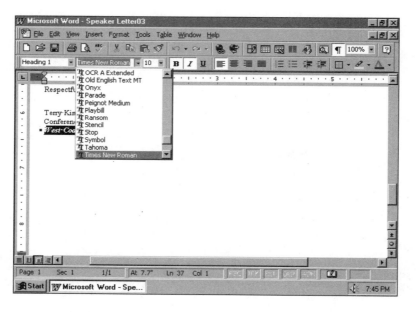

3 On the list of fonts, click Arial.

You might have to scroll up to Arial. The selected text changes to Arial.

4 To display a list of font sizes for the font you've selected, click the Font Size down arrow.

5 On the list of font sizes, click 9.

46

Copy formatting to text

If you plan to use the same formatting in different places in your document, you can save time by copying the formatting with the Format Painter. Double-click the Format Painter button if you're going to copy formatting to several locations, or just click the button if you're going to copy formatting only once.

Format Painter

1 In the signature block, verify that the line "West Coast Sales" is selected.

2 On the Standard toolbar, double-click the Format Painter button to store formatting information.

The mouse pointer now has a paint brush icon next to it. You are going to copy the formatting of the signature line.

3 Press CTRL+HOME to move to the beginning of the document.

4 Drag the pointer across the text "West Coast Sales" in the first body paragraph.

The formatting from the signature block text is applied to this text.

5 Drag the pointer across the text "West Coast Sales" in the "Corporate strategies" paragraph to apply the formatting from the signature block line to this text.

6 Click the Format Painter button to turn off the copy formatting feature.

Apply additional formatting to text

1 In the "Corporate strategies" paragraph, place the insertion point in the word "both."

To change the formatting of a single word, you do not need to select the word first.

Underline

2 On the Formatting toolbar, click the Underline button.

The word "both" is underlined.

3 In the paragraph that begins with the text "Note," select the text "immediately after the dinner."

Italic

4 On the Formatting toolbar, click the Italic button.

The text "immediately after the dinner" is italic. Click anywhere to deselect the text.

Using Additional Formatting Options

In the Font dialog box, there are additional character formatting options you can choose beyond what is available on the Formatting toolbar.

When you click the Format menu and then click Font, you can choose from the character formatting options on the Font tab. These options are described in the following table.

47

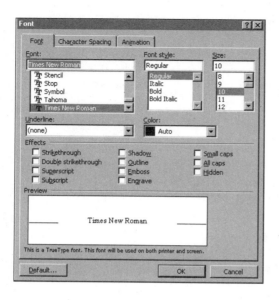

Option	Description
Font	Choose a font from the Font list. This option is the same as clicking the Font arrow on the Formatting toolbar.
Font Style	Choose a style from the Font Style list. This option is the same as clicking the Bold and Italic buttons on the Formatting toolbar.
Size	Choose or type a point size. This option is the same as clicking the Font Size arrow on the Formatting toolbar.
Underline	Choose an underline style from the Underline list by clicking the down arrow. Examples of underlining options include:

> **Single** applies a <u>single, continuous underline to the selected text</u>.
>
> **Words Only** applies a <u>single</u> <u>underline</u> <u>to</u> <u>each</u> <u>word</u> <u>and</u> <u>punctuation</u>.
>
> **Double** applies a <u>double, continuous underline</u>.
>
> **Dotted** applies a <u>dotted single continuous underline</u>|
>
> **Thick** applies a <u>thick single continuous underline</u>.
>
> **Dash** applies a <u>dashed single continuous underline</u>.
>
> **Dot Dash** applies a <u>single continuous underline composed of dots and dashes</u>.
>
> **Dot Dot Dash** applies a <u>single continuous repeating underline of two dots and a dash</u>.
>
> **Wave** applies a <u>single continuous wavy underline to the selected text</u>.

Option	Description
Color	Choose a text color by clicking the Color down arrow, and selecting a color.
Effects	Choose a font effect. Examples of effects options include:

> **Strikethrough** ~~looks like this~~
> **Double strikethrough** ~~looks like this~~
> **Superscript** looks like this
> **Subscript** looks like this
> **Shadow looks like this**
> **Outline** looks like this
> **Emboss** looks like this
> **Engrave** looks like this
> **Small caps** LOOKS LIKE THIS
> **All caps** LOOKS LIKE THIS
> **Hidden** looks like this

When you click the Character Spacing tab in the Font dialog box, you can choose from the following character spacing options.

Option	Description
Scaling	In the Scaling box, type the value by which you want to increase the width of characters.
Spacing	In the Spacing box, choose Normal, Condensed, or Expanded to adjust the amount of space between characters. In the By box, you can select the exact amount of space (measured in points) to use.
Position	In the Position box, choose Normal, Raised, or Lowered positioning to adjust the height of the characters above or below the line. In the By box, you can select the exact amount of space (measured in points) to use above or below the line.
Kerning	Click the Kerning For Font check box to specify whether you want the space between pairs of certain characters to be automatically adjusted for you based on the size of the font.

When you apply an animation effect, your text actually moves, flashes, or twinkles, depending on the effect you've applied. When you click the Animation tab in the Font dialog box, you can choose from the following animation options.

Option	Description
Blinking Background	Background around the text flashes on and off.
Las Vegas Lights	Small shapes of various colors flash and move around the text.
Marching Black Ants	A black dashed line flashes as it moves around the text.
Marching Red Ants	A red dashed line flashes as it moves around the text.
Shimmer	Text shimmers as if reflected in water.
Sparkle Text	Confetti-like colored shapes flash and move randomly around the text.

Displaying More of the Document at Once

When your work in a document focuses heavily on paragraph formatting, it is often useful to see more of the document at one time. By viewing several paragraphs (or even the entire document) at once, you can check the alignment, indentation, and spacing of the paragraphs and make additional adjustments as required. In the Zoom list, there are preset zoom settings you can use to magnify or reduce the document in the document window. You can also type in a value to change the magnification settings to whatever setting you prefer.

Change the magnification

You can adjust the magnification to get an overall view of the page width.

Zoom

1 Click the Zoom down arrow, and then click Page Width.

2 Click the Page Layout View button to the left of the horizontal scroll bar.

Your document should look like the following illustration. The actual font size does not change; only the appearance of the characters on the screen is altered.

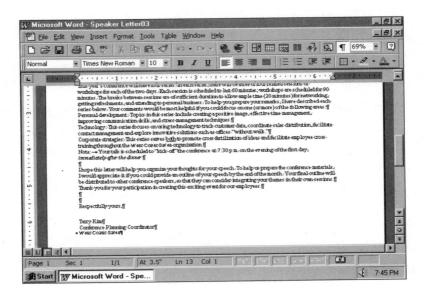

Changing Paragraph Alignment

On the Formatting toolbar, you can click a button to change the alignment or indentation of paragraphs. Using the ruler, you can customize indentation of both the left and right sides of a paragraph. Additional paragraph formatting options, such as adjusting line spacing and the space between paragraphs, are available in the Paragraph dialog box.

 TIP To apply paragraph formatting to a single paragraph, you do not need to select the entire paragraph first. When no text is selected, Microsoft Word applies paragraph formatting to the current paragraph (the one containing the insertion point).

When you change the position of a paragraph between the left and right edges of the page, you are changing the alignment of the text. Text can be left-aligned (which is the default alignment), centered, right-aligned, or justified.

Left-aligned means that all the lines in that paragraph begin at the same point on the left side of the page, and break at different points on the right side, depending on how the lines fit ("ragged right"). Left-aligned text is often used in the body of a business letter, or a book such as this one. *Right-aligned* means that all the lines in that paragraph end at the same point on the right, and begin at different points on the left, according to how the lines fit ("ragged left"). Return addresses and dates are often right-aligned at the top of a letter. *Centered* text extends in both directions from the center of the line, as seen in announcements and invitations, and is ragged both on the right and on the left. *Justified* text starts at the same point on the left for each line in the paragraph, and ends at the same point on the right; Microsoft Word adjusts the amount of space between each word to ensure a uniform edge on both sides of the paragraph.

Right align today's date

In this exercise, you will align the date with the right edge of the page.

Align Right

1   Press CTRL+HOME to place the insertion point at the top of the document.
2   Place the insertion point anywhere in the date line.
3   On the Formatting toolbar, click the Align Right button.

    The date is now aligned at the right margin of the page.

Setting Indents

You can quickly indent the left edge of a line or paragraph by using the TAB key or by clicking a button on the Formatting toolbar.

Using the Tab Key to Indent Text

An easy way to indent a single line of text is with the TAB key. You can insert a tab in front of the first character you want to indent. The TAB indents only the line that contains the insertion point. To indent multiple paragraphs at one time, using the Increase Indent and Decrease Indent buttons is usually a better choice.

Use a tab to indent a line

In this exercise, you use TAB to indent a line.

1   Move the insertion point in front of the word "Thank" in the first body paragraph.
2   Press TAB.

Using the Formatting Toolbar to Set Indents

Using the buttons on the Formatting toolbar, you can quickly indent one or more paragraphs. Each time you click the Increase Indent button, Microsoft Word indents all lines of the selected paragraph (or the paragraph containing the insertion point) a half inch. Microsoft Word has preset, or *default,* tab stops every half inch, so you are actually indenting to the next tab stop. The Formatting toolbar also has a Decrease Indent button that decreases the indent of all the lines of a selected paragraph a half inch.

Use the indent buttons

Increase Indent

If you cannot see the Format- ting toolbar, use the right mouse button to click an open area on the Standard toolbar, and then on the shortcut menu, click Format- ting.

1 Verify that the insertion point is still in the first body paragraph.

2 On the Formatting toolbar, click the Increase Indent button.

Your indented paragraph should look like the following illustration.

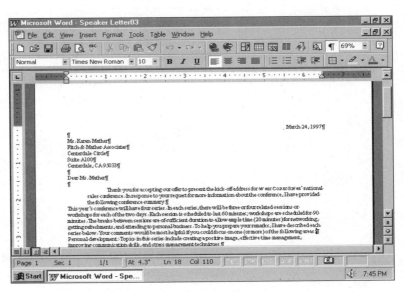

3 Click the Increase Indent button two more times.

Each time you click the button, the paragraph indents a half inch. The wordwrap feature rearranges the text to adjust to the new shorter line length.

Decrease Indent

4 On the Formatting toolbar, click the Decrease Indent button to move the paragraph left a half inch. Continue clicking the Decrease Indent until the paragraph reaches the left margin.

5 Click the Decrease Indent button again.

The text will not move past the left margin.

Indent several paragraphs

1 Select four paragraphs starting with the paragraph that begins "Personal development" and ending with the paragraph that begins "Note."

2 On the Formatting toolbar, click the Increase Indent button to indent the selected paragraphs a half inch.

3 Click anywhere to deselect the text.

Creating Bulleted and Numbered Lists

Bulleted and numbered lists are common elements in many documents. Bullets clearly separate list items from one another, emphasizing each point; numbers show sequence. The AutoFormat As You Type feature inserts a bullet and a tab whenever you type an o and two spaces (or press TAB) at the beginning of a line. To format existing text with bullets, you can click the Bullets button on the Formatting toolbar. You can also use the Numbering button to create a numbered list when you are typing new text or when you want to format existing text.

Create a numbered list

To draw attention to the paragraphs that identify the different topics covered at the conference, in this exercise, you will change three paragraphs of your document into a numbered list.

Numbering

1 Select the first three indented paragraphs, starting with the "Personal development" paragraph and ending with the "Corporate strategies" paragraph.

2 On the Formatting toolbar, click the Numbering button.

A number appears in front of each selected paragraph, and the indents adjust to separate the text from the numbers.

3 Click anywhere to deselect the text.

When the paragraph is longer than one line, the second line of text aligns with the line of text above, not with the number, as is shown in the following illustration. This paragraph formatting is called a *hanging indent*.

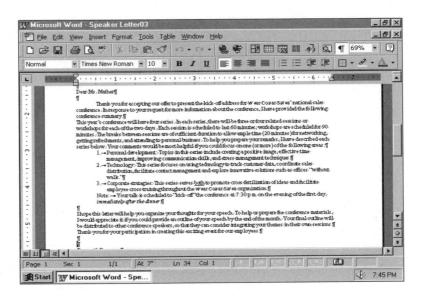

Insert another numbered paragraph

After realizing you omitted an important item in the list, you decide to insert a new numbered paragraph within the existing numbered list.

1 With the insertion point in the last line of the first numbered paragraph, press END.

2 Press ENTER.

A new blank numbered line is inserted. Notice that the remaining paragraphs are renumbered to reflect the addition of a new item in the list.

3 Type the following text: **Sales excellence: Topics in this series include prospecting, assessing customer requirements, delivering proposals, and closing the deal.**

TIP   Although using the Formatting toolbar buttons is the quickest way to create a numbered list, many more options are available through the Bullets And Numbering command on the Format menu. Use this command to change the number formatting.

Change the numbers to bullets

Because these items do not have to be presented in any particular order, you decide to list them with bullets rather than with numbers.

1 Select the numbered paragraphs.

2 On the Formatting toolbar, click the Bullets button.

The numbers are replaced with bullets.

Bullets

Create a new bullet character

The default bullet character is a simple round dot, but you can change the bullet character if you like. On the Bulleted tab in the Bullets And Numbering dialog box you can choose a new bullet character. If the bullet you want to use is not in the dialog box, you can choose from additional bullet characters. In this exercise, you change the bullet character for your bulleted list.

1 Select all the bulleted paragraphs, and click the right mouse button.

2 Click Bullets And Numbering.

3 Click the Bulleted tab, if it is not already in front.

4 Click the first box in the second row.

If you want to use a bullet character not displayed in the dialog box, you can click Customize to choose from other bullet characters.

5 Click OK.

6 On the Formatting toolbar, click the Increase Indent button.

The bullets appear as shown in the following illustration.

Increase Indent

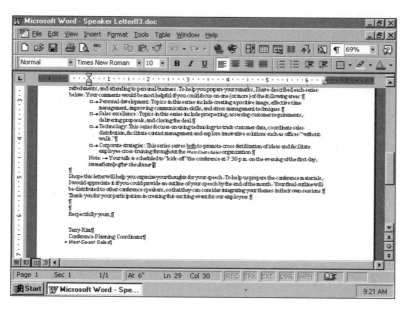

Remove bullets

You can remove the bullet in front of a line simply by clicking the Bullets button again. In this exercise, you type a new line of text and remove the bullet that Word applied.

1 With the insertion point at the end of the first bulleted paragraph, press ENTER, and type **This is our most popular series. Be sure to sign up early!**

2 On the Formatting toolbar, click the Bullets button.

The bullet is removed from the start of the line, and the text moves to the left margin.

3 On the Formatting toolbar, click the Increase Indent button twice to align the start of this line with the text above it.

Setting Custom Indents by Using the Ruler

Clicking the Increase Indent and Decrease Indent buttons is the fastest way to adjust a left indent in half-inch increments. Sometimes, however, you might want to use different indent settings. Using the ruler at the top of the document window, you can set custom indents.

For a demonstration of how to set custom indents by using the ruler, double-click the Camcorder Files On The Internet shortcut on your Desktop or connect to the Internet address listed on p. xxviii.

The markers on the ruler control the indents of the current paragraph. The left side of the ruler has three markers. The top triangle, called the *first-line indent marker*, controls where the first line of the paragraph begins; the bottom triangle, called the *hanging indent marker*, controls where the remaining lines of the paragraph begin. The small square under the bottom triangle, called the *left indent marker*, allows you to move the first-line indent marker and the left indent marker simultaneously. When you move the left indent marker, the distance between the hanging indent and the first line indent remains the same. The triangle on the right side of the ruler, called the *right indent marker*, controls where the right edge of the paragraph ends.

First-line indent marker

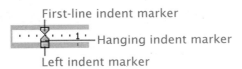 Hanging indent marker

Left indent marker

 TIP You can use the ScreenTip feature to identify the correct indent markers on the ruler.

57

Set a custom left indent

If your ruler is not already displayed, open the View menu, and click Ruler.

In this exercise, you will drag the left indent marker to adjust the entire left edge of the signature block, which will customize the indent settings for the paragraphs of the signature block in the letter.

1 Select the signature block at the end of the document, starting with "Respectfully yours."

The four lines are highlighted.

If only one marker moves, it means you dragged a triangle instead of the square. On the Standard toolbar, click the Undo button, point to the square, and try again.

2 Drag the left indent marker to the 4-inch mark on the ruler, and then release the mouse button.

Both the top and bottom triangles move. Use the dotted line to see where the new indent will be. When you release the mouse button, the text moves to align with the paragraph indent marker. Click anywhere to deselect the text.

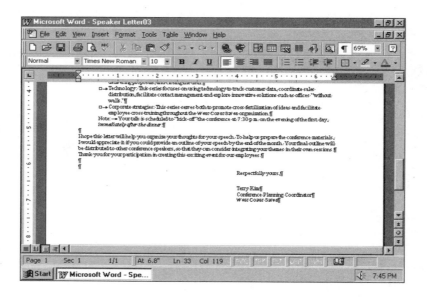

Set a right indent

1 Select the four bulleted items and the paragraph starting with the word "Note."

2 Drag the right indent marker to the 5.5-inch mark.

If you need to scroll to the right to see the right indent marker, scroll back to the left edge when you are done. Click anywhere to deselect the text.

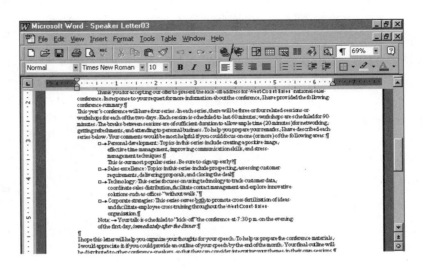

Set a hanging indent

The top triangle on the left of the ruler, the first-line indent marker, controls the start of the first line of a paragraph. To make the "Note" paragraph more distinctive, you decide to format that paragraph with a hanging indent by dragging the first-line indent marker, so that the first line of text extends to the left of the paragraph, with the rest of the paragraph "hanging" below it.

Only the top, or first-line indent, marker should move. If both markers move, it means you dragged the square instead of the top triangle. On the Standard toolbar, click the Undo button. Then point to the top triangle, and try again.

1 With the insertion point positioned in the "Note" paragraph, drag the first-line indent marker left to the .25-inch mark on the ruler.

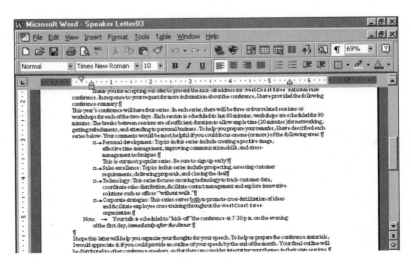

2 Drag the hanging indent marker (the bottom triangle) to the .75-inch mark on the ruler.

Make sure you click only the bottom triangle, and not the square. The first line does not move, but the "hanging" text is now aligned with the items in the bulleted list. Your screen should look like the following illustration.

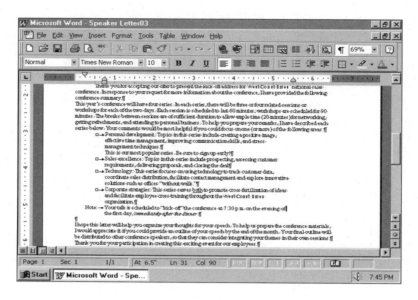

Indent the first line

If you know the exact measurements that you need for indents you can also use the Paragraph command on the Format menu.

1 Click in the paragraph starting "This year's conference."

2 Drag the first-line indent marker (the top triangle) to the .5-inch mark.

3 Repeat step 2 and indent the first line of all the remaining body paragraphs in the letter *except* the ones highlighted with bullets or the "Note" paragraph.

Aligning Text by Using Tabs

When you press TAB, the insertion point (and any text after it) moves to the first tab stop, located every half inch on the ruler. If you press TAB again, your text moves to the next tab stop. Because you can format the alignment of the tab stops to left-align, center, or right-align, you can use tabs to align text in rows and columns. You can also format tabs to align a column of numbers on their decimal point. This feature makes using TAB an easy way to, for example, create a simple table for a price list.

For a demonstration of how to create tabs on the ruler, double-click the Camcorder Files On The Internet shortcut on your Desktop or connect to the Internet address listed on p. xxviii.

Align text with tabs

To help your speaker plan an extended stay in your area after the conference, you decide to add a price list of nearby hotels to your letter. In this exercise, you will enter column headings separated by tabs.

1 Press CTRL+END to move quickly to the end of the document, and then press ENTER to create a new line at the end of the document.

2 Press BACKSPACE to left align the insertion point.

3 Type **Here is the hotel information you requested. If you would like us to make arrangements for you, please let me know.**

4 Press ENTER.

5 Press TAB, and then type **Hotel**

Left-aligned is the default formatting for a tab stop, so the left edge of your text is aligned with the first tab stop.

6 Press TAB, and then type **Description**

7 Press TAB, and then type **Rate per Night**

Create new tab stops

The defaults tab stops are located at every half-inch increment on the ruler, but you can create your own tab stops at specific locations. When you create a new tab stop, you can also specify its alignment, so that text you align with a tab is aligned the way you want. In this exercise, you want to adjust the amount of space between each column in the price list, so you create new tab stops.

Right Tab

1 Click the tab icon at the left end of the ruler until it looks like the Right Tab icon.

With this tab alignment selected, you place a right-aligned tab stop.

2 On the ruler, click the 1-inch mark.

A tab marker appears in the ruler, indicating the location of the first stop. The word "Hotel" is right-aligned on this new tab stop.

Center Tab

3 Click the tab icon at the left end of the ruler until it looks like the Center Tab icon.

With this tab alignment selected, you place a center tab stop.

4 On the ruler, click the 3-inch mark.

A tab marker appears in the ruler, indicating the location of the next stop. The word "Description" is centered on this new tab stop.

Decimal Tab

5 Click the tab icon at the left end of the ruler until it looks like the Decimal Tab icon.

With this tab alignment selected, you place a decimal tab stop.

6 On the ruler, click the 4.5-inch mark.

A tab marker appears in the ruler, indicating the location of the next stop. The text "Rate per Night" is right-aligned on this new tab stop. When you align text with the decimal tab, the text is right-aligned. Numbers will be aligned on the decimal point, starting from the right.

TIP In this exercise, you do not need to be concerned if you do not place the tab stops in the exact location. Simply drag the marker to the location you want. To remove the tab marker, you can drag the marker from the ruler. You can also use the Tab command on the Format menu to place tab stops more precisely.

Type text in the price list

With the tab stops established in the current paragraph, you can type the remaining lines of text in the price list. Each line will be aligned according to the tab stops you created.

1 Press ENTER to create a new line.

Like other paragraph formatting, the tab stops you've created are carried forward to the next paragraph when you press ENTER.

2 Press TAB, and then type **Plaza Arms**

3 Press TAB, and then type **200, 4-star restaurant**

4 Press TAB, and then type **275.50**

5 Press ENTER to create a new line.

6 Complete the remainder of the price list with the following information. Remember to press ENTER at the end of each line and to press TAB to move to the next tab stop.

City Suites	**large, studio-style rooms**	**171.15**
Country Views	**quiet rooms, golf course, pool**	**199.79**
Anna's Inn	**bed and breakfast, in-room whirlpools**	**179.25**

For a demonstration of how to add leaders, double-click the Camcorder Files On The Internet shortcut on your Desktop or connect to the Internet address listed on p. xxviii.

Add leaders to the price list

To make your text easier to follow, you can insert leaders in the price list.

1 Select all the columns in the price list.

2 On the Format menu, click Tabs to open the Tab dialog box.

3 In the Tabs Stop Position list, click 1". In the Leader area, be sure the None option is selected.

You don't want leaders to precede the first column.

4 Click Set.

5 In the Tabs Stop Position list, click 3.5". In the Leader area, select the 2 option, and then click Set.

6 In the Tabs Stop Position list, click 4.5". In the Leader area, select the 2 option ,and then click Set.

7 Click OK.

The Tab dialog box closes. Leaders are inserted between the first and second columns and the second and third columns.

NOTE Decimal tab alignment is especially useful when you are aligning numbers formatted with a proportional spaced font. A *proportional spaced font* means that some characters take up more space than others. For example, a 9 takes up more space than a 1. Most of the fonts on your computer are proportional fonts, so you should use a decimal tab whenever you are aligning numbers with tabs.

Adding Borders to a Paragraph

To create a line above, below, around, or on each side of a paragraph, you can use the Outside Border button. By using the Outside Border button, you can choose the parts of the paragraph to which you want to add a border.

Add an outside border to a paragraph

To draw even more attention to the "Note" text, you can add a box border around the paragraph.

Outside Border

➤ With the insertion point in the "Note" paragraph, click the Outside Border button.

The "Note" paragraph is surrounded by a thin black border as shown in the following illustration.

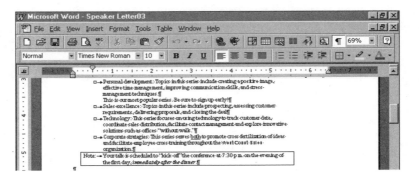

Tables And Borders

NOTE Additional border options (such as line style and weight) are available on the Tables And Borders toolbar. You can display this toolbar by clicking the Tables And Borders button on the Standard toolbar. You can use the Borders And Shading command on the Format menu to apply a variety of preset border options. From the Borders and Shading dialog box, you also have the option to display the Tables And Borders toolbar.

Changing Paragraph Spacing

Often a document is easier to read if there is additional space between lines and between paragraphs. By using the Paragraph command, you can change the line spacing of a paragraph and the space between paragraphs, as well as other paragraph formatting options.

Instead of pressing ENTER to add blank lines before and after text, you can specify the exact spacing between paragraphs. This method gives you more flexibility and precision, because you can increase spacing by a fraction of a line—for example, by .5 or 1.75 lines—instead of by whole lines.

Add spacing after a paragraph

To set off the second body paragraph from the bulleted list, you can increase the space after the paragraph.

1   Place the insertion point in the second body paragraph.
2   On the Format menu, click Paragraph.
3   In the Spacing area, click the After up arrow twice so that 12 pt appears.

In the Preview box, you can view the formatting before you apply it.

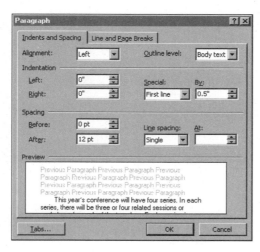

4   Click OK.

5   Place the insertion point in the last body paragraph, which starts with "I hope."

6   On the Edit menu, click Repeat Paragraph Formatting to repeat your last editing command.

Add spacing before and after paragraphs

You can increase the spacing before and after each paragraph in the bulleted list to better identify each item.

1   Select the four bulleted items and the "Note" paragraph.

2   On the Format menu, click Paragraph.

3   In the Spacing area, click the Before up arrow once so that 6 pt appears.

4   Press TAB and, in the After box, type **3**

These settings will insert 6 points of space before and 3 points of space after each selected paragraph.

5   Click OK.

Change the line spacing within a paragraph

By default, Microsoft Word creates single-spaced lines. If you want to provide more space between lines (for easier reading or to leave room for written notes), you can change the line spacing.

1   Place the insertion point anywhere in the first body paragraph, and then on the Format menu, click Paragraph.

2   Click the the Line Spacing down arrow to display the spacing options.

3   Select 1.5 Lines.

4   Click OK.

Your paragraph should look like the following illustration.

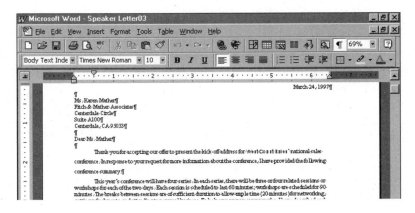

5 Repeat steps 1 through 4 for all body paragraphs, except the bulleted items and "Note" paragraphs.

6 On the Standard toolbar, click the Save button.

Save

 NOTE If you'd like to build on the skills that you learned in this lesson, you can do the One Step Further. Otherwise, skip to "Finish the lesson."

One Step Further: Creating an Instant Resume by Using the Resume Wizard

The Resume Wizard guides you through the process of creating an attractively formatted resume. Using this wizard, you can choose the style of resume you want and select other options. After you have established the basics of the document, you can type the text and edit the document as you wish. As you edit the resume document, examine the different kinds of paragraph and character formatting used throughout the document.

Start the Resume Wizard

In your role as a conference planner, you have asked potential speakers to provide resumes so you can include their profiles in the conference program. Use the Resume Wizard to create a resume of your own that the speakers can use as a model.

1 On the File menu, click New.

2 Click the Other Documents tab, and then double-click the Resume Wizard icon.

3 Answer the questions in the wizard dialog boxes to create a resume (of any type you prefer).

Save the resume

1 On the File menu, click Save.

The Save As dialog box appears.

Look In Favorites

2 Click the Look In Favorites button, and then double-click SBS Word.

3 Drag to select all the text in the File Name box, and then type **Model Resume03**

4 Click Save, or press ENTER, to close the dialog box and save the file.

Your file is saved with the name Model Resume03 in the SBS Word folder.

Finish the lesson

1   To continue to the next lesson, on the File menu, click Close for each document you have open.

2   If you are finished using Microsoft Word for now, on the File menu, click Exit.

Lesson Summary

To	Do this	Button
Set indents	Select the paragraphs to format, and click the Increase Indent button or the Decrease Indent button.	
Create bulleted lists	Select the paragraphs to format, and then click the Bullets button.	
Create numbered lists	Select the paragraphs to format, and then click the Numbering button.	
Set custom indents	Click in the paragraph to be indented, and then drag the triangular indent markers on the ruler to set the first line, left, and right indents.	
Add a border to a paragraph	Click in the paragraph, and then click the Outside Border button on the Formatting toolbar.	
Adjust spacing between paragraphs	On the Format menu, click Paragraph. Select the spacing you want in the Spacing area.	
Adjust line spacing within a paragraph	On the Format menu, click Paragraph. Select the line spacing you want from the Line Spacing list.	
View entire page width	Click the Zoom down arrow, and then click Page Width.	100%

For online information about	On the Help menu, click Contents And Index, click the Index tab, and then type
Adding borders	**borders**
Setting indents	**indentation**
Creating bulleted or numbered lists	**bullets and numbering**

Printing Your Document

Estimated time
35 min.

In this lesson you will learn how to:

- Examine a document in the Print Preview window.
- View multiple pages in the Print Preview window.
- Edit text in the Print Preview window.
- Insert page breaks.
- Print an entire document.
- Print individual pages and multiple copies of a document.
- Print an envelope.

After you create a document and get it to look the way you want, you frequently want to print the results of your efforts. In this lesson, you'll examine the layout of a document before printing the document. After you edit text and change the flow of text across pages, you'll print your document. You'll also learn how to print only the pages you want and how to print multiple copies. In addition, you'll learn how to print envelopes.

If you don't have a printer, you can still complete all the exercises in this lesson, except those that involve the actual printing.

Start the lesson

Follow the steps below to open the 04Lesson practice file, and then save it with the new name Speaker Letter04.

Open

1 On the Standard toolbar, click the Open button.

Be sure that the Winword SBS Practice folder is in the Look In box. If not, click the Look In Favorites button, and then double-click the folder.

2 In the file list, double-click the file named 04Lesson to open it.

3 On the File menu, click Save As.

The Save As dialog box appears.

Look In Favorites

4 Click the Look In Favorites button, and then double-click the SBS Word folder.

5 In the File Name box, type **Speaker Letter04**

6 Click Save, or press ENTER.

If you share your computer with others, the screen display might have changed since your last lesson. If your screen does not look similar to the illustrations as you work through this lesson, see Appendix B, "Matching the Exercises."

Speaker Letter04 is similar to the document used the previous lesson. It contains some additional text and formatting revisions to better illustrate the features covered in the exercises in this lesson.

Previewing Your Document

To get a better idea of how your document will look when you print it, you can use the Print Preview window. In the Print Preview window, you can see the overall appearance of one page, or you can see all the pages. You can see where text falls on a page and where it continues on the next page. After examining your document, you can make additional revisions to get everything just right. Previewing the document can save you time and paper, because it reduces the number of times you print the document before it looks exactly the way you want.

Preview the document

You want to get an idea of what the letter to the keynote speaker for next year's conference looks like before you print it, so you preview the document.

➤ On the Standard toolbar, click the Print Preview button.

Your document in the Print Preview window should look like the following illustration.

Print Preview

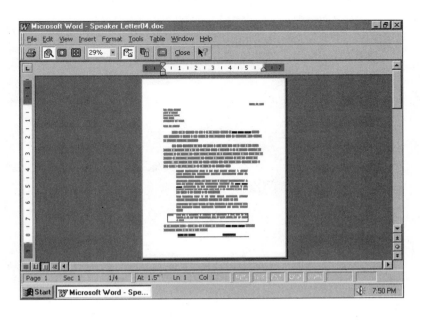

One Page

> **NOTE** If your screen does not match this illustration, on the View menu, choose Ruler to display the ruler in Print Preview. Click the One Page button if you see more than one page of the document.

The current page of your document is displayed in the Print Preview window. The Print Preview toolbar contains the buttons you use to preview the document; the menu bar still contains the same Microsoft Word menu items.

View other pages

Multiple Pages

➤ On the Print Preview toolbar, click the Multiple Pages button, move the pointer across the first two boxes in each row to select them, and then click the mouse button.

Now you can see all four pages of your document at once, as shown in the following illustration.

71

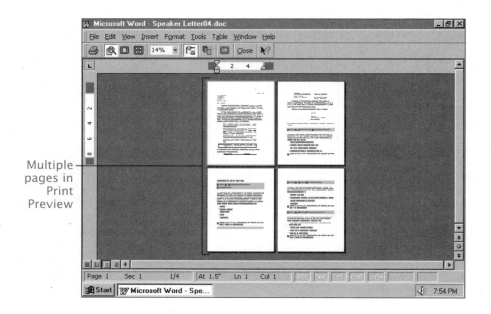

Multiple pages in Print Preview

Editing Text While Previewing

When you're in Print Preview and discover you need to make changes to your document, such as inserting, deleting, or formatting text, you do not need to return to the document window. You can make simple changes to the text directly in the Print Preview window. However, because nonprinting characters are not displayed in the Print Preview window, you should use Normal view, Online Layout view, or Page Layout view to complete more extensive editing or formatting tasks.

Edit text in Print Preview

You decide to add a brief comment to the beginning of the letter, so you zoom in on this part of the page. You do this by clicking the pointer near the text you want to magnify. Notice that the pointer changes shape to look like a magnifying glass as you move the pointer over the currently selected page.

1   Use the magnifier pointer to click near the first body paragraph on page 1 to get a magnified view of the page.

    Your screen should look similar to the following illustration.

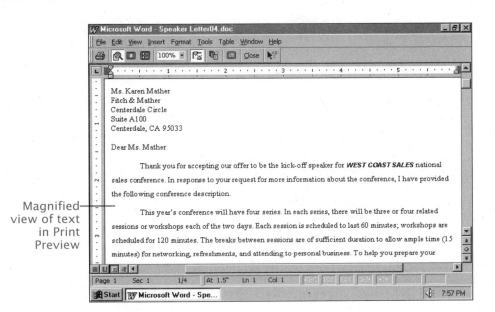

Magnified view of text in Print Preview

Magnifier

2 On the Print Preview toolbar, click the Magnifier button to change the magnifier pointer to the insertion bar.

3 To position the insertion bar, click immediately in front of the sentence that begins "In response to your request."

4 Type **After hearing your comments on a recent radio broadcast, I am looking forward to hearing your address at next year's conference.**

5 Press the SPACEBAR.

Inserting Page Breaks

For a demonstration of how to insert page breaks, double-click the Camcorder Files On The Internet shortcut on your Desktop or connect to the Internet address listed on p. xxviii.

Word inserts a *soft page break* automatically when you've typed as much text as will fit on a page. If you add or delete text somewhere on the page, the placement of the soft page break changes. Soft page breaks are indicated in Normal view by a dotted line across the screen. You cannot select or delete soft page breaks. If you are satisfied with the way Microsoft Word has arranged your text flow across pages, you can leave the soft page breaks as they stand. However, if you want to improve the balance of text across pages, or if you want to make sure that the page break remains exactly at the same point, even when you change computers or printers, you can insert manual page breaks (also called *hard page breaks*), either in the document window or in the Print Preview window. After you insert a hard page break, Microsoft Word repaginates the docu-

You can delete hard page breaks, but not soft page breaks.

ment, and changes any soft page breaks in the document as necessary. You can use hard page breaks anywhere in your document. If your document needs extensive editing or rewriting, you should not insert hard page breaks until the text is relatively final to avoid removing and reinserting page breaks as your text changes.

You can also control the flow of text across pages by using the Text Flow options available as part of the Paragraph command. You use Text Flow options to determine the flow of text for individual paragraphs. For example, you can format an individual paragraph so that it always appears on the same page as the next paragraph. You can also specify that the lines of a paragraph should appear together. These options are especially useful when you are writing text that you do not want separated by a page break.

Insert a page break

In this exercise, you will insert a page break to separate the letter part of the document from the conference program material.

Zoom

1   On the Print Preview toolbar, click the Zoom down arrow, and then click Page Width.

2   Scroll to the bottom of the second page, and then click to place the insertion point immediately after the period in the postscript at the end of the letter.

3   Press CTRL+ENTER.

This inserts a hard page break, and the following text moves to the next page.

4   On the Print Preview toolbar, click the Multiple Pages button, move the pointer across the first two boxes in the first row to select them, and then click the mouse button.

5   On the Print Preview toolbar, click the Close button.

Multiple Pages

6   Scroll down to see the new page break at the bottom of page 2.

In Normal and Page Layout views, the hard page break is represented by a dotted line labeled "Page Break." Neither the line nor the label appears in a printed document. Your screen should look similar to the following illustration.

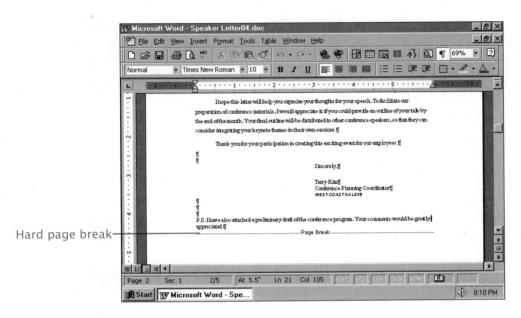

Hard page break

7   Save the document.

Controlling Text Flow

Depending on your printer, the way text flows across pages might be different. To make sure that the text you want to keep together on the same page or the text you want to separate on different pages always flows as you want it to, even on different equipment, you can apply specific text flow formatting to individual paragraphs.

Keep lines within a paragraph together

To ensure that all the lines within each paragraph in the table of names are never separated by a soft page break, you can use the Keep Lines Together option. For example, you want to make sure that the text "Duncan Mann" is never separated from the line *"West Coast Sales Award of Excellence."*

1   Select all the lines in the Name and Award table, except the table heading.

2   On the Format menu, click Paragraph.

3   Click the Line And Page Breaks tab.

The Line And Page Breaks tab moves to the front.

4   Click the Keep Lines Together check box to select it, and click OK.

A small square icon to the left of each line of the paragraph indicates that text flow formatting is applied to the text. The paragraph moves to the next page if necessary to keep the designated lines together.

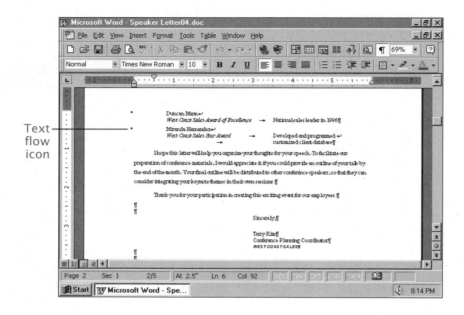

Text flow icon

Display paragraphs together

So that the paragraph that precedes the table never appears at the bottom of the page without the table, you can format the paragraph so that it is always on the same page as the table. To ensure that the paragraphs remain together and are never separated by a soft page break, you can use the Keep With Next option.

1   Select the table heading paragraph and the one that precedes it.

2   On the Format menu, click Paragraph.

    The Paragraph dialog box appears.

3   Select the Keep With Next check box, and click OK.

    The paragraphs move to next page to keep these paragraphs together.

NOTE   An orphan line occurs when the first line of a paragraph appears at the bottom of a page and the remaining lines appear on the next page. A widow line occurs when the last line of a paragraph appears at the top of page by itself. By default, Word prevents widows and orphans from occurring in your documents. If you prefer to control widows and orphans yourself, you can turn off the Widow/Orphan option on the Line And Page Break tab in the Paragraph dialog box.

Printing Your Document

Now that you have finished making changes, you are ready to print your document. You can click the Print button on the Standard toolbar to print the entire document using default settings, or you can use the Print command to select different printing options.

If you don't have a printer connected to your computer, you can skip to the end of this lesson.

> ## Printing While You Work
>
> Because Windows 95 and Windows NT are multitasking operating systems, there is no need to wait idly for your document to print. You can continue to work in Word or in other programs while your document is printing.

Print the entire document

Now that you are satisfied with the appearance of your letter, you are ready to print it. The Print button prints all pages of the currently active document on the default printer connected to your computer.

Print

1 Be sure the printer is on.

2 On the Standard toolbar, click the Print button.

The status bar displays an icon that indicates the pages are being "spooled" (sent) to the printer. The document prints on the printer connected to your computer.

Print two copies of the current page

Occasionally, you might want to print just a page or two from a long document, instead of printing all the pages. When you use the Print command, you have the option of printing only the page that currently contains the insertion point.

You can also print a document directly from the Print Preview window by using the Print button on the Print Preview toolbar or by clicking Print on the File menu.

1 Be sure the printer is on.

2 Double-click anywhere in the page number display on the left side of the status bar, and then type **1** in the Go To dialog box.

3 Click Go To to move to page 1 of your document, and then click Close.

4 On the File menu, click Print.

The Print dialog box appears.

Select the printer.

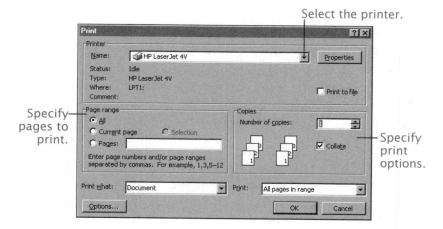

Specify pages to print.

Specify print options.

5 In the Page Range area, select the Current Page option.

6 In the Number Of Copies box, type **2**

7 Click OK to begin printing.

Printing an Envelope

If your printer can print envelopes, Microsoft Word makes it easy to address and print an envelope based on the information in an open letter. When you use the Envelope And Labels command on the Tools menu, you can specify the size of envelope or brand of label you want to print.

Print an envelope

1 Select the address block in your letter.

2 Place an envelope in your printer.

3 On the Tools menu, click Envelopes And Labels.

The Envelopes And Labels dialog box appears.

 NOTE The default envelope size is for a standard #10 business envelope. Click the Options button to select other sizes of envelopes.

4 On the envelope in the dialog box, be sure that both the return address (based on the user information you entered when you installed the software) and the recipient's address are correct. If necessary, use the dialog box to make corrections to either entry.

TIP So that you don't need to edit the return address each time, on the Tools menu, click Options. On the User Info tab, type the name and address information that you always want to use as your return address.

5 Click the Print button.

The envelope prints on your printer.

 NOTE If you'd like to build on the skills that you learned in this lesson, you can do the One Step Further. Otherwise, skip to "Finish the lesson."

One Step Further: Shrinking a Document to Fit

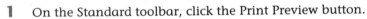

Occasionally, you may have a multiple-page document that has only a small amount of text on the last page. In Print Preview, you can use the Shrink To Fit feature to reduce the number of pages by one. Microsoft Word accomplishes this by reducing the document font sizes proportionately.

Reduce the number of pages by one

Print Preview

1 On the Standard toolbar, click the Print Preview button.

2 Click the Multiple Pages button, and drag to select all six boxes to display all five pages in the Print Preview window.

Multiple Pages

3 On the Print Preview toolbar, click the Shrink To Fit button.

The document now fits on one less page.

4 Click the Close button to return to Page Layout view.

Scroll through the document to view the changes.

5 Save the document.

Shrink To Fit

Finish the lesson

1 To continue to the next lesson, on the File menu, click Close.

2 If you are finished using Microsoft Word for now, on the File menu, click Exit.

Lesson Summary

To	Do this	Button
Display a document in Print Preview	On the Standard toolbar, click the Print Preview button.	
View multiple pages of the document at one time	On the Print Preview toolbar, click the Multiple Pages button. Drag across the number of pages you want to see at one time within the window.	
Display a document close up in Print Preview	Position the pointer on the document. When the mouse pointer changes to a magnifying glass, click the area of the document you want to view close up.	
Edit text in print preview	On the Print Preview toolbar, click the Magnifier button to change the pointer to the insertion bar.	
Insert a page break	Place the insertion point where you want the page break. Press CTRL+ENTER.	
Print all pages of a document to the default printer	Click the Print button on the Standard toolbar or on the Print Preview toolbar.	
Print a document using dialog box options	On the File menu, click Print. Select the options you want in the Print dialog box.	

For online information about	On the Help menu, click Contents And Index, click the Index tab, and then type
Previewing text	**print preview**
Printing documents	**printing**

Review & Practice

Estimated time
20 min.

You will review and practice how to:

- Create and save a document.
- Open and modify a document.
- Format characters and paragraphs.
- Preview and print a document.

In this Review & Practice section, you have an opportunity to practice the document creation and formatting techniques you learned in Part 1 of this book. Use what you have learned about creating and opening documents, and copying, moving, and formatting text, to create and modify the document in this scenario.

Scenario

West Coast Sales has launched a new product line as a result of acquiring a new company, The Terra Firm. In your role as the manager of corporate communications at West Coast Sales, you are charged with the task of creating documents designed to welcome The Terra Firm managers to the West Coast Sales organization. First, you will create a letter of welcome to The Terra Firm president. Then, you will modify a document that informs West Coast Sales managers of the new acquisition.

Step 1: Start Word, and Create a New Document

1 Start Microsoft Word.

2 Type a letter in the document. Use whatever name and address you wish. Be sure to include the date, several sentences in two different paragraphs, and a signature block at the end of the letter.

 TIP For a fast start, use the Letter Wizard, described in the Lesson 1 One Step Further.

For more information about	See
Creating a document	Lesson 1
Typing and inserting text	Lesson 1

Step 2: Save a Document

➤ Save the document with the name Review Letter01.

For more information about	See
Saving a document	Lesson 1

Step 3: Modify the Appearance of the Letter

1 Change the font size of all the text in the document to 12 points.

2 Center the date at the top of the page.

3 Indent the first line of the first and second body paragraphs to the first tab stop.

4 Indent all the lines of the signature block so that the left edge of the signature block is aligned with the left edge of the date.

5 Apply the correct text flow paragraph formatting so the lines of the signature block can never be separated by a soft page break.

For more information about	See
Changing character formatting	Lesson 3
Changing paragraph formatting	Lesson 3
Changing text flow	Lesson 4

Step 4:   *Preview and Print the Letter*

1   View the document in the Print Preview window.

2   Save and print the document.

3   If your printer can print envelopes, print an envelope to the recipient.

For more information about	See
Previewing a document	Lesson 4
Printing a document	Lesson 4
Printing envelopes	Lesson 4

Step 5:   *Open and Edit an Existing Document*

1   Open the document called 01Review, and save it as Review Memo01.

2   In the first paragraph of the memo (after the headings), move the second sentence of "Thanks to all..." to follow the last sentence in the "Get Ready to Sell" paragraph.

3   Copy the text "Terra Firm" in the cc: heading line, and then paste the text to replace the text "the Acquisition" in the "Getting Ready to Sell" paragraph.

4   Format all text occurrences of the words "West Coast Sales" and "The Terra Firm" to be Arial, bold, italic, and 10 points. Apply the small caps effect to this text as well. Do not apply this formatting to the headings.

5   Format all the italic headings as Arial, bold, and 12 points.

6   Create a bulleted list for the four items listed under the heading "Get Ready to Celebrate." Format the bulleted list so that there are 3 points of space before and after each paragraph. Indent the bulleted list to the first tab stop.

7   Insert a hard page break before the text "Acquisition Profile."

8   On the second page, format each of the four paragraphs that describe The Terra Firm products with hanging indents.

For more information about	See
Opening a document	Lesson 2
Moving text in a document	Lesson 2
Copying text in a document	Lesson 2
Changing paragraph formatting	Lesson 3
Inserting a page break	Lesson 4

Step 6: Preview and Print the Document

1 View the document in the Print Preview window.

2 Save the document, and then print only the last page of the document.

For more information about	See
Printing a specific page	Lesson 4

If you want to continue to the next lesson

1 On the File menu, click Close for each open document.

2 If a message appears asking whether you want to save changes, click Yes.

If you want to quit Microsoft Word for now

1 On the File menu, click Exit.

2 If a message appears asking whether you want to save changes, click Yes.

Part 2

Everyday Tasks Made Easy

Increasing Editing Productivity

Estimated time
50 min.

In this lesson you will learn how to:

- Identify and replace text.
- Find and replace word forms.
- Store and insert frequently used text.
- Check grammar and spelling.
- Locate objects in a document.
- Look up alternative words.

After you finish drafting a document, you might want to refine the existing text. With the Microsoft Word Find feature and the Replace feature, you can search for and replace both text and formatting. You can search for a onetime occurrence of a word, or you can search globally, which means for all occurrences of the word in the document. If you often repeat the same phrases in your document, you can work more productively by using the AutoText feature to store and insert frequently used text. In addition, every document draft can be checked for spelling and grammatical or stylistic errors. By using the Spelling and Grammar features, you can be sure your documents are letter perfect. And by using the built-in Thesaurus, you can get help choosing the exact words to convey precisely what you mean in your document.

Start the lesson

Follow the steps below to open the practice file called 05Lesson, and then save it with the new name Program Highlights05.

Open

1   On the Standard toolbar, click the Open button.

2   Be sure the Winword SBS Practice folder is in the Look In box. If not, click the Look In Favorites button, and then double-click the folder.

3   In the file list, double-click the file named 05Lesson to open it.

4   On the File menu, click Save As to open the Save As dialog box.

Look In Favorites

5   Click the Look In Favorites button, and then double-click the SBS Word folder.

6   Select the text in the File Name box, and then type **Program Highlights05**

7   Click Save, or press ENTER.

Program Highlights05 is similar to the document used in the previous lesson. Some text and formatting changes have been made to better illustrate the features covered in the exercises in this lesson.

Display nonprinting characters

To make it easier to see exactly where you are moving text in your document, you can display nonprinting characters.

Show/Hide ¶

 If paragraph marks are not already displayed, click the Show/Hide ¶ button on the Standard toolbar.

If you share your computer, the screen display might have changed since your last lesson. If your screen does not look similar to the illustrations as you work through this lesson, see Appendix B, "Matching the Exercises."

> **IMPORTANT**   To disable Automatic Spell Checking, click Options on the Tools menu, and then click the Spelling & Grammar tab. Click the Hide Spelling Errors In This Document check box to clear the selection. You can hide any green, wavy lines, which identify grammatical and punctuation errors, by clearing the Hide Grammatical Errors In Current Document check box.

Identifying and Replacing Text

In your role as the conference coordinator for the upcoming West Coast Sales conference, you are continuing your efforts to perfect the conference program. You can use the Find and Replace features to quickly find—and, if necessary, replace—all occurrences of a certain word or phrase. For example, you might want to find every instance of an outdated company name in a brochure and substitute the new name. You can make all the changes at once, or you can accept or reject each change individually. Either method ensures that the change is made consistently throughout the document.

Identify text to find and replace

The program document you opened refers to "series" for each set of sessions and workshops at the conference. However, each set should be called a "program" instead. In this exercise, you'll use the Replace command to locate the word "series" and replace it with the word "program." Before you begin replacing text, you'll make sure that no other options are in effect.

1   On the Edit menu, click Replace.

The Find And Replace dialog box appears with the Replace tab in front. For a simple replace, you can use the options available in this basic dialog box. However, for more advanced options, you can click the More button.

2   In the Find What box, type **series**

3   In the Replace With box, type **program**

If text is already in the Replace With box, select the text, and then type **program**

4   Click the More button.

The Find And Replace dialog box expands to show additional options.

5   Be sure that All is in the Search box.

If not, click the Search down arrow, and then select All. Word will search the entire document, rather than just up or just down in the document. Your completed dialog box should look like the following illustration.

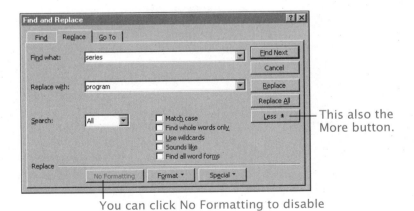

This also the More button.

You can click No Formatting to disable finding or replacing formatting.

6   To replace all occurrences of the word "series," click Replace All.

The changes are made, and a message indicates the number of changes.

7   Click OK to return to the Replace dialog box.

8   On the Replace dialog box, click the Close button to return to your document and view the changes.

Scroll through the document. The word "program" has replaced the word "series" throughout the document.

 NOTE   If you want to selectively decide when to replace a word, you click the Replace button to locate the first occurrence, and then click the Replace button (rather than the Replace All button) to make the specific change, *or* you click the Find Next button to skip the current selection and find the next occurrence of the word.

Finding and Replacing Formatting

While the Replace dialog box is open, you can also type the key combination for the formatting you want to find, such as pressing CTRL+SHIFT+H to search for hidden formatting.

You can locate text that has a specific format, such as bold or underline, and change the formatting as well as the text. You can also search for and change only the formatting without changing the text. For example, suppose you underlined division names in your document but now you want to make them italic and bold instead. With the Replace command, you can quickly find any underlined text and change the underline to italic and bold.

If the formatting you want to use is available on the Formatting toolbar, while the Replace dialog box is open, you can make your formatting selections by clicking the buttons on the toolbar. If the formatting you want to search for or replace is not available on the Formatting toolbar (such as Small Caps), you can click Format at the bottom of the Replace dialog box, and select the type of formatting you want to locate or replace.

 NOTE   In the Replace dialog box, some check boxes are dimmed by default. This means that Word won't search for the presence or the absence of this formatting. Each time you click such a check box, it toggles among the three options of not selected, selected, and selected but dim.

Finding and Changing Tenses of a Word

When you want to change a verb in your document, it is easy to forget to change other tenses of the same word. For example, if you want to change every "deliver" in your document to "bring," you also need to change "delivered" to "brought." Using the Find All Word Forms option in the Replace dialog box, you can use Microsoft Word to look for and correctly replace all forms and tenses of a word.

 IMPORTANT The Setup program you use to install Microsoft Word gives you the option to install or not install the Find All Word Forms option. You need to have this feature installed to see it in the Replace dialog box. If this option does not appear in the Replace dialog box, you can run the Microsoft Word Setup program again and specify that you want to install the Find All Word Forms feature only.

Change all tenses of a verb

In the conference program document, you want to replace "talk" or "talked" with the proper form of the word "speak." In this exercise, you will again use the Replace command, but this time you will also enable the Find All Word Forms option. When you use this option, you should not use the Replace All feature. Instead, you use the Replace command so that you can locate and examine each occurrence individually.

1　Press CTRL+HOME to move the insertion point to the start of the document.

2　On the Edit menu, click Replace. If the No Formatting button does not appear in the dialog box, click the More button.

3　In the Find What box, select the text and type **talk**

4　In the Replace With box, select the text and type **speak**

5　Be sure that All is in the Search box.

　　If not, click the Search down arrow, and select All.

6　Select the Find All Word Forms check box.

　　Your dialog box should look like the following illustration.

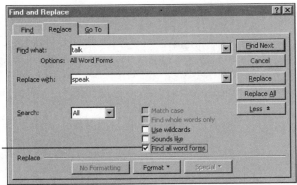

Click to search for all tenses of a word.

TIP If you are working on several documents in which you want to replace the same text, you can click the Find What down arrow and Replace With down arrow to select any text you searched for or replaced during the current Word session.

7 To locate the first occurrence, click the Find Next button.

Word finds the first occurrence of the word and displays a list of possible word forms.

8 Click the Replace button to make the change to the default word form and to locate the next occurrence. Repeat this step for each occurrence in the document.

9 Click the Close button to return to the document and view the changes.

TIP You can specify the direction in which you want Word to search for and replace text or formatting. For example, if the insertion point is at the end of the document, you can click the Search down arrow and choose Up to search and replace back through the document, from the end to the beginning.

Storing and Inserting AutoText Entries

You can use the AutoText feature to insert frequently used text. In addition to the common words and phrases Word provides as AutoText entries, you can also create your own AutoText entries, such as your company name or logo. When you create an AutoText entry, you have the option of assigning it to a menu or you can assign it an AutoText name, which allows you to type a few characters and then insert the entry by pressing F3. Because you can include symbols, graphics, numbers, and formatting, AutoText entries are particularly useful when entering serial numbers or text that requires complicated formatting.

Creating an AutoText Entry

You can begin creating an AutoText entry by selecting the text you want to store. Then, with the AutoText command on the Insert menu (you can also press ALT+F3), you can assign it an AutoText entry name. To minimize the amount of typing you need to do, use short names when naming AutoText entries.

Create an AutoText entry

As a special incentive to encourage employees to focus on specific programs at the conference, West Coast Sales is offering a "Bonus Bucks" promotion. Because Bonus Bucks is a term you expect to use frequently as you develop conference documents, you decide to create an AutoText entry.

1   In the paragraph below the first bulleted list, select the text "Bonus Bucks" (include the space after the text in your selection).

2   On the Insert menu, point to AutoText, and then click New.

   The Create AutoText dialog box appears.

3   Replace the existing text by typing **bb**

4   Click OK.

Inserting an AutoText Entry

If you prefer to insert AutoText entries from a toolbar, you can display the AutoText toolbar by clicking any toolbar with the right mouse button and then clicking AutoText.

You can insert an AutoText entry from the AutoText menu (on the Insert menu). You can also type the AutoText entry name and press F3, and Microsoft Word inserts the rest.

TIP   You can create a toolbar of AutoText entries by "tearing off" the command from the Insert menu. Point to AutoText, click the gray bar at the top of the cascaded menu, and then drag the bar to the location you want.

Use AutoText to insert text

In this exercise, you will type new text in the document and insert your new AutoText entry "Bonus Bucks."

1   Place the insertion point at the end of the paragraph under the bulleted list, type **For about 1000** and then press the SPACEBAR.

2   Type **bb**

3   Press F3.

   Word inserts the text "Bonus Bucks" as shown in the following illustration.

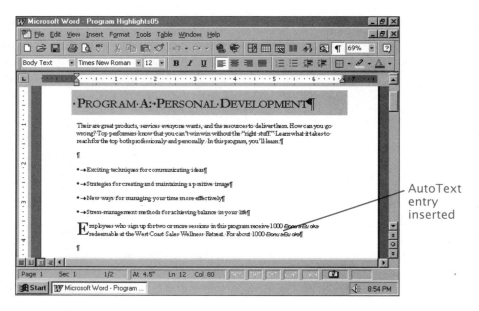

AutoText entry inserted

4   Type **you can enjoy a half-day stay at the retreat.**

5   Place the insertion point at the end of the paragraph under the next bulleted list, and type **For about 4000** and a space.

6   Type **bb**

7   Press F3.

8   Type **you can buy a laptop computer.**

9   Save the document.

Checking Spelling and Grammar

When you click Options in the Spelling dialog box, you can specify that you want Word to ignore certain types of words, including words in uppercase, words with numbers, and Internet and file addresses.

The Spelling And Grammar command identifies misspelled words or unknown words (that is, words that are not in Word's dictionary) and sentences that have possible grammatical errors or a nonstandard writing style. For many types of errors, the Grammar feature suggests ways to correct the sentence. You can choose the correction you want to make, or you can make your own changes directly in the document.

Although the Spelling And Grammar command provides a quick and convenient way to find many common spelling and grammatical errors, remember that no proofing tool can replace reading a document carefully.

Start the Spelling and Grammar tools

Microsoft Word normally checks the entire document, beginning at the insertion point. Although you can start proofing from any point in a document, in this exercise, you will position the insertion point at the top of your document.

IMPORTANT The Setup program you use to install Microsoft Word gives you the option to install or not install the Microsoft Word proofing tools, which include the Thesaurus and the Spelling And Grammar tool. You must have installed these components for them to appear on the Tools menu. If these components do not appear on your Tools menu, you can run the Microsoft Word Setup program again and specify that you want to install the proofing commands only.

1 Press CTRL+HOME to move the insertion point to the beginning of the document.

Spelling And Grammar

2 On the Standard toolbar, click the Spelling And Grammar button.

This button starts the Word spelling and grammar tools. The first high-lighted error is a grammatical error: the use of "their" instead of "there." Microsoft Word suggests considering "there" instead of "their."

Respond to the grammar and spelling errors

Microsoft Word provides explanations for the suggestions that it makes. In this ex-ercise, you learn about a grammar rule, delete repeated words, and check spelling.

Office Assistant

1 With the suggested grammar replacement still displayed in the dialog box, click the Microsoft Office Assistant button.

The Office Assistant displays an explanation of the grammatical rule concerning the usage of commonly confused words.

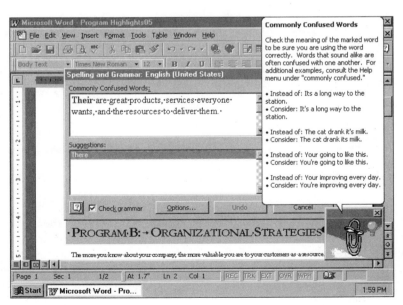

95

2 Click the Close button on the Office Assistant to close the explanation and hide the Office Assistant.

3 Click Change to insert the correct word.

The word is corrected, and the grammar checker identifies a repeated word.

NOTE Each time the grammar checker finds a sentence with a possible error, you can click the Ignore button or the Next Sentence button if you don't want to change anything. If you click Ignore, Microsoft Word ignores this occurrence of the "error" and continues checking the sentence. If you click Next Sentence, Microsoft Word skips to the next sentence. Click the Options button to specify which writing style you want to use. Click Settings in the Options dialog box to select which grammatical and stylistic rules you want to apply to your document.

4 Click Delete.

The next error is a misspelled word, "professionaly."

5 Click Change to insert the first suggested spelling.

6 For each possible error Word finds, do the following:

The problem	The solution
Whether to use "a" or "an"	Click the Office Assistant button, and review the explanation. Then, click Change to correct the error.
The word "companys" is misspelled	Select the word "company's" in the Suggestions box, and then click Change.
The word "youcan" is not in the dictionary	In the document, insert a space after the u, and then click Change.
The word "ByteComp" is misspelled	Click Add to add this word to the dictionary.
Whether "participants" is possessive or plural	This word is used properly. Click Ignore.

Locating Specific Parts of a Document

The Select Browse Object button near the bottom of the vertical scroll bar helps you locate a specific item or part of your document. After you click this button you choose the part of the document you want to locate. After Word finds the object you selected, you can move from occurrence to occurrence by clicking the Next Page and Previous Page buttons on the vertical scroll bar. For example, you can click the Select Browse Object button to specify that you want to move among the document headings, pages, sections, tables, or other objects in your document. Other options available when you click the Select Browse Object button include displaying the Go To and Find dialog boxes.

Find text

In the Program Highlights document, you want to find the word "environment" so you can further examine how it is used to describe the dynamic and turbulent sales industry.

Select Browse Object

1 Near the bottom of the vertical scroll bar, click the Select Browse Object button.

Select Browse Object pop-up menu

Find

2 Click the Find button.

The Find And Replace dialog box appears. This is the same dialog box you see when you click the Find command on the Edit menu.

3 In the Find What box, type **environment**

4 Click Find Next to locate this word.

Word selects the word in the document.

5 Click Cancel to return to the document.

Replacing a Word by Using the Thesaurus

You can use the Thesaurus to add variety and accuracy to your choice of words in a document. In the Thesaurus, you can look up alternative words for a selected word or expression. You can also locate antonyms to find words with the opposite meaning.

Look up an alternative word

The selected word "environment" does not have the exact meaning you want in your document. In this exercise, you will use the Thesaurus feature to look up an alternative word.

1 With the word "environment" still selected, on the Tools menu, click Language, and then click Thesaurus.

The Thesaurus dialog box appears.

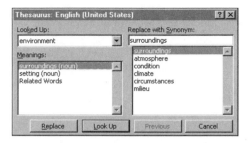

2   In the Replace With Synonym list, click milieu.

3   Click Replace.

The word "milieu" replaces the word you selected.

NOTE   If you'd like to build on the skills that you learned in this lesson, you can do the One Step Further. Otherwise, skip to "Finish the lesson."

One Step Further: Finding and Replacing Special Characters

You can use the Find And Replace feature to help you replace special characters, such as paragraph marks, tab characters, and manual page breaks in your document. For example, if you want to remove extra spacing between paragraphs in your document, you can use the Special button to locate two paragraph marks in a row and replace them with one paragraph mark.

Find and replace the paragraph marks

1   On the Edit menu, click Replace.

2   Click More if you do not see all the Replace options.

If the Special button is not available, clear the Find All Word Forms check box.

3   With the insertion point in the Find What box, click the Special button, and select Paragraph Mark.

Microsoft Word inserts a code that represents a paragraph mark.

4   Click the Special button, and select Paragraph Mark again.

5   Click the No Formatting button to clear any formatting specified from a previous search.

6   With the insertion point in the Replace With box, click the Special button, and select Paragraph Mark.

7   Click the No Formatting button to clear any formatting specified from a previous search.

8 Be sure that All is in the Search box. If not, click the Search down arrow, and then select All.

9 To replace all occurrences of double paragraph marks, click the Replace All button.

A message indicates how many changes were made.

10 Click OK to return to the Replace dialog box.

11 Click the Close button to return to the document and view the changes.

12 On the Standard toolbar, click the Save button.

Save

Finish the lesson

1 To continue to the next lesson, on the File menu, click Close.

2 If you are finished using Microsoft Word for now, on the File menu, click Exit.

3 If you see a message asking whether you want to save changes to Normal and you share your computer with others, click No. Your AutoText entries will not be saved.

Click Yes if you are the only one who uses your computer and you want to save the AutoText entries you created in this lesson.

 NOTE When you create AutoText entries, they are stored in a template document called Normal. This document contains information about the default settings in effect when you work in Microsoft Word. The options you enable (or disable) and your AutoText and AutoCorrect entries are saved in this template as well. This means that the entries you create in this document will be available in all your documents.

Lesson Summary

To	Do this
Find and replace text	On the Edit menu, click Replace. Type the text you want to find and the replacement text. Click Replace to move to the first word you want to change, and click Replace to replace each occurrence and move to the next. *or* Click Replace All to change all the words at once.

To	Do this	Button
Find and replace formatting	On the Edit menu, click Replace. Type the text you want to find and the replacement text. Use the buttons and options available in the Replace dialog box to specify the kind of formatting to find and the replacement formatting to apply.	
Create an AutoText entry	Select the text for the entry. On the Insert menu, click AutoText and click New. Type a name for the entry. Click OK to return to the document.	
Insert an AutoText entry	Type the name of the entry, and press F3.	
Check spelling and grammar in a document	On the Standard toolbar, click the Spelling And Grammar button. When Word highlights possible grammar or spelling errors, make the suggested changes or ignore them.	ABC ✓
Clarify a grammar rule	In the Spelling And Grammar dialog box, click the Microsoft Office Assistant button.	?

For online information about	On the Help menu, click Contents And Index, click the Index tab, and then type
Finding and replacing text	**find and replace**
Finding and replacing formatting	**find and replace character formatting**
Inserting frequently used text	**insert an AutoText entry**
Checking spelling and grammar	**proofing tools**

Establishing the Look of a Page

Lesson

6

Estimated time

45 min.

In this lesson you will learn how to:

- Set up margins for the entire document.
- Establish the paper size and orientation for a page.
- Create a header or footer that prints on every page.
- Work with alternating headers and footers.
- Specify a unique header or footer for each part of the document.
- Add footnotes to a document.

When you create multiple-page documents in Microsoft Word, it is easy to give all the pages of your document a consistent and polished appearance. In this lesson, you will first learn how to set the margins for the entire document. You'll change the orientation of a page in one section of the document. Finally, you will learn how to print additional information on every page in headers and footers and adjust the footers for different parts of the document.

Start the lesson

Follow the steps below to open the 06Lesson practice file, and then save the file as Program Highlights06.

Open

1 On the Standard toolbar, click the Open button.

101

*Look In
Favorites*

2 Be sure that the Winword SBS Practice folder is in the Look In box. If not, click the Look In Favorites button and then double-click the folder.

3 In the file list, double-click the file named 06Lesson to open it.

4 On the File menu, click Save As.

The Save As dialog box opens.

5 Click the Look In Favorites button and then double-click the SBS Word folder.

6 Select and delete any text in the File Name box, and then type **Program Highlights06**

7 Click Save, or press ENTER.

Program Highlights06 is similar to the document used in Lesson 5. Some text and formatting changes have been made to better illustrate the features covered in the exercises in this lesson.

Display paragraph marks

Show/Hide ¶

➤ If you cannot see the paragraph marks, click the Show/Hide ¶ button on the Standard toolbar.

If you share your computer with others, the screen display might have changed since your last lesson. If your screen does not look similar to the illustrations as you work through this lesson, see Appendix B, "Matching the Exercises."

Setting Up Document Pages

By using the Page Setup command on the File menu, you can define your margins, select your paper size, establish your paper source, and choose an orientation for your document. You also have the option of changing these settings for selected text, for the entire document, or from the current position of the insertion point to the end of the document.

Set document margins

The current version of the West Coast Sales conference program uses the default margins settings. To allow extra *white space* (a blank area) for graphics and other dramatic text effects that you plan to add later, you can increase the margins for the entire document.

1 On the File menu, click Page Setup.

The Page Setup dialog box appears.

2 Be sure the Margins tab is displayed.

3 In the Top box, click up arrow until 1.5" appears in the box.

This setting increases the distance between the top edge of the paper and the top edge of the document text, as shown in the Preview box.

4 In the Left box, increase the left margin to 2".

5 In the Right box, decrease the right margin to 1".

6 Click OK to return to the document.

 TIP You can also adjust the left and right document margins by using the ruler in Page Layout view. Position the mouse pointer near the gray edge of the ruler and when the mouse pointer changes to a double-headed arrow, drag to change the margins. To see the measurements for the margins, hold down the ALT key as you drag.

Preview the document

Print Preview

1 On the Standard toolbar, click the Print Preview button.

2 Click the Multiple Pages button, and then drag across all the squares.

Multiple Pages

Selecting all the panes displays all the pages of the document. When you are previewing multiple pages, the number of squares you select corresponds to the number of pages shown in the preview.

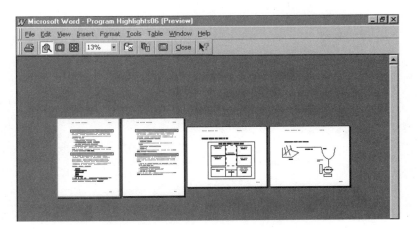

3 On the toolbar, click the Close button to return to Page Layout view.

Change the orientation of specific pages

The maps on pages 3 and 4 no longer fit properly within the new document margins you set. Although you can adjust the margins for just these pages, another solution is to change the setup of these pages so that the pages are displayed in *landscape orientation* (wider than they are tall) rather than the default *portrait orientation* (taller than they are wide). You can change the orientation on the Paper Size tab in the Page Setup dialog box.

1   Place the insertion point in front of the text "Getting Where You Want to Be" on the third page.

2   On the File menu, click Page Setup.

3   Click the Paper Size tab.

4   In the Orientation area, click Landscape.

    You can see the results of your change in the Preview box.

5   Click the Apply To down arrow, and choose This Point Forward.

6   Click OK to return to Page Layout view.

7   On the Standard toolbar, click the Save button.

    Microsoft Word saves the changes you made in this document.

Save

Delete the extra page break

Whenever you choose different page setup settings in different parts of a document—as, for example, when you choose This Point Forward in the Apply To list—Word inserts a section break between the two parts. This separation allows you to format each document section individually. When you change an option on the Paper Size, Paper Source, or Layout tabs, by default Word inserts a section break that begins on the next page.

This break is indicated by a dotted line labeled "Section Break (Next Page)." As a result, the existing hard page break (indicated by a dotted line labeled "Page Break") in the conference program is no longer needed.

1   Click the Normal View button to switch to Normal view.

2   Scroll down to the heading "Getting Where You Want to Be" to view the hard page break and the section break.

Normal View

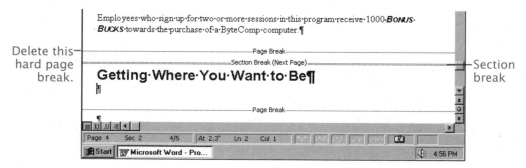

The graphics on the last two pages of the document are not visible at the moment.

3   Select the hard page break, and press DELETE.

Adjust the margins for a single page

Now that you have changed the orientation of pages 3 and 4 to landscape, you can adjust the margins for these pages as well.

1 Click the top of the third page, and make sure the insertion point is in section 2.

The status bar should indicate Page 3 Section 2

Page Layout View

2 Click the Page Layout View button to switch to Page Layout view.

3 On the File menu, click Page Setup.

4 Click the Margins tab.

5 In the Top box, change the top margin to 1.5".

6 In the Left box, change the left margin to 2".

7 In the Right box, change the right margin to 1".

Be sure This Section appears in the Apply To box. If not, click the Apply To down arrow, and then choose This Section from the list.

8 Click OK to return to the document.

Preview the document

Print Preview

1 On the Standard toolbar, click the Print Preview button.

2 Click the Multiple Pages button, and then drag across four boxes to display all the pages of the document.

Your document looks like the following illustration.

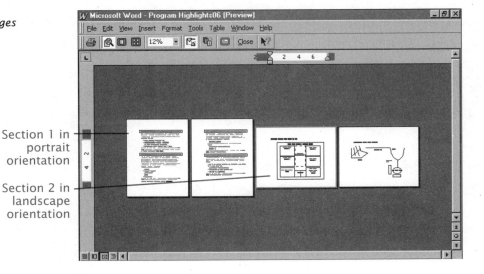

Section 1 in portrait orientation

Section 2 in landscape orientation

Multiple Pages

3 On the toolbar, click the Close button to return to Page Layout view.

4 Press CTRL+HOME to move the insertion point to the beginning of your document.

Creating Headers and Footers

In Microsoft Word, you can specify the information you want to appear on every page in the headers and footers. Text appearing at the top of every page is called the *header*; text appearing at the bottom of every page is called the *footer*. Headers and footers can contain whatever text you want, but you usually see information such as the date, the page number, or the document name.

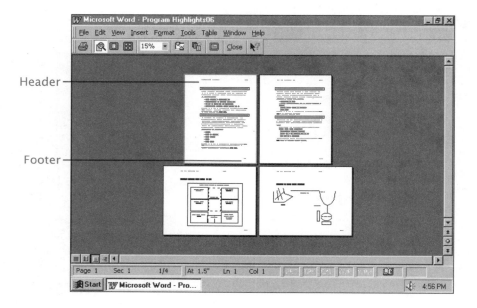

Viewing Headers and Footers

In Normal view, you cannot see headers or footers; in Page Layout view, the text in the header and footer areas appears in light gray. To create or edit headers and footers, you need to display the header or footer area by clicking the Header And Footer command on the View menu. You use the Header And Footer toolbar to help you add and modify headers and footers quickly.

When you view headers and footers, the header and footer areas are enclosed in a dotted box, and the body text is dimmed on the page. As a result, you cannot edit the body text while you are viewing and editing the headers or footers. You can use buttons on the Header And Footer toolbar to switch between the header area and the footer area, and insert the date, time, and page number.

There is also a button that hides the dimmed text if you find it distracting. If you want to modify the page setup, you can click the Page Setup button for quick access to the Page Setup dialog box.

View header and footer information

In Page Layout view, you can double-click the header or the footer to display it.

1   On the View menu, click Header And Footer.
    Your document looks like the following illustration.

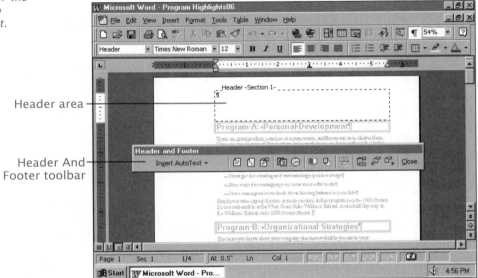

Header area

Header And Footer toolbar

TIP   If the Header And Footer toolbar obscures part of the document window, drag the title bar of the toolbar to dock (position) the toolbar anywhere in the document window. You can also double-click a gray area in the Header And Footer toolbar to dock the toolbar above the top ruler.

2   Click the Close button on the Header And Footer toolbar.

Creating Simple Alternating Footers

There are two ways to create headers or footers in a document. When you want to insert a page number on every page, you can use the Page Numbers command on the Insert menu. This command includes options to hide the number on the first page, and create alternating headers or footers. This means that all the odd-numbered pages have the same header or footer, while all the even-numbered pages have headers or footers that are different from the odd-numbered pages. When you want additional information to be included in the header or footer, you can work directly in the header or footer area and use the Headers And Footers toolbar to create customized headers and footers.

Insert page numbers

1   On the Insert menu, click Page Numbers.

    The Page Numbers dialog box appears.

2   Clear the Show Number on First Page check box.

3   Click OK.

4   Scroll to the bottom of each page and notice that no page number appears on the first page, but the page number does appear on the subsequent pages.

Create an alternating footer

In this exercise you will create footers that show the page number on the right side of odd-numbered pages and on the left side of even-numbered pages.

1   On the File menu, click Page Setup.

2   Click the Layout tab.

3   Click the Different Odd And Even check box.

4   Click OK.

5   On the Insert menu, click Page Numbers.

6   Click the Alignment down arrow, and then choose Outside.

7   Click OK.

8   Scroll to the bottom of each page and notice that no page number appears on the first page, but the page number does appear the outside edge on the subsequent pages.

Preparing for the Next Part of the Lesson

To insert additional information in a header or footer, it is best to remove the page numbers you created with the Page Number command. Because you will not be creating alternating headers and footers in the next part of the lesson, you can also disable this feature in the Page Setup dialog box.

Remove the existing page numbers

1   Double-click the page number at the bottom of page 2.

    The Header And Footer toolbar appears, and the footer area is active.

2   Select the page number.

    Shading appears over the number.

3 Click the edge of the shading.

Sizing handles appear on the shading.

4 Press DELETE.

5 Click the Close button on the Header and Footer toolbar.

The page numbers are removed.

Remove the alternating footer option

1 On the File menu, click Page Setup.

2 Click the Layout tab.

3 Clear the Different Odd And Even check box.

4 Clear the Different First Page check box.

5 Click OK.

Creating Customized Headers and Footers

By using the Header And Footer command, you can insert a page number as well as a date, time, text, and fields that contain document information. *Fields* are special instructions you insert in a document that tell Microsoft Word to supply specific information about the document or computer system. You can use the Page Numbers command to specify the starting page number and select a format for the numbers, such as uppercase and lowercase Roman numerals.

Enter text in the header

In this exercise, you will insert text and a date in the header.

If the insertion point is not in the header area, click the Switch Between Header And Footer button on the Header And Footer toolbar.

Insert Date

IMPORTANT If the page number appears in the document as {PAGE}, press ALT+F9 to turn off the display of field codes.

---

1 Make sure the insertion point is in the header area, and then type **West Coast Sales National Expo**

2 Press TAB twice to move the insertion point to the right margin.

3 On the Header And Footer toolbar, click the Insert Date button.

In the header area, the right-aligned tab marker is set to the right margin before you change the page orientation.

4 Drag the right-aligned tab marker in the ruler so that it is aligned with the 5.5-inch mark.

The header looks like the following illustration.

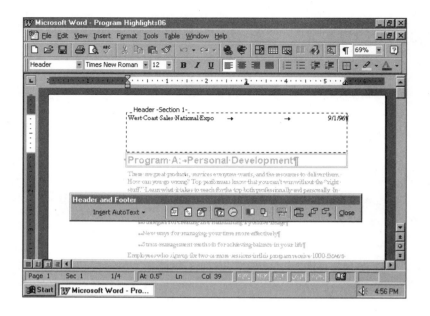

Enter text in the footer

Entering information in the footer is identical to entering information in the header. After moving the insertion point to the footer area, you can type and format text that you want to appear with the page number you will insert.

Switch Between Header And Footer

1   On the Header And Footer toolbar, click the Switch Between Header And Footer button.

2   Type **Page** and press the SPACEBAR.

Insert Page Number

3   On the Header And Footer toolbar, click the Insert Page Number button.

The page number appears next to the word "Page."

4   On the Formatting toolbar, click the Align Right button.

Align Right

5   On the Header And Footer toolbar, click the Close button to return to Page Layout view.

You can also double-click the gray document text when viewing the header or footer to exit the header or footer area.

  TIP   The Header And Footer toolbar includes an AutoText button. Click this button to insert common expressions and information in your headers or footers. See the One Step Further exercise at the end of this lesson to practice using the AutoText entries on the Header And Footer toolbar.

Preview the document

Print Preview

1   On the Standard toolbar, click the Print Preview button.

Your document looks like the following illustration.

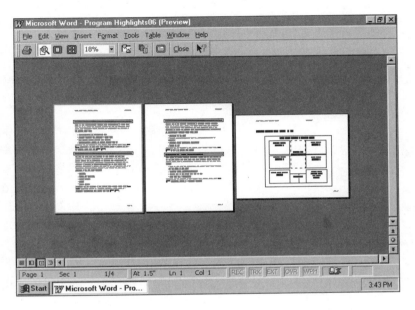

2   On the toolbar, click the Close button to return to the document in Page Layout view.

3   Save the document.

Numbering Different Parts of a Document

In longer documents, it is common to see different parts of the document numbered differently. For example, the table of contents pages might be numbered i, ii, iii, and so on. The second section would have a different numbering pattern and might be numbered as "Page 1-1, Page 1-2," and so on. To number parts of the same document differently, you first separate the document into sections by inserting section breaks for the different parts. Then, you can format the numbering in each section independently.

Break the link between sections

When you divide a document into sections, the header and footer information carries over from the previous section by default. To create unique headers and footers or page numbering for each section, you must break the connection between sections before you adjust the headers and footers. You break the connection between sections by clicking the Same As Previous button, which is depressed by default on the Header And Footer toolbar.

In this exercise, you will change the footer and page numbering of the second section, the pages containing the maps. Your document is already divided into sections for the pages you want to number differently, so you can proceed by breaking the link between sections.

Switch Between Header And Footer

1   Click to position the insertion point on page 3 (the first page of the second section of the document), and on the View menu, click Header And Footer.

2   On the Header And Footer toolbar, click the Switch Between Header And Footer button to move the insertion point to the footer area for this section.

In this example, the header remains the same in both sections.

Same As Previous

3   On the Header And Footer toolbar, click the Same As Previous button.

The button is no longer depressed. This means that the current section can have a different footer from that in the previous section.

Number the second section

Now that the document is separated into sections and the connection between footers is broken, you can format the page numbering of each section. You can also create unique headers or footers in each section. For the last two pages of the document, you will use the Roman numeral page number format.

Format Page Number

1   On the Header And Footer toolbar, click the Format Page Number button.

The Page Number Format dialog box appears.

2   In the Page Number Format dialog box, click the Number Format down arrow, and choose I, II, III.

3   In the Page Number Format dialog box, click the Start At button.

The numbering in this section is set to start at I.

4   Click OK to return to the Header And Footer toolbar.

The page number on the first page of this section is I, even though it is the third page of the document.

Modify the text in the footer

To make the footer in section two even more distinct from the footer in section one, you can modify the text next to the page number.

1   Position the insertion point in front of the word "Page" in the footer, type **Maps** and press the SPACEBAR.

2 On the Header And Footer toolbar, click the Close button to return to Page Layout view.

Preview your footers

Print Preview

Multiple Pages

1 Press CTRL+HOME to go to the top of document.

2 On the Standard toolbar, click the Print Preview button.

3 Click the Multiple Pages button, and drag horizontally across two boxes if two pages are not displayed.

4 Double-click near the bottom of page 2 in the second section to get a magnified view of the footer; scroll through the document to examine each of the footers on each page.

5 Click the Close button to close the Print Preview window.

6 Save the document.

Inserting Footnotes

In addition to footers, *footnotes* are another kind of text that can appear at the bottom of a page. When you want to make a reference to additional information in a document, you insert a footnote reference mark (or you can have Microsoft Word assign a number), and then you enter the text. If you add or delete a footnote, Microsoft Word renumbers the footnotes. Although you don't see the footnotes in Normal view, you can see them in Page Layout view and Print Preview, as well as when you print the document.

 TIP To edit a footnote in Normal view, double-click the footnote marker in the document. To edit a footnote in Page Layout view, double-click the footnotes pane of the document.

Insert a footnote

Normal View

To create an endnote, in the Footnotes dialog box, click the Endnote button. An endnote is placed at the end of a document instead of at the bottom of a page.

1 Click the Normal View button at the lower left of the window.

2 Move the insertion point to the end of the fourth bulleted item on page 2.

3 On the Insert menu, click Footnote.

4 Click OK.

5 In the footnotes pane, type **The Personal Effectiveness Hospitality room is available on both days of the conference.**

Your text in the footnotes pane looks like the following illustration.

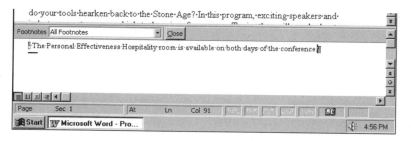

6 On the footnotes pane, click Close.

7 Click the Page Layout View button, and scroll down to see the footnote.

8 Save the document.

*Page Layout
View*

 NOTE If you'd like to build on the skills that you learned in this lesson, you can do the One Step Further. Otherwise, skip to "Finish the lesson."

One Step Further: Inserting AutoText Entries by Using the Header And Footer Toolbar

The Header And Footer toolbar includes AutoText entries that make it easier for you to create your document. These entries insert common expressions and information you frequently see in document headers and footers, such as the name of the author, the date the document was printed, the word "Confidential," and the filename.

Display the header and footer for the first section

In the Program Highlights document, you decide to include the author's name and the document filename to help you locate the document on your computer when you need to edit it in the future. You will add this information only to the first section of the document.

1 Press CTRL+HOME to move the insertion point to the beginning of your document.

2 Double-click the footer area on the first page.

The footer area opens for the first section of the document.

Insert AutoText in the footer for the first section

1 On the Header And Footer toolbar, click the Insert AutoText button.

A list of header and footer AutoText entries is displayed.

2 Click Filename, and press the SPACEBAR.

The filename of the document appears in the footer. Word inserts a space following the filename.

3 On the Header And Footer toolbar, click the Insert AutoText button, click Created by, and then press the SPACEBAR.

The text "Created by" followed by the author's name appears after the filename.

4 Click the Close button to return to the document text.

5 Save the document.

Finish the lesson

1 To continue to the next lesson, on the File menu, click Close.

2 If you are finished using Microsoft Word for now, on the File menu, click Exit.

Lesson Summary

To	Do this	Button
Establish margins in a document	On the File menu, click Page Setup. On the Margins tab, set the desired margins.	
Create a header or footer	On the View menu, click Header And Footer. In the Header Or Footer area, type the text or click the buttons for the data you want.	
View page numbers and headers or footers	On the View menu, click Page Layout.	
Break a link between sections	On the Header And Footer toolbar, click the Same As Previous button to deselect it.	
Insert a footnote	Click to position the insertion point where you want the footnote reference to be. On the Insert menu, click Footnote. Select the footnote option, and click OK. In the footnotes pane, type the text of your footnote, and then click the Close button.	

To	Do this	Button
Insert a date in a header or footer	On the Header And Footer toolbar, click the Date button.	
Insert a page number in a header or footer	On the Header And Footer toolbar, click the Page Number button.	
Create a simple header or footer	On the Insert menu, click Page Numbers. Click OK.	
Create an alternating header or footer	On the File menu, click Page Setup. On the Layout tab, in the Header And Footer area, click the Different Odd And Even check box. On the Insert menu, click Page Numbers. Click the Alignment down arrow, and then click Outside. Click OK.	

For online information about	On the Help menu, click Contents And Index, click the Index tab, and then type
Adjusting document margins	**margins**
Inserting and formatting page numbers	**page numbers**
Creating headers and footers	**headers and footers**

Using Styles

In this lesson you will learn how to:

Estimated time
45 min.

- Apply styles to text and paragraphs.
- Create a combination of formats as a character style.
- Store a combination of formats as a paragraph style.
- Apply styles quickly using AutoFormat.
- Use the Style Gallery to apply attractive formatting to an entire document.
- Change the definition of a style.

When editing and formatting a document, you might decide that all product names should be bold and italic or that paragraphs in a list should have a specific line spacing and right-indent setting. Instead of formatting every product name or paragraph in a list individually, you can save time and reduce the risk of errors by using *styles* to quickly apply a collection of format settings. By applying styles, you ensure fast and consistent formatting of text and paragraphs throughout your document. And when you modify a style, you save time because all text in that style is automatically reformatted.

In this lesson, you'll learn how to create and modify character styles to format characters, and you'll create and modify paragraph styles to format entire paragraphs. You will also learn how to use AutoFormat and the Style Gallery to apply a collection of a consistent group of styles to your document.

Start the lesson

Follow the steps below to open the practice file called 07Lesson, and then save it as Program Highlights07.

Open

1 On the Standard toolbar, click the Open button.

2 Be sure that the Winword SBS Practice folder is in the Look In box. If not, click the Look In Favorites button, and then double-click the Winword SBS Practice folder.

3 In the file list, double-click the file named 07Lesson to open it.

Look In Favorites

4 On the File menu, click Save As.

The Save As dialog box appears.

5 Click the Look In Favorites button, and then double-click the SBS Word folder.

6 Select any text in the File Name box, and then type **Program Highlights07**

Program Highlights07 is similar to the document used in Lesson 6. However, most of the formatting has been removed to better illustrate the AutoFormat features covered in this lesson.

7 Click Save, or press ENTER.

Display paragraph marks

Show/Hide ¶

➤ If you cannot see the paragraph marks, click the Show/Hide ¶ button on the Standard toolbar.

If you share your computer with others, the screen display might have changed since your last lesson. If your screen does not look similar to the illustrations as you work through this lesson, see Appendix B, "Matching the Exercises."

Formatting by Using Character Styles

Suppose you want to emphasize certain words, such as the name of each seminar in a conference brochure. So the name looks different from the surrounding text, you might format the seminar names in small caps, bold, and italics. Although you can separately locate and select each of these settings for each seminar name (a slow, tedious, and error-prone process), it is far easier to create a *character style*, which is a specified combination of any of the character formats.

By storing combinations of character formats—such as bold, italic, underline, *font* (typeface), and *font size* (type size)—as character styles, you save time and ensure that the formatting is consistent throughout your document.

Apply character formatting

The easiest way to create a new style is to take the style from text that is already formatted the way you want. In this exercise, you'll begin by formatting selected text to appear the way you want.

1 Select the text "Aspen Room" in the heading "Program A: Day One – Aspen Room."

2 On the Format menu, click Font to open the Font dialog box.

3 In the Font Style dialog box, click Bold Italic.

4 In the Effects area, click Emboss and click Small Caps.

5 Click the Color down arrow, and choose Turquoise.

6 Click OK to close the dialog box and return to the document.

Create a character style

After the selected text is formatted the way you want, you can create a character style based on that formatting.

1 On the Format menu, click Style to open the Style dialog box.

2 Click the New button to create a new style.

The New Style dialog box looks like the following illustration.

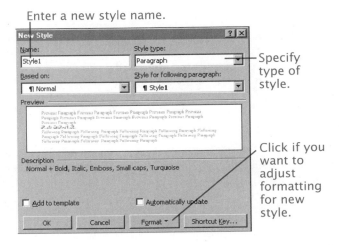

3 In the Name box, type **Room**

4 Click the Style Type down arrow, and then select Character.

This selection ensures that your style will be applied only to selected text, not entire paragraphs.

5   Click OK to return to the Style dialog box.

Your new style has been added to the list of styles in this document. The list of styles also includes the default styles provided by Microsoft Word. Character styles are identified by the letter a in the list.

Your Style dialog box looks like the following illustration.

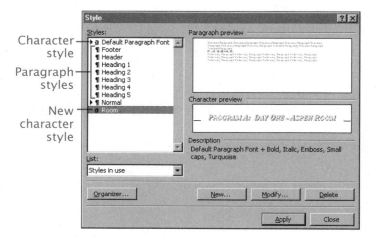

6   Click Apply to apply the Room style to the selected text and return to your document.

NOTE   You can give your style a name that is up to 255 characters long, including numbers, letters, and spaces; however, you cannot use the characters / \ ? : < > |. Two styles cannot have the same name.

Applying Character Styles

Once you've created a character style, you can apply it to any text you want formatted that specific way. After you apply a style, the selected text contains the same formatting as the text upon which you based the style.

NOTE   To create and modify character styles, you must use the Style command on the Format menu.

Apply the new character style

In this exercise, you will locate another room name in the document and apply the new character style to it.

1   Select the next room name in the document, "Aspen Room Annex."

If the Formatting toolbar is not displayed, click Toolbars, and then select the Formatting check box.

2   At the far left of the Formatting toolbar, click the Style down arrow.

Styles available in this document

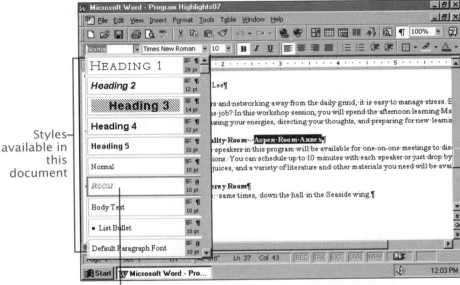

Room character style

3   Choose the Room style.

You might need to scroll through the list to locate this style. Notice that character styles are identified by the symbol **a** in the Styles list. You can also get a quick look at the formatting of the style when you click the Style down arrow.

You can also press the repeat key (F4) to repeat the last operation.

4   Locate the next room name, "Monterey Room," select the name, and then repeat steps 2 and 3.

When you complete applying styles, your document looks like the following illustration.

121

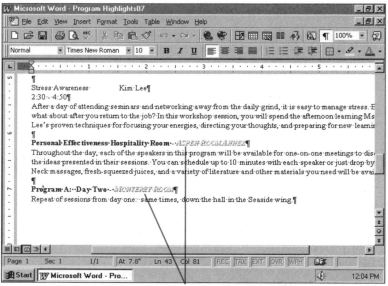

Formatting applied by using styles

Formatting by Using Paragraph Styles

For a demon-stration of how to apply for-mats, double-click the Camcorder Files On The Internet shortcut on your Desktop or connect to the Internet ad-dress listed on p. xxviii.

A *paragraph style* is a collection of both paragraph and character format set-tings that you want to apply to an entire paragraph. Remember: A paragraph is any text separated by a hard return (when nonprinting characters are dis-played, a hard return looks like this: ¶). In a paragraph style, in addition to specifying the appearance of text, you can select the alignment, paragraph spacing, and line spacing of paragraphs. You can create paragraph styles for each kind of paragraph in a document, and then apply the different styles to ensure consistent paragraph formatting for the same kinds of paragraphs in a document. For example, you might want bold, 18-point, centered text to em-phasize a heading paragraph for one of the main ideas in a document. If you create a style that has these settings and name it Heading 1, you can apply all these settings to each heading for the other main ideas. All you need to do is apply the Heading 1 style.

NOTE Heading styles also make it easy to perform advanced para-graph numbering, display the document as an outline, and create a table of contents. Some basic styles (such as heading styles) are al-ready provided in Word. You can apply these styles, modify them, or create your own.

Applying Paragraph Styles by Using AutoFormat

You can use the AutoFormat command to quickly review the existing text and formatting in a document and to enhance the appearance of the document by applying default styles to headings, body paragraphs, and paragraphs formatted as lists. For example, when you apply AutoFormat, hyphens at the start of each item in a list are changed to bullets. Using AutoFormat is a quick way to apply default styles to headings and lists in a document.

 TIP To see all the settings in effect for a specific section of text, you can choose What's This from the Help menu. This feature changes the shape of the pointer. When you click the What's This pointer on formatted text, you can see a description of the format settings currently in effect for the selected text. Choose the What's This command again to turn this feature off.

Apply styles by using AutoFormat

You decide to improve the appearance of the entire document using the AutoFormat command.

 NOTE The default styles are the built-in styles provided in the default template called Normal. There are a variety of additional templates that provide collections of built-in styles for different kinds of documents. Later in this lesson, you will learn about templates for creating other kinds of documents.

If you choose the AutoFormat And Review option, Microsoft Word will prompt you to accept or reject each formatting change.

1 Press CTRL+HOME to move the insertion point to the beginning of the document.

2 On the Format menu, click AutoFormat.

The AutoFormat dialog box appears.

3 Be sure the AutoFormat Now option button is selected.

4 Be sure that General Document is the type of document selected.

5 Click OK.

Microsoft Word applies paragraph formatting to the entire document using the default styles. Your screen should look like the following illustration.

123

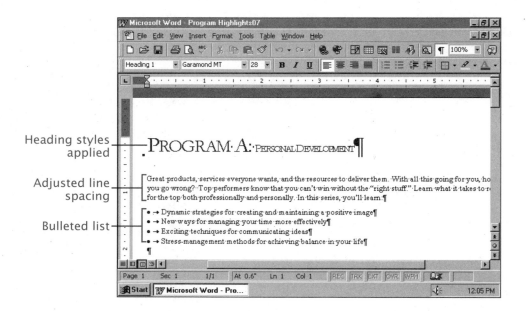

Heading styles applied

Adjusted line spacing

Bulleted list

Creating a New Paragraph Style

Creating a paragraph style is similar to creating a character style. In the New Style dialog box, you specify a set of characteristics for the paragraph style. You can also use a procedure that does not require you to use the Style dialog box. This means you can create paragraph styles more quickly.

Format a paragraph

In this exercise, you will format selected text with the font called Arial Black, center the text, and put extra space before and after the heading.

1 If paragraph marks are not currently displayed, click the Show/Hide ¶ button on the Standard toolbar.

Show/Hide ¶

2 Select the entire paragraph containing the seminar name "Image Strategies," as well as the next line containing the time. Be sure that the paragraph markers for *both* lines are selected.

3 On the Format menu, click Paragraph.

4 Click the Alignment down arrow, and select Centered.

5 Press TAB until you select the Spacing Before box, and then type **3**

This setting creates 3 points of spacing before the heading.

6 Press TAB to select the Spacing After box, and then type **3**

This setting creates 3 points of space after the heading.

7 Click OK to return to the document.

8   On the Formatting toolbar, click the Font down arrow, and select Arial Black.

Your selected formatted text should look like the following illustration.

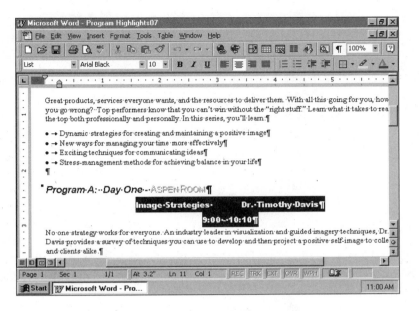

Create a paragraph style for seminar headings

When you have the paragraph formatted the way you want, you can create a new style based on the formatting in your selection.

You can also press CTRL+SHIFT+S to move to the Style box and select the current style.

1   Be sure both paragraphs are selected. On the Formatting toolbar, click in the Style box.

2   In the Style box, type **Session**

The name of the style is Session.

3   Press ENTER.

Nothing changes in the document, but when you press ENTER, Microsoft Word stores the formatting of the paragraphs as the Session style.

Applying Paragraph Styles

You can apply a paragraph style to any number of paragraphs in the document. Applying a paragraph style gives a paragraph the same formatting as the paragraph that served as the model for that style. If you do not select any text, applying a paragraph style affects entire paragraphs. If you apply a paragraph style to selected text in a paragraph, any character formatting included

125

in the style will be applied to the selected text, but the paragraph formatting is not applied. To apply formatting to the entire paragraph, do not select any text in the paragraph.

Apply a paragraph style to headings

In this exercise, you will apply the Session style to all the text paragraphs that consist of a seminar name, speaker, and time.

1 To see more of the headings, scroll down until the formatted heading "Time & More" is at the top of the screen.

2 Select the heading "Time & More" and the next line containing the time.

3 Click the Style down arrow to display the list of styles.

This displays the styles you've created and some of the default styles that Microsoft Word provides (for example, the Heading 1, Heading 2, and Heading 3 styles).

4 Scroll to and select the Session style name.

Notice that paragraph styles are identified by the symbol ¶ in the Styles list. Microsoft Word applies the formats stored in this style to the selected text. For a better look at the formatting, click outside the selection.

5 Repeat steps 3 and 4 twice to format the remaining paragraphs containing the seminar names, speakers, and times.

After you complete applying styles, your document looks like the following illustration.

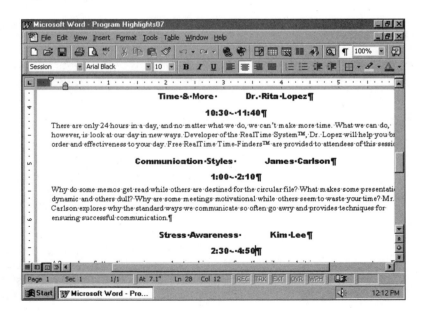

Displaying styles in a document

To see all the styles that have been applied to individual paragraphs in a document, you can display the Style Area in the document window. The Style Area option is available only when you are in Normal view.

Normal View

To view the style name and all of the formatting that is applied to your text, click the Help button, and then click on the text.

1   To the left of the horizontal scroll bar, click the Normal View button.

2   On the Tools menu, click Options.

3   Click the View tab to select it.

4   In the Style Area Width box, type 1"

    This action creates a 1-inch strip, called the Style Area, along the left side of the document window.

5   Click OK.

    The left side of the document window displays the name of the style applied to each paragraph, although character styles are not shown. You can adjust the width of the Style Area by dragging the vertical line that separates the Style Area from the document.

6   Use the up scroll arrow to scroll line by line to the top of the document, noting the formatting and styles as you go.

Using the Style Gallery

You can open the Style dialog box by double-clicking the style name in the Style area.

You can use the Style Gallery command on the Format menu to further enhance the appearance of your document. Using the Style Gallery, you can view different document styles and apply styles to your document by using the most appropriate template. In the Style Gallery, you can choose from a list of preformatted, professionally designed templates. *Templates* are master copies of standard document types that contain the styles and formatting that are appropriate for a variety of documents, including letters, resumes, newsletters, and memos. The Style Gallery includes a Preview box where you can see how your document will look when formatted in the styles of different templates.

NOTE   Templates also provide boilerplate text, graphics, document settings, and other features that are standard in certain types of documents. Lesson 8, "Saving Time by Using Templates and Forms,"discusses these other aspects of templates.

Apply the styles from another template

1   Press CTRL+HOME to place the insertion point at the top of the document.

2   On the Format menu, click Style Gallery.

    The Style Gallery dialog box appears.

3   In the Template box, click Professional Memo.

A sample of the document formatted by using the Professional Memo template styles appears in the Preview box.

4   Click OK.

Microsoft Word applies the styles contained in the Professional Memo template to the document. Among other formatting changes in the document, the text formatted in the Heading 1 style is shaded and the body text font changes to Arial. Your screen should look like the following illustration.

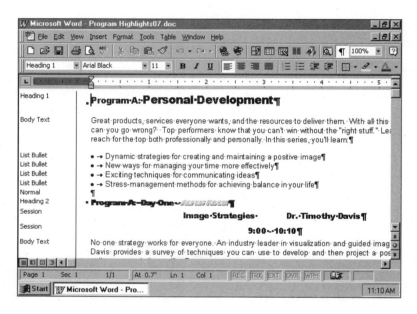

5   On the Standard toolbar, click the Save button.

Save

Apply a style

1   Place the insertion point in the heading "Image Strategies."

2   On the Formatting toolbar, click the Style down arrow, and then select the Heading 3 style.

Changing a Style

Suppose that after viewing the conference brochure, you decide to apply formatting to the Heading 3 style by changing the space before and after the heading. Instead of reformatting every heading separately, you can change the style definition. By redefining the style, you change the formatting of every paragraph formatted in that style.

In these exercises, you will make quick adjustments to the paragraph formatting before redefining the style.

Reformat a paragraph style

1 Be sure the insertion point is in the heading "Image Strategies."
2 On the Format menu, click Paragraph.
3 Click the Alignment down arrow, and click Centered.
4 In the Indentation area, click the Indent down arrow until 0 is displayed.
5 In the Spacing area, click the Before up arrow until 6 is displayed. Click the After up arrow until 6 is displayed.
6 Click OK to return to the document.

Redefine the style

1 Be sure the insertion point is in the Images Strategies line.
2 On the Formatting toolbar, click the Style down arrow, and then select the Heading 3 style.

   The Modify Style dialog box appears.
3 Be sure that the Update The Style To Reflect Recent Changes option is selected, and then click OK.

   Every paragraph formatted in the Heading 3 style changes to reflect the new formatting.

 TIP   If you want the style settings to always reflect every change you make to text formatted with this style, select the Automatically Update The Style From Now On box in the Modify Style dialog box.

4 Apply the Heading 3 style to each of the remaining session headings.
5 Click the scroll down arrow to scroll through the document line by line to view the results of this change, or decrease your zoom magnification to see more of the document. Your document should look like the following illustration.

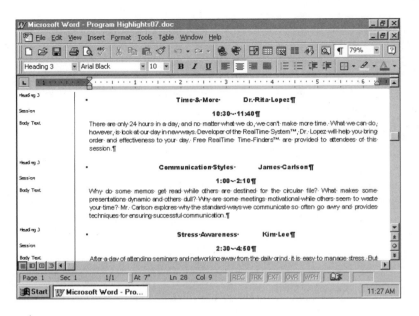

6 Save the document.

The current version of the document is saved in place of the previous version.

NOTE To make applying styles even easier and faster, you can also specify a keyboard shortcut as an alternative to applying a style from the Formatting toolbar. You can assign a keyboard shortcut to a style by clicking the Modify button in the Style dialog box and then clicking the Shortcut Key button. Press the keyboard combination you would like to assign to the current style. Then, click Assign, and close the dialog boxes.

Hide the Style Area

You can hide the Style Area by dragging the vertical line all the way to the left of the document window.

▶ Position the mouse pointer over the vertical line that separates the Style Area from the document text; when the pointer shape changes to a two-headed arrow, drag the line to the far left of the document window.

NOTE If you'd like to build on the skills that you learned in this lesson, you can do the One Step Further. Otherwise, skip to "Finish the lesson."

One Step Further: Using Background AutoFormatting

When you create new text, the AutoFormat As You Type feature will do much of the formatting for you. For example, if you type a lowercase o followed by a space or a tab at the beginning of a line (and press ENTER at the end of the line or paragraph), the AutoFormat As You Type feature will change the o to a bullet and format the paragraph so that the second and succeeding lines of a paragraph are left-aligned with the text (after the bullet) in the first line. Other AutoFormat As You Type features include changing "1st" to "1ST," (TM) to ™, and automatically formatting headings.

Create a new document

New

➤ On the Standard toolbar, click the New button.

Select AutoFormat As You Type settings

As with many Microsoft Word background features, you can specify options for the AutoFormat As You Type feature.

1 On the Format menu, click AutoFormat.

2 In the AutoFormat dialog box, click the Options button.

3 In the AutoCorrect dialog box, click the AutoFormat As You Type tab, and click any check boxes that are not already selected on this tab.

4 Click OK to return to the AutoFormat dialog box.

5 Click OK to close the AutoFormat dialog box.

Format your document as you type

1 Type **Sign Up for the 3rd Annual West Coast Sales Conference**

The rd is superscripted automatically when you press the SPACEBAR after typing rd.

2 Press ENTER twice.

When you insert two blank lines after the first paragraph in a document, Word applies the Heading 1 style to this paragraph.

3 Type the following text to continue entering text and formatting your document. Be sure to press TAB after typing the first lowercase o. The AutoFormat feature automatically inserts the bullets and tabs in each subsequent line.

We are pleased to bring you four exciting programs of seminars and workshops, including:

o **Personal Development**

o   **Organizational Strategies**

o   **Sales Excellence**

o   **New Technologies**

4   Press ENTER twice to stop the automatic formatting of bulleted paragraphs.

5   Type a series of three hyphens, and then press ENTER to create a border that spans the width of the page.

6   Type **Register by May 25th and get a free Time Finder(TM) portfolio in your conference packet.**

The date and the trademark symbol are automatically formatted.

Name and save the document

1   On the Standard toolbar, click the Save button.

2   Click the Look In Favorites button, and then double-click the SBS Word folder.

3   In the File Name box, type **One Step07**

4   Click Save.

5   On the Format menu, click AutoFormat, and then click Options.

6   On the AutoFormat As You Type tab, clear the Define Styles Based On Your Formatting check box.

7   Click OK to close each open dialog box.

Save

*Look In
Favorites*

Finish the lesson

1   To continue to the next lesson, on the File menu, click Close for each open document.

2   If you are finished using Microsoft Word for now, on the File menu, click Exit.

Lesson Summary

To	Do this
Create a character style	Select the formatted text, and then click Style on the Format menu. Click New, and then enter a new style name. Select the Character style type. Click OK, and then click Apply.

To	Do this
Apply a character style	Select the text you want to format. On the Formatting toolbar, click the Style down arrow, and then select the style name.
Apply automatic formatting to a document	On the Format menu, click AutoFormat.
Create a paragraph style	Select the formatted paragraph. In the Style box on the Formatting toolbar, type the style name, and then press ENTER.
Apply a paragraph style	Select the paragraphs you want to format. On the Formatting toolbar, click the Style down arrow, and then select the style name.
Display the Style Area	Be sure you are in Normal view. On the Tools menu, click Options, and click View. In the Style Area Width box, type the size of the area.
Hide the Style Area	Position the pointer over the vertical line that separates the Style Area from the document text; when the pointer changes shape to a two-headed arrow, drag the line to the left edge of the document window.
Redefine a paragraph style	Apply the desired formatting to one of the paragraphs containing the style you want to change. Reapply the style, be sure the first option is selected, and then click OK.
Apply styles from a predefined template	On the Format menu, click Style Gallery. Choose a template.

133

For online information about	On the Help menu, click Contents And Index, click the Index tab, and then type
Defining, naming, applying, and changing character styles	**characters, formatting**
Defining, naming, applying, and changing paragraph styles	**styles, paragraph**

Saving Time by Using Templates and Forms

In this lesson you will learn how to:

- Design a memo based on a template.
- Create a custom template.
- Gather information using electronic forms.
- Make an electronic form.
- Create a table in a form.
- Use an electronic form.
- Create an instant fax.

If you work with specific kinds of documents (such as proposals, memos, letters, and so on), each requiring its own set of formatting and styles, you can save time by using wizards and templates. You can copy styles and AutoText entries you've already created in other documents and templates and use those styles in new documents and templates. By fine-tuning the templates to meet your needs, you can create your own custom templates. By using a template, one special kind of document you can create is a form. Combining forms with the Word table feature allows you to create attractive, easy-to-use forms that you can print or publish on the Internet or on your company intranet.

In this lesson, you'll create a template and an electronic form. Then you will fill out the form, and, if you wish, send it as an instant fax.

> **Adding Power to Your Forms**
>
> In addition to the simple forms you can create by using the controls on the Forms toolbar, you can create more powerful forms (like the ones you see on the World Wide Web) by using ActiveX controls. When the power of the Visual Basic programming language is combined with the innovative technology of ActiveX, you can create exciting forms and pages that are attractive and easy to use. For more information, on the Help menu, click Contents And Index, and on the Index tab, type **ActiveX**

Creating a Memo Based on a Template

A *template* is a special kind of Word document that can assist you in creating specific kinds of documents (such as memos, press releases, and letters). Although it is similar to a wizard (because it helps you create different kinds of documents quickly, providing the details of the design and format), a template gives you the ability to develop the document you want without having to respond to a series of wizard dialog boxes. You simply choose the template that corresponds to the type of document you want to create and start editing. The template takes care of the character, paragraph, and page formatting, and you can enter and edit text directly in the document. Placeholder text in the template makes it easy for you to enter text in the proper locations.

Create a new memo

As part of your responsibilities as the conference coordinator for West Coast Sales national conference, you need to get an accurate idea of the technical and audiovisual equipment you'll need at the conference. You plan to create a survey to gather that information from your presenters, but first you should send last year's survey to your technical support person for his evaluation. To explain what the evaluation should discuss, you quickly create a cover memo using a memo template.

1   On the File menu, click New.
2   On the Memos tab, double-click the template called Professional Memo.

    A new document window opens, ready for you to create a new memo.

Adjust the magnification

Zoom

➤ On the Standard toolbar, click the Zoom down arrow, and then click Page Width.

    The memo document looks like the following illustration.

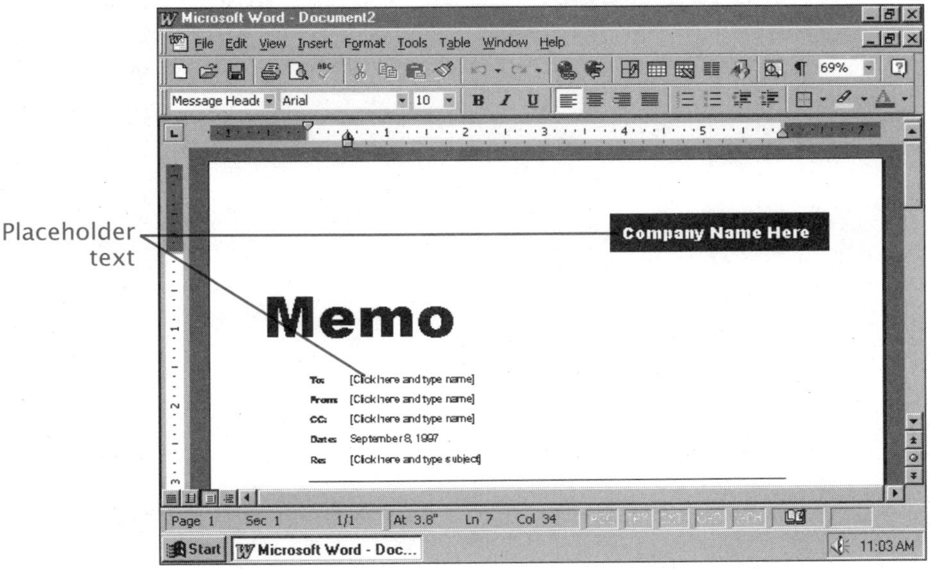

Show paragraph marks

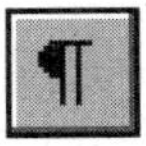

Show/Hide ¶

➤ To display paragraph marks, click the Show/Hide ¶ button.

Enter text in the document

Enter the text of the memo in the document by selecting the existing placeholder text and typing your own.

1. Select the text in the black box in the upper right, and then type **West Coast Sales**; *do not* press ENTER after typing this text.
2. In the To line, click the word "here" to select the entire line, and then type **Eric Bustos, Technical Support Services**
3. In the From line, click the word "here" to select the entire line, and then type **Terry Kim** (or type your own name), **Communications and Conference Planning**
4. Select the CC line, and then press DELETE.

   You are not sending a copy of the memo to anyone.
5. In the Re line, click the word "here" to select the entire line, and then type **Last year's survey**

   The first part of the memo looks like the following illustration.

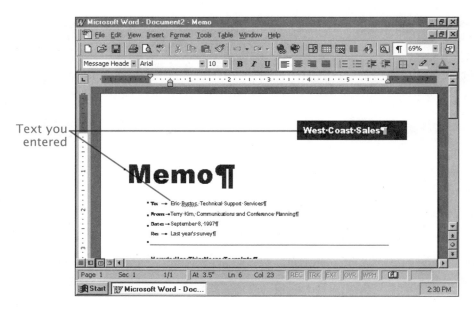

Text you entered

6 Select the body paragraph of placeholder text and type:

I've attached a copy of last year's speaker's equipment survey. Because I will use this survey to create a new electronic form for speakers to complete, please make any changes you would like to see in this year's form. I need your reply by the end of the week.

7 Delete the line "How to use this memo template."

Name and save the document

Save

1 On the Standard toolbar, click the Save button.

The Save As dialog box appears.

2 Click the Look In Favorites button, and then double-click the SBS Word folder.

Look In Favorites

3 Select any text in the File Name box, and then type **Equipment Memo08**.

4 Click Save, or press ENTER.

Designing a Custom Template

Microsoft Word provides several templates for business documents, including letters and memos. If none of these templates provides the kind of document you want, you can create your own template. An easy way to create a template is to start with a document that already has many of the formatting features you want.

Edit the document

The memo you just created contains many of the formatting features you like. Because you frequently communicate with the Technical Support Services department, you decide to create a template based on your memo. However, before you do, you want to make a few changes that will be reflected in all your memos to Technical Support Services.

1   Place the insertion point after the text "Memo," and then type **randum**

2   On the Format menu, click Change Case.

3   Be sure that Uppercase is selected, and click OK.

4   Select the four heading lines (TO/FROM/DATE/RE), click the Font Size arrow, and then select 12.

5   Select the text in the Re line, and then type **memo topic goes here**

6   Select the body paragraph, and then type **text body goes here**

7   Press ENTER twice, type **Action Item 1** and then press ENTER.

8   Type **Action Item 2** and then press ENTER twice.

You can also press SHIFT+CTRL+> twice to increase the size of the selected text by 2 points.

Save the document as a template

Now that your document contains the standard text and formatting you want for standard memos, you can save the document as a template. Microsoft Word adds the DOT template extension to the document name when you save the file. You do not see this extension unless you have disabled the Hide MS DOS extensions option in Windows Explorer.

1   On the File menu, click Save As.

2   In the File Name box, type **Tech Memo08**

3   Click the Save As Type down arrow, and then select Document Template.

4   Click Save.

The template is stored in the Templates subfolder.

5   On the File menu, click Close.

Gathering Information by Using Electronic Forms

Paper forms are known for being difficult to fill in and are sometimes difficult to read after they are completed. An electronic form minimizes many of the disadvantages of paper forms. By using Microsoft Word, you can design an electronic form to ensure that your forms are completed quickly and accurately. Because a user fills in your form electronically, you won't have to decipher someone's handwriting. Using what you have learned about templates, you can create a form you can fill out as a Microsoft Word document.

In addition, if your computer is connected to a network or an *intranet*—a powerful corporate information and collaboration system used as an internal corporate Web site—electronic forms can be filled out and shared in the same way you share any other documents, possibly eliminating the need for certain paper forms. If you have a site on the World Wide Web, you can post electronic forms to your Web site to collect customer information, survey product offerings, and even take orders from customers.

Making an Electronic Form

You create a form by first creating a template that contains the arrangement of text and fields you want for your form. A *field* is an area where the user can enter a response to a prompt or question on the form. You specify the types of fields you want and apply formatting to the form. Finally, before you save the template, you protect the form so that when people work on the form, they can supply information in the fields but cannot change the text or format of the form.

Create an electronic form

As part of your responsibilities as the conference coordinator for West Coast Sales national conference, you need to get an accurate idea of your technical and audio-visual equipment needs for the conference. To gather this information, you can create a form that the conference presenters can complete electronically.

 NOTE   You do not need to be connected to a network to complete an electronic form. You simply need to open the form in Microsoft Word.

1   On the File menu, click New.

2   On the General tab, be sure that the Blank Document template is selected.

3   In the Create New area, select the Template option.

    Your electronic form is a template document.

4   Click OK.

5   On the Standard toolbar, click the Save button.

6   In the File Name box, type **Form Template08**

    Microsoft Word stores the template in the Templates folder in the Microsoft Office folder. All templates must be stored in this folder so that the name of the template appears in the New dialog box. If you change the default location of your Templates folder, the new location appears in the Save As dialog box.

7   Click Save.

Save

Design your form

Using the following illustration as a guide, enter text for the top part of the form. Later, you can format the text to make your form more attractive.

1   At the insertion point, type **West Coast Sales** and then press ENTER.

2   Type **National Sales Conference** and then press ENTER.

3   Type **Presenters Survey** and then press ENTER twice.

Display the Forms toolbar

The buttons available on the Forms toolbar make it easy to create a form.

> Use the right mouse button to click anywhere on any toolbar, and then click Forms.

The Forms toolbar is displayed. So the toolbar does not obscure your view of the document window, you can double-click the title bar to move the Forms toolbar above the workspace, or you can drag the toolbar to a new position.

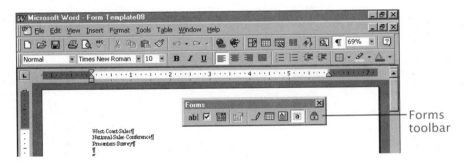

Forms toolbar

Creating a Table

Tables play an important role in formatting and arranging text and fields in a form. In Microsoft Word, a *table* is a grid of rows and columns containing boxes (called *cells*) of text or graphics. Unlike a table that you might create using tabs, you can easily add or delete text in a grid-based table without affecting the arrangement of text in columns.

Inserting a Blank Table

When you insert a table, Microsoft Word outlines each cell with a thin border. You can apply different borders, or you can remove them entirely. If you do remove the borders from the table, you see dotted gridlines that indicate the table cells. These gridlines do not appear when you print the table. Just as a paragraph mark ends every paragraph, an *end-of-cell mark* shows the end of every cell. At the end of each row, there is an *end-of-row mark* that identifies the end of the row. End-of-cell marks and end-of-row marks do not print.

Insert a table

Insert Table

You can also click the Insert Table button on the Standard toolbar to insert a table.

You can create more complex tables by using the Draw Table button on the Forms toolbar. Click the Draw button to "draw" lines where you want to divide the cells.

For a demonstration of how to insert a blank table, double-click the Camcorder Files On The Internet shortcut on your Desktop or connect to the Internet address listed on p. xxviii.

1 On the Forms toolbar, click the Insert Table button to display the grid.

2 Click the upper left square, and drag across the grid to select seven rows down by three columns across, as shown in the following illustration.

As you drag down and select rows at the bottom of the grid, the grid will display more rows, one at a time, to accommodate your dragging, all the way down to the bottom of your screen.

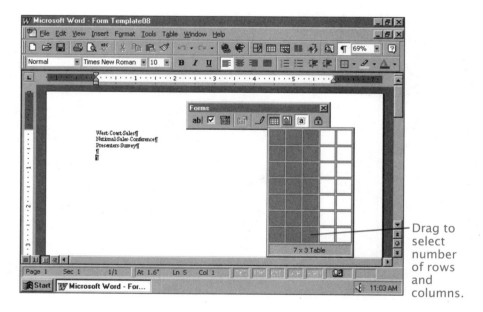

Drag to select number of rows and columns.

3 Release the mouse button.

When you release the mouse button, Microsoft Word inserts an empty table that contains the number of columns and rows that you selected.

Gridlines   End-of-cell marks   End-of-row marks

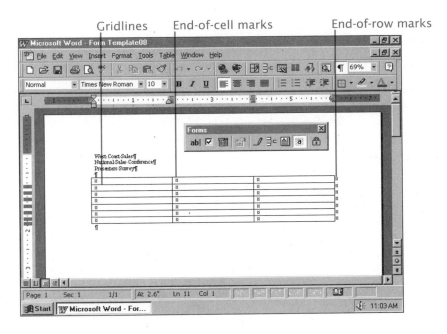

Add text to the table

1   Click in the first cell, and then type **Name:**

This text is the label for the field you create in the next step.

To move to the previous cell, press SHIFT+TAB. To indent text in a table using tabs, press CTRL+TAB.

2   Press TAB to move to the next cell in the table.

Inserting Fields and Controls

For each field on your form, you display a control. A *control* is a type of field used to enter responses to questions or provide information. Text fields, drop-down lists, and check boxes are all examples of controls you can add to a form. *Text fields* (the equivalent of the blank lines you fill in on paper forms) can be a fixed length or an unlimited length. A *list field* provides a list of valid options from which to choose. For "yes" or "no" responses, you can create *check box fields* in which the user can place an "X" by clicking in the box. To make the form even easier to complete, you can also specify the "default" answer in specific fields.

143

Insert a text field

A *text field* is a field in which the user can enter text. You can allow users to enter an unlimited amount of text, or you can restrict the number of characters they are able to enter. In this exercise, you will create a text field in this cell in which users can enter a name.

Text Form Field

1   On the Forms toolbar, click the Text Form Field button.

Five small circles appear in the cell. This is a text field.

2   Double-click the text field.

Double-clicking a text field displays the Text Form Field Options dialog box. In this dialog box, you specify the options you want for the field.

Field length—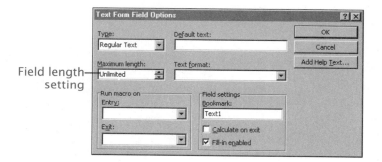
setting

3   Be sure that Unlimited is in the Maximum Length box.

If it is not, use the arrows to select Unlimited. This selection allows the user to enter an unlimited amount of text in the field.

4   Click OK.

You won't see any change to the field in the table.

5   Place the insertion point in the second row of the first column.

Insert text and another text field

1   Type **Extension:**
2   Press TAB to move to the next cell in the table.
3   On the Forms toolbar, click the Text Form Field button.
4   Double-click the text field.

5 Use the Maximum Length up arrow to select 4.

This selection allows the user to enter only four characters in this field when filling out the form. If the user attempts to enter more characters, the program beeps.

6 Click the Type down arrow, and then select Number.

This selection ensures that the user enters a number (not a letter). If the user attempts to enter a character that is not a number, a message indicates that a number is required.

7 Click OK to return to the form.

8 Place the insertion point in the third row in the first column.

Insert text and another text field

1 Type **Title:**

2 Press TAB to move to the next cell in the table.

3 On the Forms toolbar, click the Text Form Field button.

4 Double-click the text field.

5 In the Maximum Length box, type **30**

This selection allows the user to enter up to 30 characters in this field. If the user attempts to enter more characters, the program beeps.

6 Click OK to return to the form.

Add text to the form

Next, you will enter a label that describes the fields in the next part of the form.

1 Place the insertion point in the fourth row in the first column.

2 Type **I will need this equipment:**

3 Press the DOWN ARROW key to place the insertion point in the cell below (the fifth row in the first column).

Insert a check box field and text

When you want the user to specify a Yes or No response in a form, you can insert a check box field.

1 On the Forms toolbar, click the Check Box Form Field button.

A shaded check box appears in the cell.

*Check Box
Form Field*

2   Press TAB to move to the cell in the next column.

3   Type **Overhead projector**

Insert two check box fields and text

1   Place the insertion point in the first cell of the next row.

2   On the Forms toolbar, click the Check Box Form Field button.

     A shaded check box appears in the cell.

3   Press TAB to move to the cell in the next column, and then type **Slide projector**

4   Place the insertion point in the first cell of the next row.

5   On the Forms toolbar, click the Check Box Form Field button.

     A shaded check box appears in the cell.

6   Press TAB to move to the cell in the next column, and then type **Computer**

7   On the Standard toolbar, click the Save button to save the work you have completed so far.

     Your screen should look like the following illustration.

Save

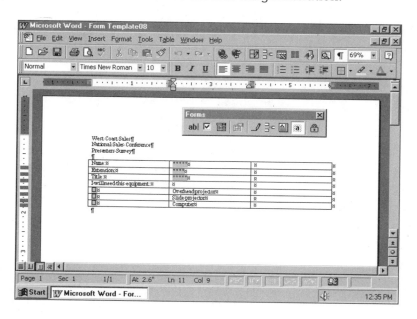

Add text to the form

In this exercise, you enter a label that describes the field you will create next.

1 Place the insertion point in the cell at the first row of the third column.

2 Type **Division:**

3 Press the DOWN ARROW key to place the insertion point in the cell below (the second cell in the third column).

Insert a drop-down list field

To make it easy for the user to specify the division name to which he or she belongs, you can create a list of selections. The user clicks this drop-down field to make a selection from the list.

Drop-Down Form Field

1 On the Forms toolbar, click the Drop-Down Form Field button.

2 Double-click the list field you just created.

Double-clicking a drop-down form field displays the Drop-Down Form Field Options dialog box. In this dialog box, you specify the options you want for the field.

Specify selections in a list field

In this exercise, you enter the list of choices available for the user to complete the form.

1 In the Drop-Down Item box, type **Corporate**

You can also press ENTER.

2 Click the Add button.

The item "Corporate" appears in the list to the right. The first item in the list is the default selection.

3 Type **Finance**

4 Click Add.

The item "Finance" appears in the Items In Drop-Down List box to the right.

5 Type **Marketing and Communications** and then click Add.

6 Type **Sales** and then click Add.

7 Type **Systems and Technology** and then click Add.

8 Click OK.

Your form looks like the following illustration.

147

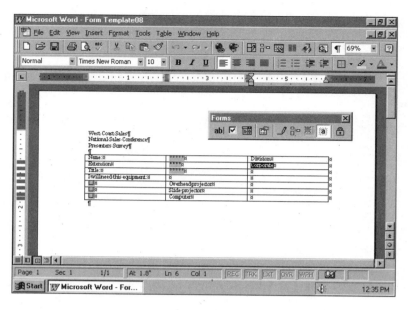

9 Save the document.

Improving the Appearance of a Table

Just as you can format text in paragraphs, you can format text in a table. In addition to the font and paragraph formatting options, you can use special table-formatting commands to make creating a table that has borders and shading even easier. By using the Table AutoFormat command, you can choose from many preset formatting options to instantly create attractive tables.

Format the table

In this exercise, you will use the Table AutoFormat command to make the table more attractive and easier to read. You will also center the table horizontally on the page.

1 Use right mouse button to click anywhere in the table, and then click Table AutoFormat on the shortcut menu.

2 In the Formats list, scroll down and select the List 5 format.

3 Clear the Heading Rows check box, and then click OK.

4 On the Table menu, click Cell Height And Width.

In the Cell Height And Width dialog box, you can specify the alignment of the entire table.

5 Click the Row tab, if it is not displayed.

6 In the Alignment area, select the Center option button, and then click OK.

Format cells

In this exercise, you will use the Align Right button on the Formatting toolbar to align the text and fields in the first column. You will also change a cell's text style to bold and hide paragraph marks and gridlines.

Align Right

Bold

Show/Hide ¶

1 Position the pointer near the top edge of the first column.

2 When the pointer shape changes to a down arrow, click to select the first column.

3 On the Formatting toolbar, click the Align Right button.

4 Click the first-row cell in the third column (the one that contains the text "Division:"), and then, on the Formatting toolbar, click the Bold button.

5 On the Standard toolbar, click the Show/Hide ¶ button to hide nonprinting characters. Click anywhere in the text to clear the selection. Your form looks like the following illustration.

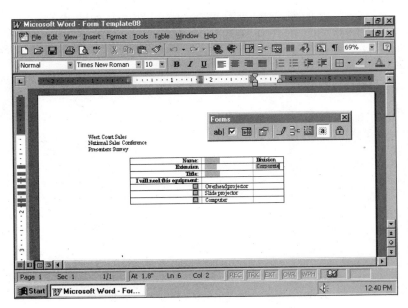

Insert a new column

1 Position the pointer near the top edge of the first column.

2 When the pointer shape changes to a down arrow, click to select the first column.

Insert Columns

3 On the Standard toolbar, click the Insert Columns button.

A new blank column appears to the left of the columns in the table. The new column is the same width as the column you selected.

Merge cells in a column

1 Make sure the first column is still selected, use the right mouse button to click the first column, and then click Merge Cells.

A single cell appears down the length of the table.

2 Type **Equipment Request Form**

Align the text vertically

1 On the Format menu, click Text Direction.

The Text Direction–Table Cell dialog box appears.

2 In the Orientation area, click the far left Text box. Click the left box that displays the text formatted vertically, reading from bottom to top.

3 Click OK.

Your form looks like the following illustration.

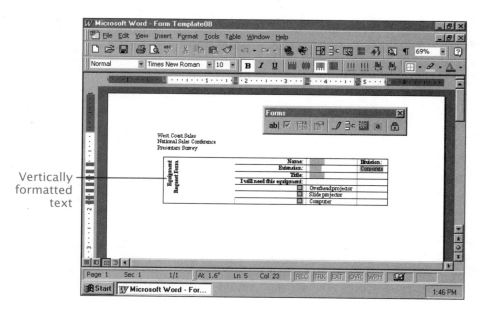

Vertically formatted text

Format the form title

Center

1 Select the three lines of text at the top of the document (outside the table), and click the Center button on the Formatting toolbar.

Bold

2 Be sure the text is still selected, and then on the Formatting toolbar, click the Bold button.

3 On the Formatting toolbar, click the Font Size down arrow, and select 18.

4 Click in the new column you created earlier.

5 Drag the left column boundary for the first column to the 1-inch mark on the horizontal ruler.

6 On the Formatting toolbar, click the Outside Border down arrow, and then click the Right Border button.

Outside Border

Hide form shading

By default, the fields are shaded. You can hide the shading to improve the appearance of the form.

Form Field Shading

➤ On the Forms toolbar, click the Form Field Shading button to hide the shading.

Your form looks like the following illustration.

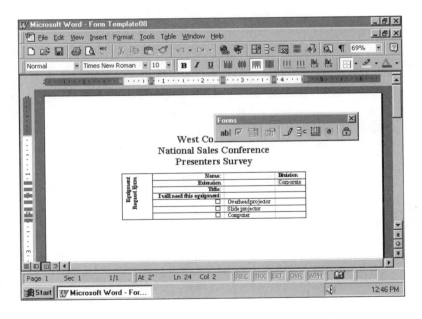

Protect the form

So that people do not inadvertently change the form when they complete it electronically, you should protect the form.

Protect Form

➤ On the Forms toolbar, click the Protect Form button to protect the form.

Hide the Forms toolbar

You are finished using the Forms toolbar in this lesson.

➤ On the Forms toolbar, click the Close button, or click on the View menu, point to Toolbars, and select Forms to hide the Forms toolbar.

Save and close the form

1 On the File menu, click Close.

2 When a message appears, asking whether you want to save changes, click Yes.

Your form is saved as a template.

If You Want to Create a Web Document in Microsoft FrontPage

If you plan to publish a form or another type of document as a Web page using Microsoft FrontPage, you need to save the document in a special format called HTML. HTML, a special formatting language, allows the document to be formatted correctly when it appears on your Web site. To save a document in HTML, on the File menu, choose Save As HTML and name the file. After the document is saved in the HTML format (or in *.htx or *.idc), you can open the document in FrontPage and publish the document as part of your Web site.

To get a head start creating Web documents, use the Word Web Page template or the Word Web Page wizard. Just click the New button on the Standard toolbar to create a new document. In the New dialog box, click the Web Pages tab and either choose the template or use the wizard.

Using an Electronic Form

Now that you have created a form, you can use Microsoft Word to fill it out. To complete an electronic form, you create a new document based on the form's template. Each completed form is a Microsoft Word document.

Open an electronic form

You want to start your presentation planning on the right track. In this exercise, you will fill out an electronic form to identify what you need for your presentation.

1 On the File menu, click New.

2   On the General tab, select Form Template08.

3   Be sure that the Document option is selected.

4   Click OK.

Complete the form online

To move from field to field, you can press TAB. Because the form is protected, you cannot move to cells that do not contain fields.

1   In the Name field, type **Terry**

2   Press TAB to move to the next field.

3   In the Extension field, type **4321** and then press TAB to move to the next field.

4   Click the Division down arrow.

The drop-down list appears. Your screen should look like the following illustration.

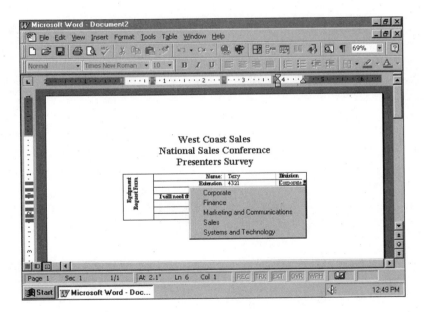

5   On the Division list, select Corporate.

6   Press TAB to move to the Title field, and then type **The Internet: Cyber Where?**

7   Click both the Overhead Projector and the Computer check boxes to select them.

Save

Look In Favorites

Save your completed form

1   On the Standard toolbar, click the Save button.

2   Click the Look In Favorites button, and then double-click the SBS Word folder.

3   In the File Name box, type **Tech Form08** and then click Save.

Your responses in the form are saved in this document. The original form template is unchanged.

Creating an Instant Fax

If you want to fax a currently open Microsoft Word document, you can do so without exiting from Word. You can use the Fax Recipient command on the Send To submenu that starts the Fax Wizard. Then, you answer the Wizard's questions regarding the style of cover page and other faxing options. Word creates a document based on your choices. After the basics of the cover page are established, you can type any additional text or edit the cover page as you wish.

Send a fax

In your role as conference planner, you would like to fax a draft of the form you created. Use the Fax Wizard to create an attractive cover page for the current document that you want to fax.

1   On the File menu, point to Send To, and then click Fax Recipient.

The Fax Wizard dialog box appears. On the left side of the dialog box, you see your current point in the process of completing the wizard. On the right side, you enter your preferences to the choices provided by the wizard.

2   Click the Document To Fax button. Be sure The Following Document and With A Cover Sheet options are selected and that Tech Form08.doc is in The Following Document box.

These options are already selected by default unless you have already run this wizard and chosen other options.

3   Click Next to display the next dialog box.

4   Click the I Want To Print My Document So I Can Send It From A Separate Fax Machine option to print this fax and send it later.

 NOTE   If you choose the Microsoft Fax option or the option to use another fax software package, Microsoft Word will send the fax immediately after you complete the wizard and save the document.

5   Click Next to display the next dialog box.

The Recipient dialog box appears.

6   In the Name box, type **Julie Rogers**

7   In the Fax Number box, type 1-999-555-1234.

8   Click Next to display the next dialog box.

9   Choose a cover sheet style based on the style you prefer.

10   Click Next to display the next dialog box.

11   In the Sender Information dialog box, complete the name and address information for yourself and your company.

12   Click Finish to complete the wizard and display the fax cover page.

Faxing to a Name in the Address Book

You can click the Address Book button in the Recipient dialog box to choose a name you have already entered in your Address Book.

Save the fax cover page

1   On the Standard toolbar, click the Save button.

The Save As dialog box appears.

2   Click the Look In Favorites button, and then double-click the SBS Word folder.

3   In the File Name box, type **Program Fax02**

4   Click Save, or press ENTER, to close the dialog box and save the file.

> **NOTE** If you'd like to build on the skills that you learned in this lesson, you can do the One Step Further. Otherwise, skip to "Finish the lesson."

One Step Further: Providing Help Information in a Form

To make it easier for a user to enter the correct information in a field, you can provide information as a message that appears on the status bar or as a Help window that appears when the user presses F1. In this exercise, you will create a message on the status bar for the current field, clarifying how many characters are allowed in the title of the speech.

Open the form

Open

1 Click the Open button.

2 Click the Look In box down arrow, double-click C, double-click Program Files, double-click Microsoft Office, and then double-click Template.

3 At the bottom of the Open dialog box, click the Files Of Type down arrow, and then click Document Templates.

4 Double-click the Form Template08 template.

Unprotect the form

To add help information to a field, you will be modifying it. Because the form is protected, you need to unprotect the form before you continue.

1 Click the right mouse button on any toolbar, and then click Forms to display the Forms toolbar.

2 Click the Protect Form button.

You can now edit the form.

Protect Form

Assign help to a field

1 Double-click the Title field (not the Title label).

2 In the Text Form Field Options dialog box, click Add Help Text.

3 In the Form Field Help Text dialog box, be sure that the Status Bar tab is in front.

4 Select the Type Your Own button.

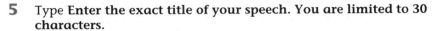
5 Type **Enter the exact title of your speech. You are limited to 30 characters.**

This message will appear in the status bar when the user moves to this field in the form.

6 Click OK to return to the Text Form Field Options dialog box.

7 Click OK to return to the form.

8 On the Forms toolbar, click the Protect Form button.

9 Save the form.

Finish the lesson

1 To continue to the Review & Practice, on the File menu, click Close for each open document.

2 If you are finished using Microsoft Word for now, on the File menu, click Exit.

Lesson Summary

To	Do this
Create a template	Save the document as a template by clicking Save As on the File menu and selecting Document Template on the Save As Type list.
Create a new document using a template	On the File menu, click New. Click the tab for the type of document you want to create. Double-click the template.
Create a form	On the File menu, click New. On the General tab, select Blank Document, and click the Template option. Click OK, and then use the Save As command to rename the form.
Display the Forms toolbar	On the View menu, click Toolbars, and then select the Forms check box. *or* Use the right mouse button to click on any toolbar, and then click Forms.

To	Do this	Button
Insert a table	On the Standard toolbar or on the Forms toolbar, click the Insert Table button, and then drag to select the number of columns and rows you want.	
Move to the next table cell	Press the TAB key. *or* Use the arrow keys.	
Move to the previous table cell	Press SHIFT+TAB. *or* Use the arrow keys.	
Insert a text field	On the Forms toolbar, click the Text Form Field button. Double-click the text field. Specify the desired options in the dialog box, and click OK.	
Insert a check box	On the Forms toolbar, click the Check Box Form Field button.	
Insert a drop-down list field	On the Forms toolbar, click the Drop-Down Form Field button. Double-click the text field. Specify the desired options in the dialog box, and click OK.	
Protect a form	On the Forms toolbar, click the Protect Form button.	
Complete an electronic form	On the File menu, click New, and then select a form template.	

For online information about	On the Help menu, click Contents And Index, click the Index tab, and then type
Using templates	**templates**
Creating forms	**forms**
Creating tables	**tables**

Review & Practice

You will review and practice how to:

Estimated time
25 min.

- Create a document from a template.
- Search for and replace text.
- Add AutoText entries.
- Check spelling and grammar.
- Make and apply new styles.
- Utilize an electronic form.
- Design a table in a document.

In this Review & Practice, you have an opportunity to fine-tune the editing and formatting skills you learned in Part 2 of this book. You can use what you have learned about inserting repeated text, proofing, applying stored formatting, and creating documents with a template to develop a press release that describes the acquisition of The Terra Firm by West Coast Sales. You will also create an order form that can be filled out electronically.

Scenario

As a corporate communications manager, you have many responsibilities at West Coast Sales, including developing press releases announcing major events in the company. With the acquisition of The Terra Firm, you must prepare a press release that announces West Coast Sales' new relationship with The Terra

Firm. To save time in the future, you will also create a customized press release template. In conjunction with the acquisition of West Coast Sales, customers can place orders for The Terra Firm's products, and you will also create an electronic form for the sales team.

Step 1:   *Create a Press Release Template*

1   On the File menu, choose New. On the Memos tab, double-click the Elegant Memo template.

2   Specify Document Template as the file type to save the document, and then name the new template Press ReleaseRP2.

For more information about	See
Creating a template	Lesson 8

Step 2:   *Modify Template Text*

1   Select the text in the heading at the top of the page, and then type **Press Release**

2   Select all the text in the TO: line, and then delete it.

3   In the next line, change the text "FROM" to "CONTACT." Click the placeholder text, and then type your name and phone number.

4   Select all the text in the CC: line, and then type **FOR IMMEDIATE RELEASE**

5   Select the first line under the thin border, and then type **Insert Headline**

6   Delete the remaining lines.

For more information about	See
Modifying a template	Lesson 8

Step 3:   *Add AutoText Entries*

1   Create AutoText entries for the following words and phrases. Do not include the paragraph mark when you select the text for the entry. Create your own abbreviations for the entry names.

West Coast Sales
The Terra Firm

2   Save and close the template.

For more information about	See
Using AutoText	Lesson 5

Step 4: *Customize the Press Release Template*

1   On the File menu, choose New. Be sure Document is selected in the Create New area, and then double-click the Press ReleaseRP2 template on the General tab.

2   Save the document as **Terra Press Release**

3   Click in the SUBJECT line, and then type **West Coast Sales/Terra Firm merger**

4   Click in the DATE line, and Word automatically inserts the current date.

5   Replace the headline placeholder with the following text. Use the appropriate AutoText entries as you type.

The Terra Firm recognizes West Coast Sales market leadership and worldwide distribution network.

6   Add the following body text. Use the appropriate AutoText entries as you type.

Effective immediately: The Terra Firm, an innovator in lawn care solutions, is now a division of West Coast Sales. Senior management in both organizations determined that the long-standing relationship between these companies could be improved with a corporate consolidation. West Coast Sales expects to benefit from The Terra Firm's innovative line of lawn care products (a perfect complement to the outdoors-oriented, environmentally conscious retailer), while The Terra Firm expects to achieve greater distribution of its products and increased market awareness by the alliance. New offerings include:

7   Press ENTER, and then type the following text:

TerraTek, a powerful landscape design software package for novice and advanced gardeners. Helpful Garden Sprites guide you through the process of choosing the correct plantings based on soil type, moisture, geographical location, amount of sun, size, and plant color.

TerraLink, a communications program that connects you to The Terra Firm's web site for the latest on gardening information. It also supplies information (based on a satellite feed) to your TerraTek database for foolproof plant selection.

TerraUltimate, the complete lawn care solution that combines the information in your TerraTek database with the software that controls the sprinkling and fertilizer distribution for your landscape.

For more information about	See
Creating a document from a template	Lesson 8

Step 5: Proof Your Document

1 Use the Spelling and Grammar features to correct any grammatical and spelling errors in the document.

2 If you are working on your own computer, add AutoCorrect entries for words you misspell frequently.

For more information about	See
Correcting errors	Lesson 5

Step 6: Apply, Create, and Modify Styles

1 Apply bullets to the last paragraph of text.

2 Use the Bullets And Numbering command to change the bullet symbol to diamonds.

3 Indent the paragraph .5 inch from the left and right margins.

4 Create a new paragraph style called Product Bullet, based on the current selection.

5 Apply this new style to the last three paragraphs on this page.

6 Select one of the paragraphs, and add 6 points space above and below.

7 Reapply the Product Bullet style, and then modify the style based on the currently selected text. Apply the modified style to the last three paragraphs.

8 Create a new character style called Product Name to format selected text in bold, italics, small caps. Apply this new style to each occurrence of a product name in the press release.

9 Save your changes.

For more information about	See
Creating styles	Lesson 7

Step 7: Create an Electronic Form

1 Create a new template based on the Blank Document template.

2 Type **Order Your Terra Firm Products Today!** and press ENTER.

3 Format the title as centered, 18-point, Arial bold. Use the Outside Border button to put a border around the title.

4 Add three lines of space below the bordered text, type **Select the products you want to order:** and then format the line as 10-point Arial, bold.

5 Display the Forms toolbar, and insert a table that is five rows high by three columns wide. In the first column, enter the field names (TerraTek, TerraLink, TerraUltimate, TerraNet, and TerraGreen) and the five check boxes.

6 In the first row of the second column, type **Choose a delivery option:**

7 In the fourth row of the second column, type **Enter your TerraFirm Key Code:**

8 In the last row of the second column, type **Check here to receive a confirmation call:** Then right-align the text in the middle column.

9 In the first row of the third column, create a drop-down list for each of the delivery options: XferExpress (next day), Xfer Courier (two day), and Xfer Economy (5 day).

10 In the fourth row of the third column, create a text field that is 5 characters long and that can accept only numbers.

11 In the last row of the third column, create a check box that is enabled by default.

12 Turn off form field shading.

13 Protect the document so that the user can modify only the form fields.

14 Save the form template as New TemplateRP2 in the Templates folder.

For more information about	See
Creating an electronic form	Lesson 8

Step 8: *Complete an Electronic Form*

1 Create a new document based on the New TemplateRP2 template that you created in the last exercise.

2 Complete the form using the information in the following illustration.

3   Save the form document as Order FormRP2 in the SBS Word folder.

For more information about	See
Completing an electronic form	Lesson 8

Finish the Review & Practice

1   Hide the Forms toolbar.

2   To continue to the next lesson, on the File menu, click Close for each open document.

3   If you are finished using Microsoft Word for now, on the File menu, click Exit.

Part 3

Arranging Text and Graphics

Tracking Changes in Documents

Estimated time
35 min.

In this lesson you will learn how to:

- Compare documents.
- Accept and reject changes in a document.
- Change revision options.
- Highlight changes in a document

When you want other people to review your work in a document, Microsoft Word includes a number of features that make comparing documents and reviewing changes much easier. And by changing the revision options, you can customize how changes and revisions appear in your document.

As the conference coordinator for the West Coast Sales upcoming national conference, you are in the process of completing a brochure of program highlights. To ensure that the information is accurate and comprehensive, you formed a team composed of individuals in other West Coast Sales departments. Each person has been given a copy of the program highlights document, and has been asked to add material that is specific to his or her respective department and area of expertise. Using Microsoft Word, revision tracking and document comparison tools, you can coordinate their efforts and incorporate their contributions into the document with ease.

Start the lesson

Each team member has reviewed the highlights in each part of the program, and has saved his or her work in the document. In this exercise, you will open the revised document. Follow the steps below to open the practice file called 09Lesson.

Open

1 On the Standard toolbar, click the Open button.

2 Be sure that Winword SBS Practice folder is in the Look In box. If it is not, click the Look In Favorites button, and double-click the Winword SBS Practice folder.

3 In the file list, double-click 09Lesson to open the file.

4 On the File menu, click Save As.

Look In
Favorites

The Save As dialog box appears. Be sure that the SBS Word folder is in the Save In box. If it is not, click the Look In Favorites button, and then double-click SBS Word.

5 Select any text in the File Name box, and then type **Merged Highlights09**

You can also
press ENTER.

6 Click Save.

NOTE If you want to save changes to a new version rather than to a new document, on the File menu, click Versions. Click Save Now. In the Comments dialog box, enter text to identify the version.

Comparing Document Changes

In Microsoft Word, you can use the Compare Documents command to identify changes between versions or documents. The Compare Documents command, which is located on the Track Changes submenu of the Tools menu, uses revision marks to identify changes between documents or versions. By default, Word uses strikethrough formatting to identify text that has been deleted from the original document. Underlined text means text has been inserted. In the left margin, *change lines* (vertical lines) identify lines that contain changes. Changes made by different authors appear in different colors. You can adjust the revision marks settings to suit your preferences.

Compare documents

In this exercise, you will compare the revised document with a copy of the original document.

1 On the Tools menu, point to Track Changes, and then click Compare Documents.

The Select File To Compare With Current Document dialog box appears.

If your screen does not look similar to the illustrations as you work through this lesson, see Appendix B, "Matching the Exercises."

2 Be sure that Winword SBS Practice folder is in the Look In box. If it is not, click the Look In Favorites button, and double-click the Winword SBS Practice folder.

3 In the file list, double-click 09Original to open the file.

After Microsoft Word compares these two documents, your document window looks like the following illustration.

Strikethrough indicates deleted text.

Underscore indicates inserted text.

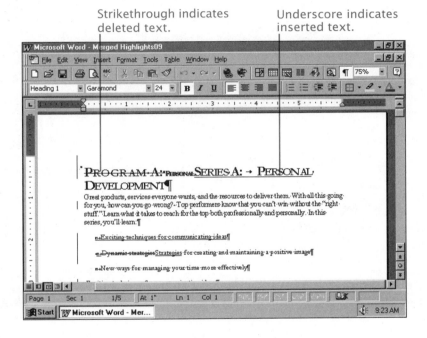

 NOTE Some changes in text formatting, such as changes in capitalization, are not identified.

Accepting and Rejecting Changes

With the changes in the document identified, you can decide whether or not to accept individual changes. After you respond to each change, Microsoft Word highlights the next change for you to accept or reject. If you change your mind about accepting or rejecting a change, you can click the Undo button in the Accept Or Reject Changes dialog box to undo the most recent change.

169

TIP You can accept or reject all changes at one time by clicking the Accept All button or the Reject All button.

Review changes

1 On the Tools menu, point to Track Changes, and then click Accept Or Reject Changes.

The Accept Or Reject Changes dialog box appears. This dialog box remains open as you review changes in a document.

Reject this change.

Reject all changes.

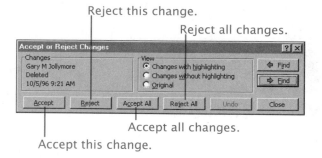

Accept all changes.

Accept this change.

2 Click ⮕Find.

Microsoft Word locates the first difference between the revised document and the original document.

Accept changes

You can accept or reject each change. The Changes section of the Accept Or Reject Changes dialog box provides additional information about the change. In this exercise, you accept the change and move on to the next change.

1 Click Accept.

The change is accepted in the document. Any revision marks are removed, and the next change is automatically selected.

 TIP The Reviewing toolbar contains many useful features for reviewing document changes. Use the right mouse button to click any toolbar, and then click Reviewing to display the Reviewing toolbar. The buttons on the Reviewing toolbar give you the ability to move between changes, insert comments, accept or reject changes, and turn revision marks on and off.

2   Click Accept.

The change is accepted in the document. Any revision marks are removed, and the next change is automatically selected.

3   Click ➡Find.

The change is skipped, and the next change is automatically selected.

Reject a change

When you do not want to accept a change, you can reject the change. If you are unsure, you can click Find Next to ignore the change for now.

➤   Click Reject.

The change is rejected in the document, restoring the text to the wording in the original document. The revision marks are removed, and the next change is automatically selected.

Undo a response to a change

➤   Click Undo.

The change you rejected in the previous step is restored.

Accept remaining changes

1   Click Accept.

The change is accepted in the document. Any revision marks are removed and the next change is automatically selected.

2   Accept each of the remaining changes in the document by pressing Accept All, and then when Word asks if you want to accept all remaining changes, click Yes.

3   Click Close to close the dialog box and return to the document window.

4   Save the document.

Identifying Changes

When you are working in a document that has a lot of changes, you might prefer not to see all the individual changes, but rather to see only the changed lines that identify the line containing changes. For example, your manager would like to see the work contributed by other team members. Instead of providing a document that identifies each and every change, you can provide a document that uses only changed lines to identify changes.

Display only changed lines

In this exercise, you will hide the revisions so that only the changed lines are displayed.

1   On the Tools menu, click Options.

    The Options dialog box appears.

2   Click the Track Changes tab to bring it to the front of the dialog box.

3   In the Inserted Text section, click the Mark down arrow, and then click (None).

4   In the Deleted Text section, click the Mark down arrow, and then click Hidden.

    Your completed dialog box should look like the following illustration.

No revision marks
for inserted or
deleted text

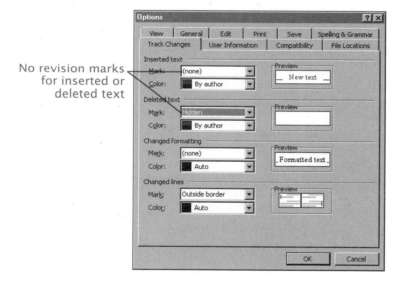

5   Click OK to close the Options dialog box and return to the document.

Compare documents

With the Track Changes options set to display only changed lines, you can once again compare the revised document with the original to produce a document that displays changes with changed lines.

1   On the Tools menu, point to Track Changes, and then click Compare Documents.

The Select File To Compare With Current Document dialog box appears.

2 Be sure that Winword SBS Practice folder is in the Look In box. If it is not, click the Look In Favorites button, and double-click the Winword SBS Practice folder.

3 In the file list, double-click 09Original.

After Microsoft Word compares these two documents, your document window looks like the following illustration.

Changed lines identify lines containing revisions.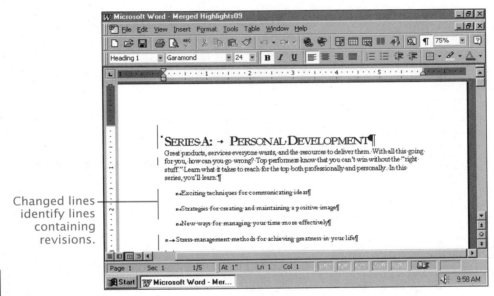

Save

5 On the Standard toolbar, click the Save button.

Highlighting Changes

You can activate the Highlight Changes feature when you want to display revision marks for the changes you make to a document. The Highlight Changes feature displays revision marks to identify additional changes you make to the document, as you make them.

Highlight new changes

1 On the Tools menu, point to Track Changes, and then click Highlight Changes.

The Highlight Changes dialog box appears.

2 Click the Track Changes While Editing check box to select it.

3 Click OK.

4 Press CTRL+ END to place the insertion point at the end of the document.

5 Type **Stress management facilities are being provided by Stress Management Strategies.**

The changed line in the margin indicates the presence of revised text in this paragraph. You might need to scroll to the left to see the changed line in the document window.

Changed line —
New text —

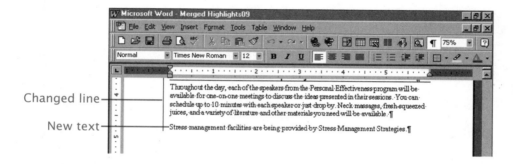

Turn off changes highlighting

In this exercise, you turn off changes highlighting, so that Microsoft Word does not continue to highlight additional changes in your document.

1 On the Tools menu, point to Track Changes, and then click Highlight Changes.

The Highlight Changes dialog box appears.

2 Clear both Highlight Changes check boxes.

3 Click OK to return to the document window.

4 Save the document.

NOTE If you'd like to build on the skills that you learned in this lesson, you can do the One Step Further. Otherwise, skip to "Finish the lesson."

174

One Step Further: Inserting Comments

In earlier versions of Microsoft Word, this feature was called Annotations.

When working on the same document with others, it is often useful to provide explanations of proposed changes, ask questions, or add editorial comments. By using the Comments feature, you can easily insert such comments without adding to the actual text of the document.

Insert a comment

When you insert a comment, a comment identifier formatted in hidden text is placed in the document. You type the text of your comment in the Comment pane at the bottom of the document window and close the pane when you are done. In this exercise, you insert a comment regarding the stress management company.

1   With the insertion point at the end of last paragraph, on the Insert menu, click Comment.

The insertion point appears in the Comment pane, which opens at the bottom of the document window.

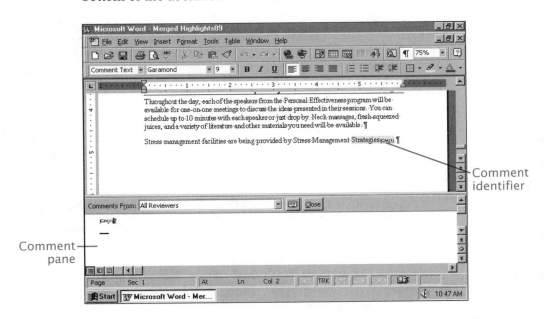

2   In the Comment pane, type **Martin: I was able to negotiate a great deal for us from this new vendor.**

3 At the top of the Comments pane, click the Close button.

The comment indicator and the last word of the line are highlighted, alerting the reader to the presence of a comment. Change the magnification as needed to get a better view of the highlighted text.

Display a comment

You can view a comment by placing the cursor over the comment mark and waiting a moment. The comment is displayed along with the reviewer's name. In this exercise, you will display the comment you just entered.

1 Place the cursor over the comment identifier and wait a moment.

The comment is displayed along with the reviewer's name.

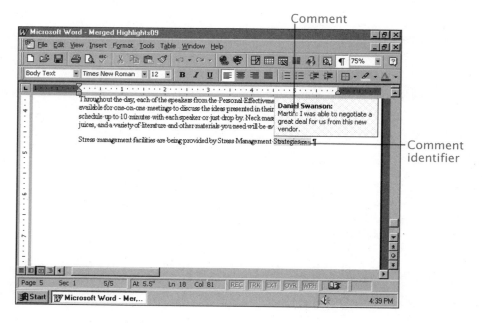

2 Move the pointer to close the comment.

3 Save the document.

 NOTE If you want to edit or annotate existing comments, you can open the Comment pane at the bottom of the screen either by double-clicking the comment mark or by using the Comments command on the View menu. Click the Close button just above the Comment pane to close it.

Finish the lesson

1 To continue to the next lesson, on the File menu, click Close.
2 If you are finished using Microsoft Word for now, on the File menu, click Exit.

Lesson Summary

To	Do this
Compare documents	On the Tools menu, point to Track Changes, and then click Compare Documents. Open the document you want to compare with the active document.
Review changes	On the Tools menu, point to Track Changes, and then click Accept Or Reject Changes. Click ➡ Find to locate first change.
Accept a change	In the Accept or Reject Changes dialog box, click Accept. Click the Accept All button to accept all changes.
Reject a change	In the Review Revisions dialog box, click Reject. Click the Reject All button to reject all revisions.
Undo a response to a change	In the Review Revisions dialog box, click Undo Changes.
Change revision options	On the Tools menu, click Options. On the Track Changes tab, select the options you want to use.
Highlight changes	On the Tools menu, point to Track Changes, and then click Highlight Changes. Use the check boxes to select your options.
Turn off changes highlighting	On the Tools menu, point to Track Changes, and then click Highlight Changes. Use the check boxes to clear the options you want to turn off.

For online information about	On the Help menu, click Contents And Index, click the Index tab, and then type
Comparing documents	**revision marks, comparing documents**
Document versions	**revision marks, document versions**
Revision marks	**revision marks, overview**

Organizing a Document by Using Outlining

Estimated time
40 min.

In this lesson you will learn how to:

- Switch to Outline view.
- Use the Outlining toolbar to promote and demote headings.
- View only selected heading levels and body text.
- Rearrange blocks of text by moving headings.
- Combine subdocuments.

When you work with a document that is several pages long and contains many different topics, or with one that has a hierarchical structure (main topics and related subtopics), the Microsoft Word outlining feature is a valuable tool for examining and adjusting the structure of your document. In this lesson, you will display a document in Outline view so that you can see how it is organized. You will also learn how to view only specific levels of the document and how to reorganize your document quickly by moving headings and promoting and demoting heading levels.

Start the lesson

Follow the steps below to open the practice file called 10Lesson, and then save it as Program Highlights10.

Open

*Look In
Favorites*

1   On the Standard toolbar, click the Open button.

2   Be sure that the Winword SBS Practice folder is in the Look In box. If it is not, click the Look In Favorites button, and then double-click the folder.

3   In the file list, double-click the file named 10Lesson.

4   On the File menu, click Save As.

   The Save As dialog box appears.

5   Click the Look In Favorites button, and then double-click the SBS Word folder.

   This folder is created in Lesson 2.

6   Select and delete any text in the File Name box, and then type **Program Highlights10**

7   Click Save, or press ENTER.

If you share your computer with others, the screen display might have changed since your last lesson. If your screen does not look similar to the illustrations as you work through this lesson, see Appendix B, "Matching the Exercises."

An associate at West Coast Sales has made changes to the Program Highlights document. Although you have already approved the changes to the text, you want to review the changes to the organization and structure of the document using the Outline view.

Working in Outline View

To use the Microsoft Word outline feature, you need to display your document in Outline view. The fastest way to switch between views, including Outline view, is to click the View buttons just above the status bar.

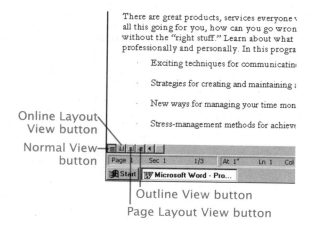

Online Layout View button

Normal View button

Outline View button

Page Layout View button

Switch to Outline view

Outline View

> In the lower left of the window, click the Outline View button.

When you are in Outline view, the Outlining toolbar appears below the other toolbars at the top of the window. Here is an overview of the buttons on the Outlining toolbar.

To	Use these buttons
Promote and demote headings	⬅ ➡
Demote heading to body text	⇨
Move heading and associated subheadings and text up or down one line	⬆ ⬇
Expand a heading to reveal its subordinate subheadings and associated text	➕
Collapse a heading to hide its subordinate subheadings and associated text	➖
Show all levels through the selected level	1 2 3 4 5 6 7 All
Show only the first line of body text in a paragraph. This button toggles to display all lines	≡
Show outline with or without formatting	A/A
Display Master Document toolbar	▢

Display formatting

Show Formatting

> On the Outlining toolbar, click the Show Formatting button to change the formatting.

Show Formatting is a toggle button. Click to turn it off, and click again to turn it on. If you don't click this button, the headings and the body text are both formatted in the same font in Outline view. By displaying headings and body text so that they are formatted differently from each other, you can more easily distinguish headings from the body text of the document. The formatting in Outline view is not the same as the formatting you see in Page Layout or Normal view.

181

NOTE In some ways Outline view and Document Map are very similar. For example, both views display headings in your document and help clarify the document's organization of ideas and structure. However, unlike the Document Map, Outline view also offers the ability to rearrange the structure of the document, as well other features that help you focus on the important ideas in your document.

Understanding Outline View

When you first display your document in Outline view, the different levels of text in your document are shown in several different ways to indicate how the text is organized. The size of the text, how it is indented, and the symbols on the left are all indicators of the text relationships in your document. If text is formatted in a heading style that has additional subheadings, it has an outline symbol (a plus sign) next to it. A minus sign next to text formatted in a heading style indicates the text has no subheadings. Lower-level headings are indented under higher-level headings. Text that is not formatted in a heading style is called *body text*. Body text is identified by a small square next to it and is usually indented under the heading that it follows. The following illustration identifies what you see in Outline view.

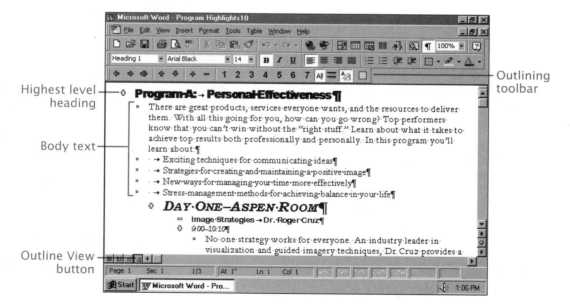

In Outline view, you see a plus sign (+) next to the text "Program A: Personal Effectiveness." The plus sign indicates that this text is formatted as a heading style, and contains subheadings. When you select the heading, the Style box on the Formatting toolbar indicates that this is a Heading 1. The text "Day One–Aspen Room" is a Heading 2, and the plus sign to the left indicates that it also has subheadings. The text "Image Strategies   Dr. Roger Cruz" is assigned Heading 3 and has no subheadings, as indicated by the minus sign.

 NOTE   The higher the level number, the lower the heading level. For example, heading level 1 is the highest level. Subsequent levels are represented by increasingly higher numbers.

Promoting and Demoting Headings

By using the Paragraph command on the Format menu, you can assign an outline level to a paragraph without formatting the paragraph in a specific style.

In Outline view, you can promote a heading to a higher level or demote it to a lower level. You can change body text to a heading level in the same way you promote or demote a heading. You can also change a heading level to body text by using the Demote To Body Text button.

Promote headings

To organize this document, you will use the Promote and Demote buttons to establish a hierarchical structure for the remaining topics.

1   Click the heading "Program B: Hot Technologies," and then click the Promote button on the Outlining toolbar.

This text is promoted from Heading 2 to Heading 1.

Promote

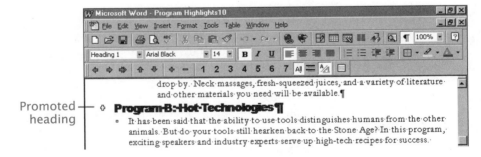

Promoted heading

You can also drag the outline symbol to the left to promote a heading or to the right to demote a heading.

2   Scroll down, and select the text "Tech Center."

You can also place the insertion point anywhere in the line that you want to promote.

3   Click the Promote button to promote this text to Heading 2.

4   Scroll down, and place the insertion point in the text "WCS SST System."

5   Click the Promote button twice to promote this text to Heading 3.

Your outline looks like the following illustration.

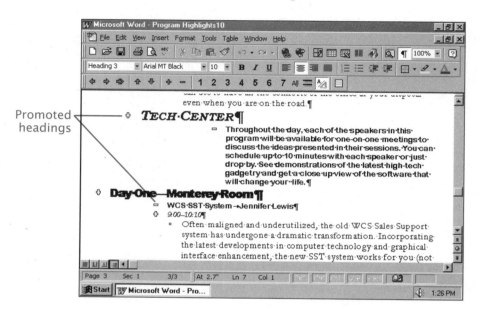

Promoted headings

Demote headings

When you want to change an existing heading level to a lower level, use the Demote button on the Outlining toolbar. In this exercise, you use Demote features to change heading levels.

1   Click the text "Day One—Monterey Room."

2   On the Outlining toolbar, click the Demote button to demote this text to Heading 2.

3   Scroll up, and then click in the text "Throughout the day...".

4   On the Outlining toolbar, click the Demote To Body Text button.

This text is now body text. Your outline looks like the following illustration.

Demote

Demote To
Body Text

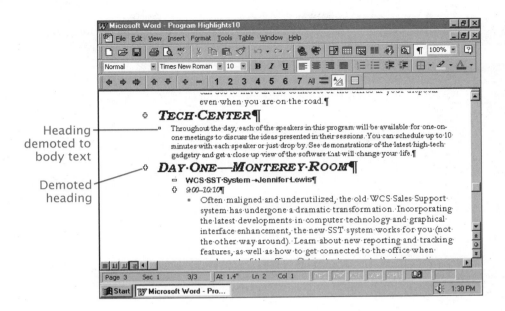

Heading demoted to body text

Demoted heading

Viewing Specific Parts of the Outline

A major benefit of using Outline view is that you can focus only on those parts of the document that are important to you at the moment. For example, to get the "big picture," you can display only Headings 1 and 2 and hide all the sub-headings and any subordinate body text—the body text immediately subordinate to the first two headings remains displayed. When you are ready to focus on the details of a topic, you can view lower-level headings and body text. You also have the option of viewing all the body text or only the first line of each paragraph.

Viewing Specified Heading Levels

When you want to focus on the higher-level structure of your document or overview information, you might want to see only the first two or three heading levels. You can click the heading level button that corresponds to the lowest level of detail you want to see. For example, if you click the Show Heading 3 button, you see heading levels 1, 2, and 3.

View first-level headings

You can click the Show Heading 1 button to get the highest level view of your document. This is useful when you want to focus on only the major elements in your document.

Show Heading 1

> Scroll to the beginning of the document, and click the Show Heading 1 button on the Outlining toolbar.

The Show Heading 1 command can be applied anywhere in your document. You returned to the beginning of the document to see the headings shown in the following illustration.

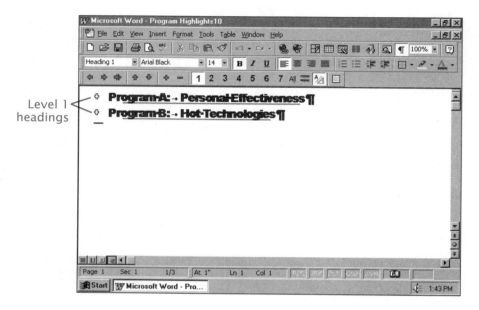

View the first three heading levels

Use lower-level settings when you want to focus on specific details or individual topics in your document. Viewing only a few levels helps you see the overall structure and focus on the organization of your document without the distraction of seeing more text than you need.

Show Heading 3

> On the Outlining toolbar, click the Show Heading 3 button.

Your document looks like the following illustration.

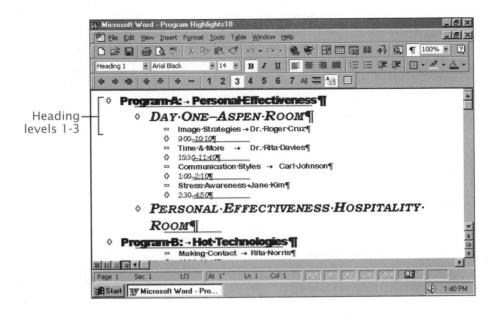

Heading levels 1-3

View all heading levels and body text

When you want to see all the information in your document, you can click the All button on the Outlining toolbar.

Show All Headings

➤ On the Outlining toolbar, click the Show All Headings button.

All heading levels and first lines of text in your document are displayed.

View two heading levels

Show Heading 2

➤ On the Outlining toolbar, click the Show Heading 2 button.

The first two levels in your document are displayed.

Expanding and Collapsing Headings

The heading level buttons on the Outlining toolbar affect the number of heading levels displayed for the entire outline. The Expand and Collapse buttons allow you to focus on selected parts of the document rather than on the document as a whole. When you want to display more heading levels under a single heading, you can *expand* that heading, and when you want to display fewer headings, you can *collapse* them. The Expand and Collapse buttons on the Outlining toolbar display (or hide) subordinate headings and text of the heading containing the insertion point.

187

Expand a heading

You can use the Expand button to see more detail about a topic in your document. Click the button repeatedly until you see all the subordinate text.

Expand

1 Scroll down, and place the insertion point in the heading "Day One—Monterey Room."

2 On the Outlining toolbar, click the Expand button.

The next level of subheading under this heading is displayed.

3 Click the Expand button again so that all subordinate text and subheadings under this heading are displayed.

The other headings in the document remain collapsed.

Level 2 heading

Subordinate text displayed

Expanded heading symbol

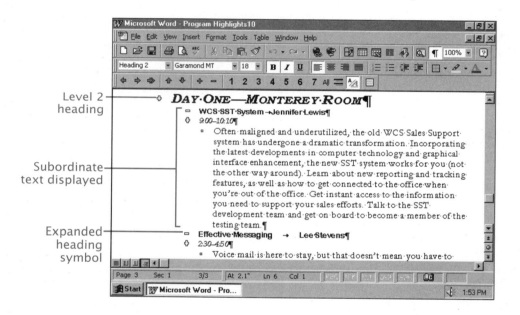

 TIP You can also double-click the outline symbol to expand and collapse headings. Double-clicking the outline symbol for an already expanded heading collapses the heading, while double-clicking the outline symbol for an already collapsed heading expands the heading.

Collapse a heading

Use the Collapse button to hide details in your document.

Collapse

➤ Make sure the insertion point is still in the heading "Day One—Monterey Room," and then click the Collapse button on the Outlining toolbar.

The lowest level of subheadings and text under this heading are hidden. You can continue clicking this button to further collapse the subheadings and text.

Viewing Body Text

When you display body text in Outline view, you can specify how much of the body text you want to see. You can choose to see all the body text, which is useful for editing. Or you can choose to see only the first line of individual paragraphs of body text, which is useful for helping you recall the content of a paragraph without displaying all the text.

Display the first line of body text

The Show First Line Only button on the toolbar toggles to display the first line of a paragraph or to display all the body text. For example, when all the body text is displayed, clicking this button hides all but the first line of text. When you click the Show First Line Only button again, all the text reappears.

1 Make sure the insertion point is still in the heading "Day One—Monterey Room," and then click the Expand button once.

2 On the Outlining toolbar, click the Show First Line Only button.

Only the first line of text in each paragraph is visible.

Show First Line Only

First line of text displayed

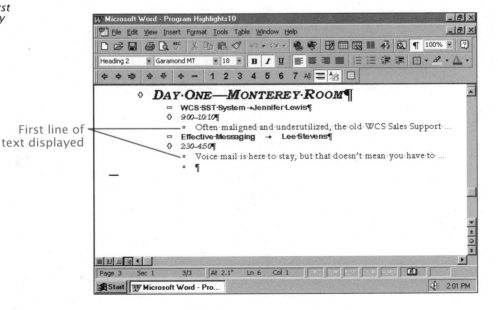

Moving Blocks of Text

For a demonstration of how to move text in Outline view, double-click the Camcorder Files On The Internet shortcut on your Desktop or connect to the Internet address listed on p. xxviii.

Using Outline view to reorganize a document ensures that all the text associated with a collapsed heading stays together if you need to move text around in your document. You can rearrange large blocks of text in your document without selecting all the text you want to move. You also avoid having to scroll extensively to move your text over a long distance. In Outline view, when you move a collapsed heading, all the subordinate headings and text, whether visible or not, move with the heading. If you move an expanded heading, however, only the selected text moves.

Move a block of text

To move a block of text in an outline, you collapse the heading so that all the subordinate headings and body text are hidden. Then you use the Move Up and Move Down buttons on the Outlining toolbar to move the heading up or down one line at a time. When you move the heading, the subordinate headings and body text move as well.

Show Heading 2

Move Down

Expand

Show First Line Only

You can also drag the outline symbol for the heading you want to move.

1 On the Outlining toolbar, click the Show Heading 2 button.

2 Select the heading "Tech Center."

3 On the Outlining toolbar, click the Move Down button to move the selected heading after the heading "Day One—Monterey Room."

4 Click the Expand button, and then click the Show First Line Only button to see that all the subordinate text also moved.

Your outline looks like the following illustration.

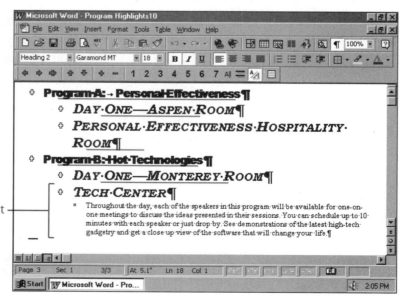

Moved text

Show Heading 3

*Show All
Headings*

5   On the Outlining toolbar, click the Show Heading 3 button.

6   Select the headings "Making Contact" and "Off-Site Tools," which are formatted in the Heading 3 style.

7   On the Outlining toolbar, click the Move Down button three times.

     Both headings move down together in the document.

8   On the Outlining toolbar, click the Show All Headings button to display all the document text.

Combining Documents

If you are working on a very large document, you can work more effectively if you divide the document into smaller pieces (subdocuments) and work on each piece separately. Using the Microsoft Word Master Document feature, you can combine the subdocuments by inserting them into a master document. When you open the master document, you can view and edit all the subdocuments at one time. You can also take advantage of outlining features to move around blocks of text, organize ideas, and promote and demote headings.

Insert a subdocument

By inserting a document into the master document as a subdocument, you can make changes to the text in the master document and to the subdocument. If someone has made changes to the subdocument, the most up-to-date version of the subdocument opens in the Master Document. In this exercise, you will insert a draft of a description of another program for the West Coast Sales conference Program Highlights document.

> **NOTE**   While a master document is open, no one else can make changes to the subdocuments. Only the user who opened the master document can open and make changes to the subdocuments.

*Master
Documents*

*Insert
Subdocument*

1   Press CTRL+END to go to the end of the document. On the Outlining toolbar, click the Master Documents button.

     The Master Document buttons are at the left end of the Outlining toolbar.

2   Click the Insert Subdocument button.

     The Insert Subdocument dialog box appears.

3   Be sure the Winword SBS Practice folder is in the Look In box. In the file list, double-click the file named 10Subdoc.

     The subdocument is inserted in the Program Highlights document. The Program Highlights document is now a master document.

NOTE Although you can edit the subdocument directly in the master document, you might prefer to edit the document in a new document window (and not in Outline view). Double-clicking the subdocument icon opens the subdocument in its own document window. When the subdocument is in its own document window, in the Master Document window you see an icon of a lock. This icon indicates that the subdocument is locked. If you want to make changes to a subdocument in Normal or Page Layout view, you must switch to subdocument window and make your changes there. When you close the subdocument window, you return to the Outline view.

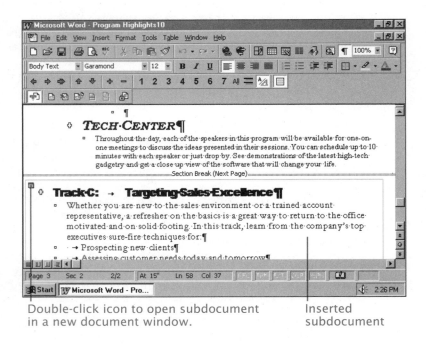

Double-click icon to open subdocument
in a new document window.

Inserted
subdocument

4 Save the document.

Switch to Normal view

Normal View

➤ In the lower left of the window, click the Normal View button.

The subdocument appears in the document window after the next page section break.

NOTE If you'd like to build on the skills that you learned in this lesson, you can do the One Step Further. Otherwise, skip to "Finish the lesson."

One Step Further: Moving Around Using Bookmarks

Another way to minimize the amount of scrolling you need to do in a large document is to use bookmarks. *Bookmarks* are invisible labels you assign to different parts of the document so you can move quickly to the part in which you want to work, just as a physical bookmark helps you find your place in a book without having to check page numbers. If you move or even edit text that is associated with a particular bookmark, you can still move quickly to that topic, no matter where it is located in the document, by using the bookmark.

Creating a Bookmark

To create a bookmark you place the insertion point where you want to assign a bookmark. You can also select text (words, phrases, lines, or entire paragraphs) that you want to mark. Using the Bookmark command, you assign that location a bookmark name. There is no limit to the number of bookmarks you can include in your document. The document already includes a previously created bookmark.

Create a bookmark

Because the name for the exhibits area of the conference has not yet been approved, you decide to create a bookmark that has a generic name for this part of the Program Highlights document.

1 Select the heading "Tech Center."

2 On the Insert menu, choose Bookmark.

Bookmark names cannot include spaces.

3 In the Bookmark dialog box, type **exhibits** in the Bookmark Name box.

Bookmark names are not case-sensitive. This means you can enter names in both uppercase or lowercase.

4 Click the Add button.

A bookmark named "exhibits" has been assigned to the selected text.

Save

5 On the Standard toolbar, click the Save button.

6 Press CTRL+HOME to move the insertion point to the start of the document.

Using Bookmarks to Move to a Location in the Document

After you create a bookmark, you can quickly move to that topic simply by using the Go To feature and selecting the bookmark to which you want to go. By creating bookmarks for areas of your document that you plan to return to later, you can quickly locate the part of the document you want.

Creating Bookmarks That Have Links

You can make moving to a bookmark location even faster by creating a link. A *link*—which is also known as a *hyperlink* or a *jump*—provides the ability to move to other locations in a document (or to a location on the World Wide Web) when you click a word or graphic. You can create links in a Word document that jump to bookmark locations.

 NOTE Creating a link also displays the Web toolbar in the program window so you can quickly get to Internet Web sites. If you do not want to use this toolbar, use the right mouse button to click the toolbar. On the shortcut menu, click Web to hide the toolbar.

1 Select the text to which you want to assign a link.

2 On the Insert menu, click Hyperlink.

3 In the bottom part of the Hyperlink dialog box, type the name of the bookmark to which you want the link to jump.

You can also click Browse to display a list of all the bookmarks in you document from which you can choose.

4 Click OK.

The link appears as red underlined text. Click the link to jump to the bookmark location.

Go to a bookmark location

To see how useful bookmarks are, you can use the Go To feature to move to an existing bookmark already saved for you in the practice document.

You can also use the Bookmark command on the Insert menu to select the bookmark you want.

1 Double-click the page number on the left side of the status bar.

The Find And Replace dialog box appears.

2 Be sure the Go To tab is in front.

3   In the Go To What box, select Bookmark.

4   Click the Enter Bookmark Name down arrow.

Specify Bookmark.

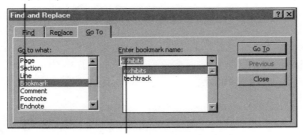

Select the bookmark you want.

5   Select exhibits.

6   Click the Go To button.

Microsoft Word moves to the text in the document identified by the exhibits bookmark.

7   Click Close. If a message asks you whether you want to save your changes, click Yes.

Finish the lesson

1   To continue to the next lesson, on the File menu, click Close.

2   If you are finished using Microsoft Word for now, on the File menu, click Exit.

Lesson Summary

To	Do this	Button
Display the document in Outline view	Click the Outline View button next to the horizontal scroll bar.	
Promote or demote a heading	Click the Promote button. *or* Click the Demote button.	
Demote a heading to body text	Click the Demote To Body Text button.	
Display specific headings for the entire document	Click the heading level button that corresponds to the headings you want to see.	

To	Do this	Button
Hide subheadings and text for selected headings	Select the heading, and then click the Collapse button.	
Display subheadings and text for selected headings	Select the heading, and then click the Expand button.	
Display all headings and body text	Click the Show All Headings button.	
Toggle the display to show the first line or all lines of body text	Expand the heading, and then click the Show First Line Only button.	
Move a collapsed heading	Select the heading, and then click the Move Up or Move Down button to move one line at a time.	

For online information about	On the Help menu, click Contents And Index, click the Index tab, and then type
Outlining	**outlines**

Creating and Printing Merged Documents

Estimated time
50 min.

In this lesson you will learn how to:

- Create a main document.
- Create a data source of names and addresses.
- Attach an existing data source to a main document.
- Merge data source information into a main document.

Suppose you want to mail out several letters that are nearly identical. Using Microsoft Word, you can create a *merged document,* which is a form letter in which customized information is combined with repetitive or boilerplate text. In this way, you can create many letters efficiently, each with a personal touch. In this lesson, you will learn how to create a main document that contains boilerplate text. Then, you will create a data source, which is the document that contains the individualized information. Finally, you will merge the main document and the data source to create your customized form letters. You'll also learn how to attach an existing data source (one already created) to a main document.

Merging Documents: Basic Techniques

Preparing any type of merged document involves two files: a main document and a data source. The *main document* contains the standardized text and graphics you want in each version of the merged document. The *data source* contains only the information that varies with each version—names, addresses, account numbers, and product codes, for example. You insert special instructions, called *merge fields*, in the main document to indicate where you want the variable information to appear. When you merge the data source and the main document, Microsoft Word inserts the appropriate information from the data source into the merge fields to create a merged document.

Whether you're printing mailing labels or personalizing a form letter, you use the same basic techniques to create the final, merged documents. The Mail Merge Helper guides you through each part of the process:

Part 1   Open a new or existing document that will be the main document.

Part 2   Attach an existing data source or create a new one.

Part 3   Insert merge field names into your main document.

Part 4   Merge the data source information with the main document.

Create a main document

Suppose you want to send letters to several people you met at a recent trade show to set up appointments on your next road trip. You can create a main document containing boilerplate text about the purpose of your visit, and later merge the appropriate names and addresses. In this exercise, you create a form letter main document.

New

To set up your screen display, see Appendix B, "Matching the Exercises."

1   If you don't have a blank document on your screen, click the New button on the Standard toolbar to create a new document.

Be sure that the Standard and Formatting toolbars and the ruler are displayed, and that Normal view is selected.

2   On the Tools menu, click Mail Merge.

The Mail Merge Helper dialog box appears.

3   Under Main Document, click Create.

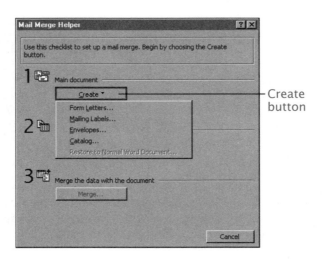

4 To open the Form Letter dialog box, click Form Letters.

5 In the Microsoft Word dialog box, click Active Window.

This selection uses the currently active document window as the main document. It does not open a new document.

Creating a Data Source

Now that you've created an empty main document, you're ready to create a data source. A data source contains all the text and graphics that change with each version of a merged document. Each set of related information (for a specific customer, for instance) makes up one *data record* in the data source. The different pieces of information in each record—for example, title, first name, last name, company, street address, city, state, postal code, and product—are called *fields*.

Understanding Data Sources and Databases

In its simplest form and most basic definition, a data source could be considered a very simple database. But a true database is so much more than a table in a Word document. A database created in Microsoft Access, for example, is a file that contains data organized in rows and columns (records and fields). A group of rows that contain related information is called a *table*. A database can contain multiple tables. It also contains information about how the tables are related. The database also contains reports and forms for use with the tables. Information stored in database records is more efficiently stored than records stored in a Word table. You can use a Microsoft Access database as a merge data source, but you have to identify Microsoft Access specifically as the data source in the Mail Merge Helper.

Each field name in a data source is identified in the header row of the data source. The field names in the header row must be unique and can have as many as 40 characters. You can use letters, numbers, and underscore characters, but not spaces. The first character must be a letter.

Acceptable field names	Unacceptable field names
FirstName	First Name (a field name cannot contain spaces)
Address1	1Address (a field name must begin with a letter)
VacationFax	SecondaryPersonalResidenceFaxTelephoneNumber (a field name cannot exceed 40 characters)

Define the field names for the header row

From the Mail Merge Helper dialog box, you can either open an existing data source or create a new one. In this exercise, you will create a new data source and select the field names to be included.

1   In the Mail Merge Helper dialog box, under Data Source, click the Get Data button.

2   Select Create Data Source.

Microsoft Word displays the Create Data Source dialog box; you can use this dialog box to specify the field names you want to include in your data source. You can start with the suggested fields already provided, delete the ones you don't want to use, or add your own.

3   For each of the following field names, first select the field, and then click the Remove Field Name button to remove the field from the list. You need to scroll down to select field names farther down in the list.

JobTitle

Address2

Country

HomePhone

WorkPhone

4   In the Field Name box, type **Product**

You can type over any text already selected in the Field Name box.

5   Click the Add Field Name button.

Your new field appears at the bottom of the Field Name list.

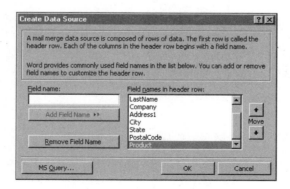

6   Click OK.

The Save As dialog box appears.

Save the data source

Now that you have defined the field names for the header row, you must save the data source file you created.

Look In Favorites

1   Click the Look In Favorites button, and then double-click the SBS Word practice folder.

2   Click in the File Name box, and type **Data Source11**

3   Click Save.

A Microsoft Word dialog box informs you that this data source has no records in it. You can start adding records immediately, or you can return to the main document and begin adding merge fields.

Entering Data Records

To begin entering records, you click the Edit Data Source button in the dialog box. Then, you can add records in the Data Form dialog box. The Data Form dialog box contains the fields you specified in the data source. You enter a set of fields (data record) for each individual to whom you want to send this letter. You can enter as many data records as you wish.

Complete the data source form

In this exercise, you will enter the name, address, and product information for the first person on your list.

1   Click the Edit Data Source button.

The Data Form dialog box appears.

If you need to return to a previous field to edit it, press SHIFT+TAB.

2   Type the following information in the form. As you complete each field, press ENTER to move to the next field.

Title	**Mr.**
FirstName	**Guy**
LastName	**Barton**
Company	**Victory Sports**
Address1	**4321 Pacific**
City	**Cascade Views**
State	**WA**
PostalCode	**98076**
Product	**camping and adventure gear**

Your completed dialog box looks like the following illustration.

201

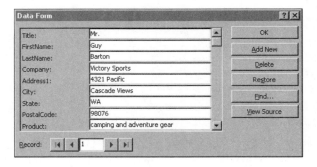

3 Click the Add New button to enter another data record.

You can also press ENTER to enter a new record.

4 Add new data records for the following individuals. For one of them, you will not enter a company name. By default, Microsoft Word will skip blank fields, so the merge is not affected if blank entries are in the data form. Remember to click the Add New button to add another data record.

Record 2

Title	**Ms.**
FirstName	**Karen**
LastName	**Nelson**
Company	
Address1	**43908 Big Sky Drive**
City	**Riverdale**
State	**WY**
PostalCode	**87087**
Product	**camping gear**

Record 3

Title	**Mr.**
FirstName	**James**
LastName	**Lee**
Company	**Fleet Feet Sports**
Address1	**Valley Heights Mall**
City	**Peach City**
State	**GA**
PostalCode	**06578**
Product	**outdoor cooking gear**

5 Click the OK button.

You return to the main document. Notice the new Mail Merge toolbar. Use the buttons on this toolbar when you are working with merged documents.

Mail Merge toolbar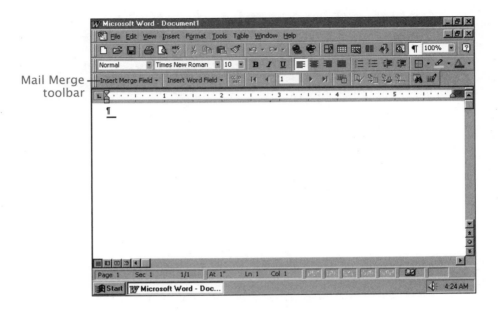

Save the main document

To attach the data source you just created to this main document, you need to save the main document. When you save the main document at this point, you are also saving the data records you entered.

Save

1 On the Standard toolbar, click the Save button.

2 Click the Look In Favorites button, and then double-click the SBS Word folder.

Look In Favorites

3 Under File Name, type **Main Document11** and then press ENTER.

After you save the document, your data source is attached to the main document.

Preparing Main Documents

Now that your data source is complete, you are ready to complete your main document. You want to type the standard text, using the correct spaces and punctuation that will print in all versions of the merged document. You also need to specify where you want your customized information to appear. To indicate where the variable information should appear, you insert merge fields that correspond to fields in the data source. When you merge the main document with the data source, Microsoft Word replaces the merge field names with the corresponding information from each data record in the data source.

Display paragraph marks

The merge field names act as *placeholders*; that is, they reserve a place for the data source information. You must insert the same spacing and punctuation between the merge field names as you would between words. Displaying paragraph marks makes it easier to see the spaces between words and the paragraphs in the document.

Show/Hide ¶

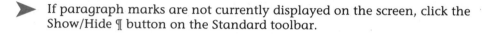 If paragraph marks are not currently displayed on the screen, click the Show/Hide ¶ button on the Standard toolbar.

Insert the date

In this exercise, you use the Date And Time command to insert the current date into the main document. If you want Microsoft Word to automatically update the information each time you print the document, you select the Automatically Update check box.

1   On the Insert menu, click Date And Time.

2   Select the date format that shows the date like this: June 28, 1997.

3   Click the Update Automatically box, and click OK.

    Microsoft Word inserts a date field into the document. Each time you print the main document, Microsoft Word will update the date field with the current date.

4   Press ENTER twice to leave a blank line below the date.

Inserting Field Names in the Main Document

When you insert the merge field names into the main document, you are telling Microsoft Word where you want the variable information from the data source to appear. Microsoft Word encloses each field name in chevrons (« »).

Insert the title, first name, and last name

1   On the Mail Merge toolbar, click Insert Merge Field.

    When you click this button, a list of the field names that you specified in the data source is displayed. You select field names to insert in the main document from this list.

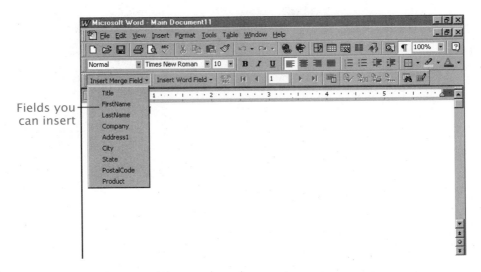

Fields you can insert

2   Click the Title merge field name to insert it into the document.

3   Press the SPACEBAR to insert a blank space between the title and the first name.

4   Click Insert Merge Field to insert the next field name, and select FirstName.

5   Press the SPACEBAR to insert a blank space between the first name and the last name.

6   Click Insert Merge Field, and then select LastName.

7   Press ENTER to move to the next line.

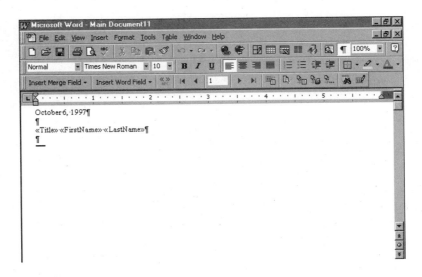

Insert the company name and address

1 Click Insert Merge Field, select Company, and then press ENTER.

2 Click Insert Merge Field, select Address1, and then press ENTER.

3 Click Insert Merge Field, and then select City.

4 Type a comma, and then press the SPACEBAR.

This creates the correct punctuation between the city and state.

5 Click Insert Merge Field, and then select State.

6 Press the SPACEBAR to insert a space between the state and the postal code.

7 Click Insert Merge Field, and then select PostalCode.

8 Press ENTER twice to leave a blank line.

Type the salutation

You can use a merge field name as many times as you want in a document. In this exercise, you type the boilerplate salutation "Dear" followed by the Title and LastName merge fields, and finally a colon.

1 Type **Dear** and then press the SPACEBAR. Do *not* press ENTER.

2 Click Insert Merge Field, and select Title.

3 Press the SPACEBAR to leave a space between the title and the last name.

4 Click Insert Merge Field, and select LastName.

If you see the Office Assistant, click Cancel to turn off the Office Assistant, and finish the letter without the help of a wizard.

5 Type a colon, and then press ENTER twice to leave a blank line.

Your document looks like the following illustration.

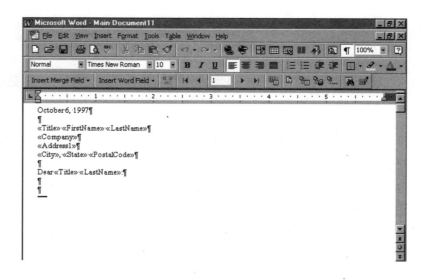

Finish typing the letter

You can use a merge field name within the body of the letter to customize the text. In this exercise, you insert the name of the city in each letter.

1 Type **Thank you for attending our trade show. We will be in**

Do *not* press ENTER.

2 Press the SPACEBAR.

A space is inserted following "We will be in."

3 Click Insert Merge Field, select City, and then press the SPACEBAR.

4 Type **next month. We would like to show you our new** and then press the SPACEBAR.

5 Click Insert Merge Field, and select Product.

6 Type a period. Then, press ENTER twice to create a blank line between the body of the letter and the closing.

7 Type **Sincerely,** and then press ENTER three times.

8 Type **Terry Kim** (or type your name).

9 On the Standard toolbar, click the Save button.

Your completed document looks like the following illustration.

Save

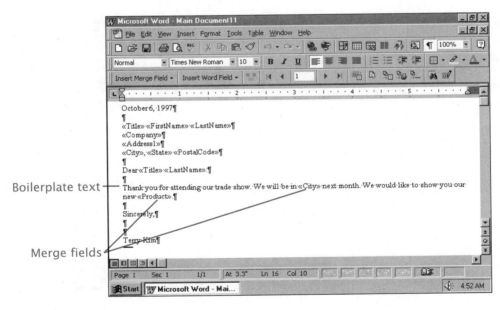

Boilerplate text

Merge fields

Merging Documents

After you've attached a data source to the main document and inserted merge field codes into the main document, you are ready to combine the main document with the data source. You have three merge choices; each is available by clicking one of the following buttons on the Mail Merge toolbar.

- Use the Check For Errors button to have Microsoft Word check the main document and the data source and alert you to errors before you merge or print.

- Use the Merge To Printer button to merge the main document with the data source and immediately print each resulting document.

- Use the Merge To New Document button to merge the main document and data source and to store the resulting documents in a new document called Form Letters1. You can then view each version of the merged document on your screen and check formatting, spacing, and other details.

 NOTE The number associated with the form letter document name increases by one each time you merge a main document with a data source. The number you see might be different.

Merge the information into a new file

In the following exercise, you will use the Merge To New Document button to merge and then view your source data.

Merge To New Document

▶ To merge the main document and the data source and store the results in a new file, click the Merge To New Document button on the Mail Merge toolbar.

Each form letter is separated by a double dotted line labeled "Section Break (Next Page)." Each section is formatted to begin on a new page.

View and edit the letters

As you scroll through the letters, verify that the second letter does not have a company address. Microsoft Word skips this field in the second letter because you left the company field blank in the data source. You can edit any of the text in the letters as you would edit any other document, including the field text.

1 Click the scroll bar down arrow to scroll down and examine each letter.

2 In the last letter, select the word "month" and type **week** instead. Then, position the insertion point at the end of the last sentence, press the SPACEBAR, and then type **Please contact Katrina Ortez to set up an appointment.**

Print the merged letters

Print

> If you have a printer connected to your computer, be sure that the printer is turned on, and then click the Print button on the Standard toolbar.

If you don't have a printer, continue with the next exercise.

Close the merged document file

1   On the File menu, click Close.

2   When a message appears asking whether you want to save this document, click the No button.

You do not need to save this file. You can quickly generate another merged document (without the changes you just made) whenever you want to print these documents. The main document called Main Document11 is still open in the document window.

Attaching an Existing Data Source

You can use other existing data sources with your main documents, provided that the data source you want to use contains the same field names in the header row that are found in the main document. For example, a co-worker also has a list of individuals to whom you want to send your letter and has already entered the data records into a data source. You can attach your main document to your co-worker's data source using the Mail Merge Helper.

Using the Address Book as a Data Source

The Address Book is a Windows 95 feature that you can use if you have installed Microsoft Exchange, Schedule+, or Outlook on your computer. Outlook is a powerful scheduling and contact management program included in Office 97. You can use the Address Book to store and then insert names, addresses, or other information into a document. You can also use the Address Book option as your data source when you click the Data Source button in the Mail Merge Helper.

Attach an existing data source

The practice files you installed include a file called 11Data. This data source contains additional data you can merge with your main document. The fields in the header row of this data source are the same as the fields in the data source you created earlier in the lesson, and are the same fields you inserted in the main document.

*Mail Merge
Helper*

1 On the Mail Merge toolbar, click the Mail Merge Helper button.

2 In the Data Source area, click the Get Data button.

3 Select Open Data Source.

4 In the Open Data Source dialog box, click the Up One Level button, and then open the Winword SBS Practice file.

5 Double-click 11Data.

6 If you see a message asking whether you want to save Data Source11, click Yes.

7 When you return to the Mail Merge Helper dialog box, click the Close button.

8 Click the Merge To New Document button.

Microsoft Word merges the main document with the data source and displays the merged letters in a new document window called Form Letters2.

*Merge To New
Document*

Close the merged document file

1 On the File menu, click Close.

2 Click the No button. You do not need to save this file.

> **NOTE** If you'd like to build on the skills that you learned in this lesson, you can do the One Step Further. Otherwise, skip to "Finish the lesson."

One Step Further: Creating Mailing Labels

As part of the preparations for an upcoming conference, you decide to create mailing labels for the conference attendee letter envelopes. Using the Mailing Labels option when you create a main document, you can select from a list of standard labels for your envelopes. After you merge the data source into the labels main document, you can print the labels.

Create a main document for the labels

New

1 On the Standard toolbar, click the New button to create a new document.

2 On the Tools menu, click Mail Merge.

3 Under Main Document in the Mail Merge Helper dialog box, click the Create button.

Clicking this button reveals a list of main document options from which you can choose.

4   Click Mailing Labels.

A Microsoft Word message asks whether you want to use the active window as the Main Document or create a new document.

5   In the dialog box, click the Active Window button.

Attach an existing data source

1   In the Data Source area, click the Get Data button.

2   Select Open Data Source.

The Open Data Source Dialog box appears.

3   In the Winword SBS Practice folder, double-click 11Data.

A message tells you that Word needs to set up your main document.

Set up the label main document

1   Click the Set Up Main Document button to return to the main document.

2   In the Label Options dialog box, scroll through the Product Number list, and choose 5260 - Address.

This selection formats your labels so that they will print correctly on this kind of label.

3   Click OK.

The Create Labels dialog box appears.

4   In the Create Labels dialog box, click the Insert Merge Field button, and click the Title merge field name to insert it into the label.

5   Press the SPACEBAR to insert a blank space between the title and the first name.

6   Click Insert Merge Field to insert the next field name, and select FirstName.

7   Press the SPACEBAR to insert a blank space between the first name and the last name.

8   Click Insert Merge Field, and select LastName.

9   Press ENTER to move to the next line.

10   Click Insert Merge Field, select Company, and press ENTER.

11   Click Insert Merge Field, select Address1, and press ENTER.

12   Click Insert Merge Field, and select City.

13   Type a comma, and then press the SPACEBAR so that the punctuation will be correct between the city and state.

14   Click Insert Merge Field, and select State.

15 Press the SPACEBAR to insert a blank space between the state and the postal code.

16 Click Insert Merge Field, and select PostalCode.

17 Click OK to return to the Mail Merge Helper, and then click Merge to display the Merge dialog box.

18 In the Merge dialog box, click Merge again.

The merged label document looks like the following illustration. You can click the Merge To Printer button to print labels, or you can save the merged labels document and print the labels later.

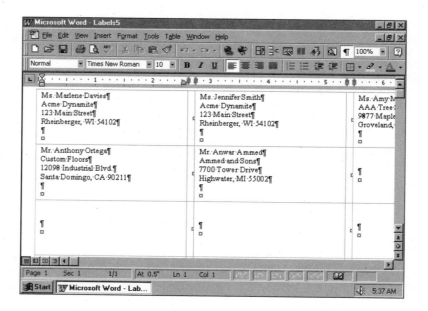

Finish the lesson

If you want to continue to the next lesson

1 Hold down the SHIFT key, and on the File menu, click Close All.

2 When a message appears asking whether you want to save changes, click No.

You do not need to save the merged labels document.

3 When a message appears asking whether you want to save changes to the next open document, click the Yes button and save the main label document using the name Label Main11 in your SBS Word folder.

4 If another message appears asking whether you want to save changes to the last remaining open document, click Yes.

If you want to quit Microsoft Word for now

1   On the File menu, click Exit.

2   When a message appears asking whether you want to save changes, click No.

   You do not need to save the merged labels document.

3   When a message appears asking whether you want to save changes to the next open document, click the Yes button and save the main label document using the name Label Main11 in your SBS Word folder.

4   If another message appears asking whether you want to save changes to the last remaining open document, click Yes.

Lesson Summary

To	Do this	Button
Create a main document	On the Tools menu, click Mail Merge. Under Main Document in the Mail Merge Helper dialog box, click Create and select a document type. Make a selection in the dialog box.	
Create and attach a data source	Be sure the document you want to use as the main document is open. On the Tools menu, click Mail Merge. Click Get Data, and select Create Data Source to open the dialog box where you add or remove field names. After you name and save the data source, click Edit Data Source to display a data form.	
Insert merge fields in a main document	With the main document open, click Insert Merge Field on the Mail Merge toolbar. Select the name of each field you want to insert.	
Merge a main document and a data source, and save the merged documents to a new file	With the main document open, click the Merge To New Document button on the Mail Merge toolbar to merge the information into one file.	

For online information about	On the Help menu, click Contents And Index, the Index tab, and then type
Merging documents	**merging documents (mail merge)**
Merging specific data records	**merging data records (mail merge), data sources**

Arranging Text and Graphics in a Document

Estimated time
60 min.

In this lesson you will learn how to:

- Create columns in a document.
- Vary the number of columns within a document.
- Insert manual column breaks, and add lines between columns.
- Position text within a text box.
- Use drop caps.
- Add lines and shapes.
- Create three-dimensional shapes.
- Use hyphenation to separate parts of words on separate lines.
- Enter text in Overtype mode.

With Microsoft Word, you can produce "snaking" columns, in which text flows from the bottom of one column to the top of the next. In this lesson, you'll format a document with a different number of columns for different parts (sections) of the document. You will also use a text box to position text precisely on the page. In addition, you will use the Drawing feature to draw lines and create three-dimensional shapes in the document.

Start the lesson

Follow the steps below to open the practice file called 12Lesson, and then save it with the new name Program Highlights12.

Open

*Look In
Favorites*

1 On the Standard toolbar, click the Open button.

2 Be sure the Winword SBS Practice folder is in the Look In box. If not, click the Look In Favorites button, and then double-click the folder.

3 In the file list, double-click the file named 12Lesson to open it.

4 On the File menu, click Save As.

The Save As dialog box appears.

5 Click the Look In Favorites button, and then double-click the SBS Word folder.

6 Select any text in the File Name box, and then type **Program Highlights12**

7 Click Save, or press ENTER.

Program Highlights12 is similar to the document created in Lesson 11. Some text and formatting changes have been made to better illustrate the features demonstrated in the exercises in this lesson.

If you share your computer with others who use Microsoft Word, the screen display might have changed since your last lesson. If your screen does not look similar to the illustrations as you work through this lesson, see Appendix B, "Matching the Exercises."

To give the program highlights document a more dramatic appearance, you decide to arrange the text creatively.

Creating Columns

You can use the Columns button on the Standard toolbar to create up to 12 columns in a document. Microsoft Word automatically breaks each column at the bottom of the page and moves the remaining text to the top of the page to start a new column. You also can use the Columns command on the Insert menu to create and format columns.

NOTE The number of columns you can create using the Columns button depends on the resolution of your monitor. The higher the resolution, the more columns you can create using this button. If the number of columns you want to create exceeds the number of columns you see when you click the Columns button, use the Columns command instead.

Display nonprinting characters

Before you begin, display nonprinting characters, if they are not already displayed.

Show/Hide ¶

➤ On the Standard toolbar, click the Show/Hide ¶ button.

Create multiple columns in a document

When you use the Columns button on the Standard toolbar, Microsoft Word formats the text of the document into the number of columns you specify.

Columns

1 On the Standard toolbar, click the Columns button.

2 Select the second column.

If a message appears indicating that you need to be in Page Layout view, click OK. Side-by-side columns now appear in your document, as shown in the following illustration. Scroll through the document to view the column formatting.

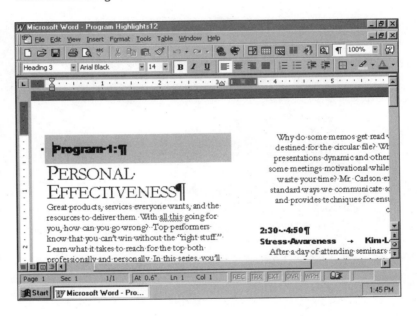

Varying Columns Within a Document

You've learned how easy it is to create columns in a document. If you need a more sophisticated page layout, you can vary how many columns appear on a page or in sections of the document. For example, you might make the headline of a brochure one column that extends across the width of the page and arrange the body of the brochure in two columns. To vary the number of columns, you insert a *section break* before you create your new columns. When you insert section breaks, you divide a document into sections, which are indicated by double-dotted, nonprinting lines.

For a demonstration of how to insert section breaks, double-click the Camcorder Files On The Internet shortcut on your Desktop or connect to the Internet address listed on page xxviii.

When you insert a section break to create differing numbers of columns on the same page, indicate that you want a *continuous break*. This means that the next section appears on the same page immediately following the preceding section. The type of section break you select is indicated by a nonprinting label in the double-dotted lines. You can then format each section separately. The following illustration shows a page divided into three sections. The second section is formatted in two columns, while the first and third sections are formatted in one column.

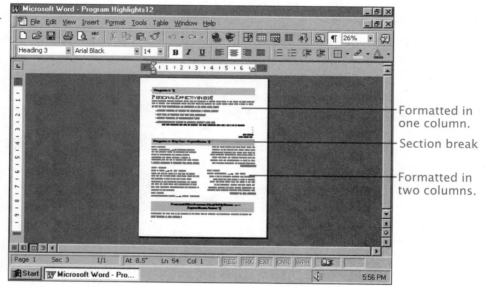

Formatted in one column.

Section break

Formatted in two columns.

Inserting Section Breaks

In Normal view, a section break appears as a double dotted line extending the width of the page, making it easy to format sections differently. After you format each section, you can switch back to Page Layout view to see how the column arrangement looks.

Switch to Normal view

Because it is easier to work with section breaks in Normal view, switch to Normal view. You want to be in Normal view to see the section breaks you are creating in the exercise.

Normal View

➤ On the far left of the horizontal scroll bar, click the Normal View button.

The text changes to one long column in Normal view.

Insert a section break

1   Place the insertion point in front of the text "9:00–10:10."

2   On the Insert menu, click Break.

The Break dialog box appears. It should look like the following illustration.

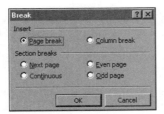

3   Under Section Breaks, select the Continuous option.

The new section will print immediately following the previous section on the same page.

4   Click OK.

Microsoft Word inserts the section break—a double dotted line labeled "Section Break (Continuous)." Now the document has two sections: one above the section break and one below the section break. The status bar indicates that the insertion point is located in section two.

Section break in document

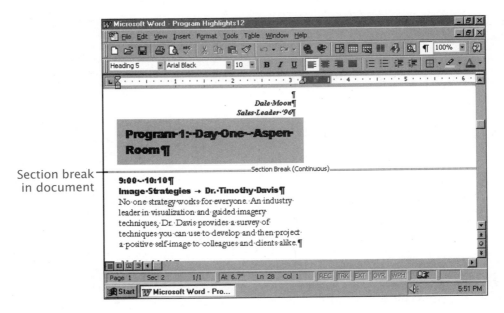

Insert another section break

A fast way to repeat the previous command is to use the Repeat command on the Edit menu. Part of the command name reflects the previous activity.

1 Scroll down, and click to position the insertion point in front of the shaded heading "Personal Effectiveness Hospitality Room."

2 On the Edit menu, click Repeat Insertion.

   Now you can format each section with the number of columns you want.

Creating Columns in Each Section

To create a different number of columns in each section, move to the section in which you want to vary the number of columns. Then, use the Columns button on the Standard toolbar to create the columns. With the document divided into sections, your column formatting affects only the section that contains the insertion point.

Format each section

1 Scroll to the top of the document.

2 Click anywhere in the first section to position the insertion point.

   Be sure that the status bar displays Section 1.

Columns

3 On the Standard toolbar, click the Columns button, and click Column 1.

4 Scroll down, and click anywhere in Section 3 to position the insertion point.

   Be sure that the status bar displays the correct section number.

5 On the Standard toolbar, click the Columns button, and click the first column to create one column in the last section.

Getting an Overview of the Layout

The Zoom button on the Standard toolbar is useful when you are working with columns. You can use the various Zoom control selections to change the magnification setting of the document. You can select one of the magnification settings, or you can type in an exact value. The value you choose depends not only on the type of monitor you are using and its resolution, but also on your personal preferences—that is, on how large or small you like your text as you work. When you change the magnification, you are changing only the way the document appears on the screen, not the size of the fonts or the length of the document.

To see even more of the document, you use the Full Screen view, which displays your document in a window that has no menus, toolbars, or scroll bars.

Adjust magnification

You can adjust the zoom magnification to see more of the page on your screen.

Zoom

1 Scroll to the beginning of the document. On the Standard toolbar, click the Zoom down arrow, and click Whole Page.

The document looks like the following illustration.

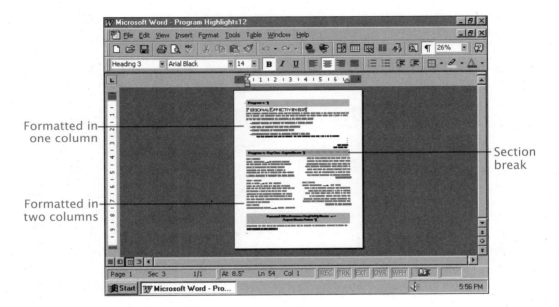

2 On the Standard toolbar, click the Zoom down arrow, and click Page Width.

Using the Page Width magnification setting, you can see both edges of the page.

3 Save the document.

Formatting Columns Within a Document

To get exactly the look you want in your document, you can take advantage of additional formatting options available in Microsoft Word. For example, to balance the amount of text in each column, you can use the Break command to specify precisely where the text should break between columns.

You can also use the Columns command, which includes special options for formatting columns. For example, you can use the Columns command to insert vertical lines between columns. You can also use this command to specify the space between columns or to create columns of unequal widths.

Insert a manual column break

In this exercise, you will insert a manual column break in the first column to balance the amount of text in each column.

1 Scroll up, and click to position the insertion point in front of the text "1:00–2:10."

2 On the Insert menu, click Break.

3 Click the Column Break option.

4 Click OK.

The text after the column break moves to the top of the next column. Your document looks like the following illustration.

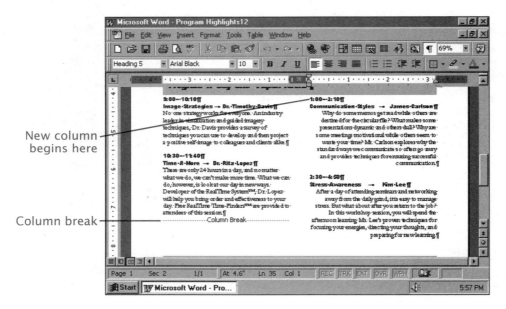

New column begins here

Column break

Modify formatting between columns

In this exercise, you will format one column to be wider than the other, increase the space between two columns, and add a vertical line to further separate the text in the columns.

1 On the Format menu, click Columns.

The Columns dialog box opens.

2 Be sure that the Equal Column Width check box is clear.

3 In the Width And Spacing area, click the Col #1 Width down arrow until 3" is in the text box.

The width of the right column automatically increases and the width of the left column decreases.

4 Click the Col #1 Spacing down arrow until 0.3" is in the text box.

5 Click the Line Between check box to select it.

The completed dialog box looks like the following illustration.

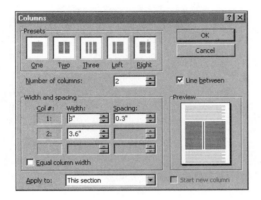

6 Click OK.

Your document looks like the following illustration.

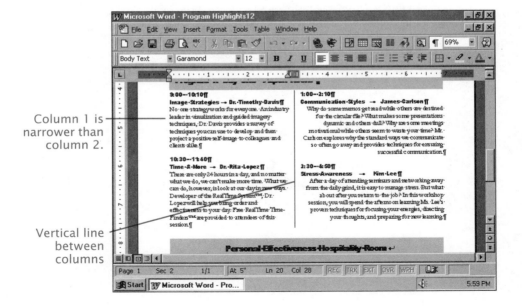

Column 1 is narrower than column 2.

Vertical line between columns

7 Save the document.

Positioning Text by Using Text Boxes

A *text box* is text surrounded by a frame that allows the text to be positioned anywhere on the page. You can specify how surrounding text wraps itself around the text box. If you resize the text box, the text rewraps within it. You can format framed text just as you format regular text, but the surrounding text is not affected. In the following exercises, you'll insert text into a text box, size and position the text box, and format the surrounding borders as well as the text within the box.

For a demonstration of how to create a text box, double-click the Camcorder Files On The Internet shortcut on your Desktop or connect to the Internet address listed on page xxviii.

Create a text frame

1 Scroll toward the middle of the document, and select the line "My sales increased 25% over the previous year after attending WCS '96. I owe it all to WCS!" and the three paragraph marks plus the name and title that follow.

2 On the Standard toolbar, click the Cut button.

The text is now on the Clipboard.

3 On the Insert menu, click Text Box.

4 With the new pointer shape, drag a 2.5-inch high by 1.5-inch wide rectangle near the area where you just deleted the text.

A blank text box appears. The box has a border that will print and sizing handles that will not print. The Text Box toolbar, which contains additional text box options, opens.

Cut

5 On the Standard toolbar, click the Paste button.

Your text box is as shown in the following illustration.

Paste

224

You can drag the toolbar out of your way if it obscures your view.

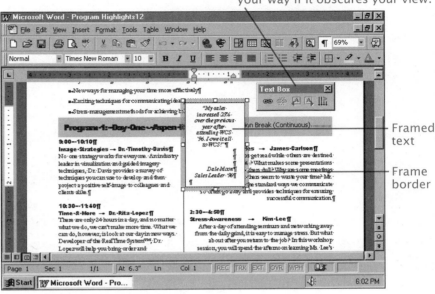

Framed text

Frame border

Size the text box

1   Place the pointer over the bottom middle sizing handle. When the pointer changes to a two-headed arrow, drag the bottom middle sizing handle up to the 2-inch mark on the vertical ruler.

2   Click outside the text box to hide the sizing handles and view the overall effect.

   The Text Box toolbar closes automatically when the text box selection is cleared.

Format the text box

You have a variety of options for changing the appearance of the text box. For example, you can control the flow of text around the text box and you can adjust the borders and shading of the box itself. You can add shading and change the style of the border. In this exercise, you will apply 25 percent shading and place a double-line border around the text.

1   Double-click the border of the text box to display the Format Text Box dialog box.

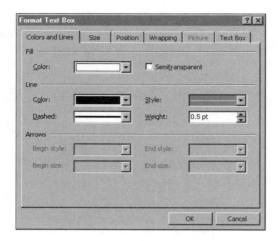

2 Be sure that the Colors And Lines tab is in front.

3 In the Fill section, click the Color down arrow, and select the lightest gray (25%).

4 In the Line section, click the Style down arrow, and select the 4½ point double-line style.

Adjust the flow of text around the text box

On the Wrapping tab in the Format Text Box dialog box, you can adjust how the text wraps around the text box. In this exercise, you will specify that you want the text that surrounds the text box to wrap around the text box.

1 With the Format Text Box dialog box still open, click the Wrapping tab to display the options on the Wrapping tab.

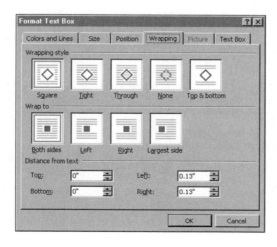

2 In the Wrapping Style area, click the Square option.

3 In the Wrap To area, click the Both Sides option.

4 Click OK to return to the document.

Position the text box to create a sidebar

A *sidebar* is specially formatted text positioned next to or at the bottom of the main article or text in a document. You can use sidebars to include text about a related topic or to provide background information about the subject of the nearby article. In this exercise, you will create a sidebar by dragging the text box into the left margin of the document.

Click the text box to display the sizing handles.

1 Be sure the sizing handles are displayed.

2 Scroll down, and then position the pointer near the frame (but not near a sizing handle) to display the four-headed pointer.

3 Drag the text box to the position shown in the illustration below. Adjust the position of the frame if necessary.

4 Click anywhere outside the text box to clear the selection. Your screen should look like this.

Drag to here.

Text flows around text box.

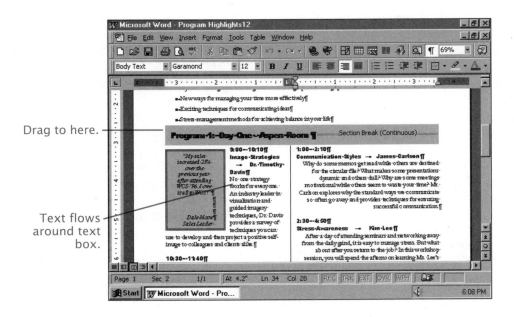

Position the text box to create a pull quote

A *pull quote* is specially formatted text positioned within an article or between columns in a document. Pull quotes are especially useful for testimonials or quotations related to an article. By dragging the text box to a position between the two columns of the document, you can create a pull quote.

1   Click the text box once to display the sizing handles.

2   Scroll down, and then drag the text box to the center of the document, positioning the framed text as shown in the following illustration. Adjust the position of the frame if necessary.

Drag to here.

Text flows around framed text.

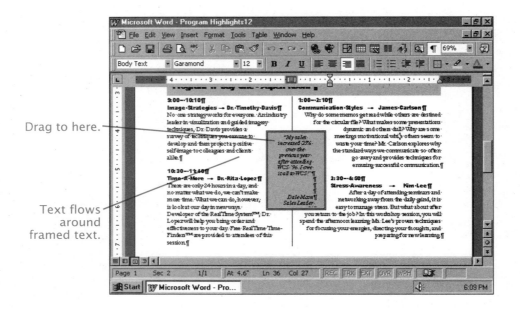

Using Drop Caps

One way of creating an additional effect in your document is to use drop caps. A *drop cap* is an enlarged, uppercase first character of a paragraph. The first line of the paragraph is aligned with the top edge of the oversized character. The Drop Caps command automatically positions the oversized framed character at the start of the current paragraph.

Insert a drop cap

In this exercise, you create a drop cap in your document.

You can format the enlarged character so that it drops up to a maximum of 10 lines.

1   Click anywhere in the paragraph below the heading "Personal Effectiveness Hospitality Room" to position the insertion point.

2   On the Format menu, click Drop Cap.

The Drop Cap dialog box appears.

3 Under Position, click the Dropped option.

4 In the Lines To Drop box, type **2**

5 Click OK.

The first character in the paragraph appears enlarged in a frame, as shown in the following illustration.

The drop cap character appears in the same font as the surrounding paragraph, but you can change the font if you want.

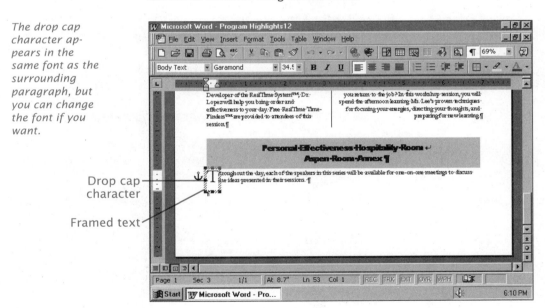

Drop cap character

Framed text

6 Save the document.

Drawing Lines in a Document

With the Drawing toolbar you can draw lines and insert shapes in your document. You can also modify the graphics objects you create by changing their color, shape, line thickness, transparency, pattern, and myriad other characteristics that enhance the appearance of your graphics.

Display the Draw toolbar

Drawing

➤ On the Standard toolbar, click the Drawing button.

The Drawing toolbar appears at the bottom of the program window.

Draw a straight line

Line

1   On the Drawing toolbar, click the Line button.

The pointer changes shape to look like a plus sign.

TIP   If you want to draw several lines, you can double-click the Line tool to keep the Line pointer active after you draw each line. Click the Line tool again (or click another tool) to disable the Line pointer.

2   Starting at the left side of the page below the two columns, drag a line across the page to the right, as shown in the following illustration.

Line in document

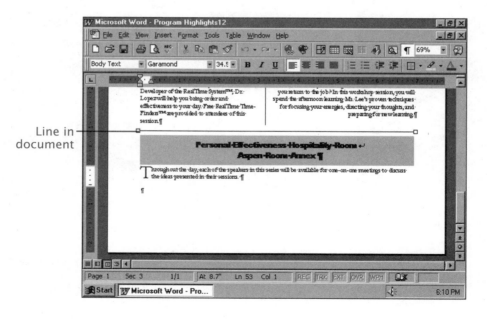

3 Click the line (not on the sizing handles at either end), and then drag the line to center it between the bottom of the columns and the following heading.

Insert an AutoShape

1 On the Drawing toolbar, click the AutoShapes button to see a menu of AutoShapes you can create.

2 On the AutoShapes menu, point to Basic Shapes.

The Basic Shapes menu offers the following shapes.

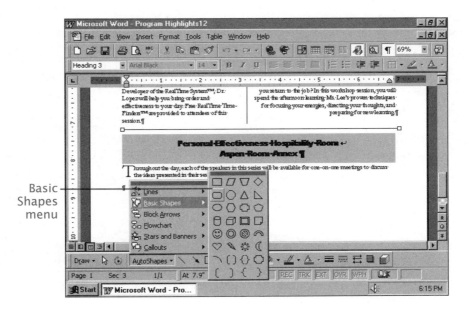

Basic Shapes menu

3 Click the Lightning Bolt shape, and then click in the blank area at the bottom of the document.

The Lightning Bolt shape appears, as shown in the following illustration.

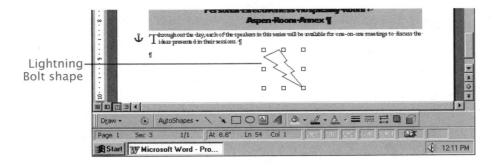

Lightning Bolt shape

Modifying Drawing Objects

After you have inserted a Drawing object in your document, you can modify the object to look the way you want. You can double-click the object to make basic changes in the object's dialog box, or you can simply click the object to select it and click the buttons on the Drawing toolbar to make even more changes, such as creating three-dimensional shapes, adjusting the orientation of a figure, or modifying the style of a line.

Create a 3-D shape

In this exercise you will apply three-dimensional (3-D) characteristics to the lightning shape.

3-D

To see additional 3-D options, click 3-D Settings at the bottom of the 3-D menu to display the 3-D toolbar.

1   With the Lightning Bolt shape still selected, on the Drawing toolbar, click the 3-D button.

The options look like the following illustration.

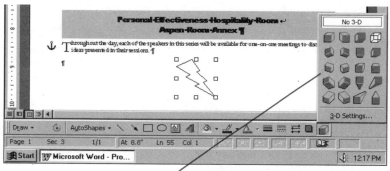

3-D options on the Drawing toolbar

2   Click the first shape in the first row.

The Lightning Bolt shape appears as a three-dimensional shape.

Fill Color

3   On the Drawing toolbar, click the Fill Color down arrow, and then click the bright yellow box.

The Lightning Bolt shape is yellow, as indicated by the shading in the following illustration.

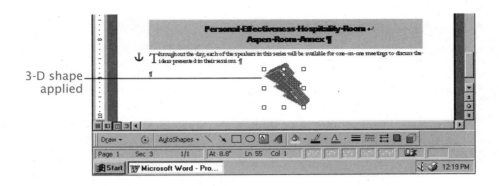

3-D shape applied

Change the orientation of a shape

In this exercise you will flip the lightning shape so that it points to the left instead of to the right.

➤ On the Drawing toolbar, click the Draw button, point to Rotate Or Flip, and then click Flip Horizontal.

Position the shape

In this exercise, you will move the Lightning Bolt shape to a new area in the document.

➤ With the Lightning Bolt shape still selected, click in the center of the shape (take care not to click a sizing handle), and drag the shape to the right of the bulleted list near the top of the document, as shown in the following illustration.

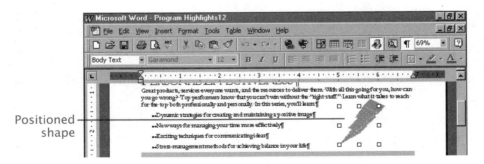

Positioned shape

Modify a line

In this exercise, you will change the thickness and style of the line you drew earlier in this lesson.

1   Click the horizontal line that is above the shaded text near the bottom of the document.

The sizing handles that appear at the ends of the line indicate the line is selected.

Dash Style

2   On the Drawing toolbar, click the Dash Style button, and then click the Square Dot line option, which is the third line from the top.

The line changes to a dotted line composed of small square dots.

Line Style

3   On the Drawing toolbar, click the Line Style button, click 4½ pt, and then click anywhere away from the line to clear the selection.

The thickness of the line changes to 4½ points, as shown in the following illustration.

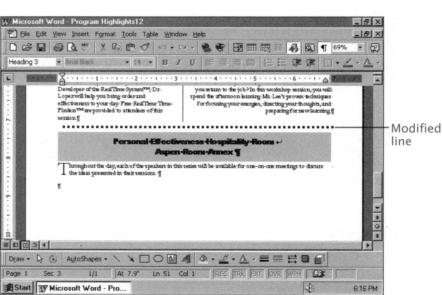

Modified line

Hyphenating Words

To improve the flow of text around framed text and in columns, you can use hyphens to separate longer words over two lines. When you want to make the hyphen optional (so that the word breaks only if it is at the end of the line), you can use a soft hyphen.

TIP When you want to make sure that text separated by a hyphen doesn't break across two lines as, for example, when you want to make sure numbers separated by a hyphen remain on the same line, you can use a nonbreaking hyphen. To create a nonbreaking hyphen, press CTRL+SHIFT+HYPHEN.

Use hyphenation

1 Place the insertion point between the "t" and the "ings" in the word "meetings" in the body text near the top of the right column.

2 Press the HYPHEN key.

   The word splits so that the characters before the hyphen appear at the end of the previous line and the characters after the hyphen appear at the start of the next line.

3 In the first paragraph in the first column, place the insertion point between the "h" and the "niques" in the word "techniques."

4 Press CTRL while you press HYPHEN.

   This creates a soft hyphen so that the word breaks only if it appears at the end of the line. For example, if you adjust the width of the column or change the width of the text box, the word might no longer require a hyphen. When you use a soft hyphen, the hyphen does not appear if the word no longer falls at the end of the line.

Work in Overtype mode

When you want to replace old text with new text, you can either delete the old text first or you can work in Overtype mode.

You can also press INSERT on the keyboard.

1 Double-click the OVR indicator in the status bar.

   The indicator becomes active.

2 Click in front of the "s" in "self-image."

3 Type **char** and press CTRL+HYPHEN

   Your typing replaces the existing text.

4 Continue typing **acter**.

   If you preview your document, you see that the word is not broken across two lines.

Turn off Overtype mode

1 In the status bar, double-click the OVR indicator to turn off Overtype mode.

2 Save the document.

Making AutoCorrect Exceptions

As you become familiar with working with Word, you might decide that you don't want AutoCorrect to make certain kinds of corrections to your capitalization. For example, after you type a period, the AutoCorrect feature usually capitalizes the next character you type. So that Word does not automatically correct the first character that follows after you type "Ltd.," you can add an AutoCorrect exception.

1 On the Tools menu, click AutoCorrect.

   The AutoCorrect dialog box appears.

2 Click Exceptions.

3 In the AutoCorrect Exceptions dialog box, be sure that the insertion point is in the Don't Capitalize After box.

4 Type **Ltd.**

5 Click Add, and then click OK.

   The Exceptions dialog box closes, and you return to the AutoCorrect dialog box.

6 Click OK.

7 Click at the end of the first body paragraph in the first column and type

   Dr. Davis is the CEO of Consultants Ltd. of Tampa, Florida.

   Notice how "of" was not automatically capitalized.

8 Save the document.

> **NOTE** If you'd like to build on the skills that you learned in this lesson, you can do the One Step Further. Otherwise, skip to "Finish the lesson."

One Step Further: Creating WordArt Special Text Effects

When you want to create interesting effects with text, you can use WordArt. This feature allows you to apply 3-D effects to text. You can orient your text at a variety of angles and display it in many shapes and patterns.

Display the WordArt toolbar

Insert WordArt

1 On the Drawing toolbar, click the Insert WordArt button.

   The WordArt Gallery dialog box appears.

2　Click the second option from the left in the second row from the top.

3　Click OK.

The Edit WordArt Text dialog box appears.

Edit and format WordArt text

1　Type **Program Highlights**

2　Click the Font down arrow, and then choose Arial Black.

3　Click the Size down arrow, and then choose 48.

4　Click OK.

The WordArt text appears in the document, and the WordArt toolbar opens.

Change the orientation of a WordArt object

Free Rotate

1　Click the Free Rotate button.

A circle arrow is at the tip of the pointer.

2　If you cannot see a green dot at each corner of the WordArt object, position the pointer over the object until the pointer changes to a four-sided arrow, and then drag to the left until the green dot appears.

3　Place the pointer over the top right green dot until the pointer changes to the circle arrow again.

4　Drag up and to the left until the WordArt object is completely vertical.

Use the dotted lines as a guide.

5　Position the pointer over the object until the pointer changes to a four-sided arrow, and then drag to the left until the object appears in the white area to the left of the text in the document

6　Click the Close button on the WordArt toolbar.

The WordArt toolbar closes.

7　Save the document.

Finish the lesson

1　Use the right mouse button to click the Drawing toolbar, and then click Drawing.

The Drawing toolbar closes.

2　To continue to the Review & Practice, on the File menu, click Close.

3　If you are finished using Microsoft Word for now, on the File menu, click Exit.

Lesson Summary

To	Do this	Button
Create columns	On the Standard toolbar, click the Columns button, and then click to select the number of columns you want.	
Divide a document into sections	Position the cursor at the point where you want to insert the section break. On the Insert menu, click Break, and then select the option you want under Section Breaks.	
Format each section in a document separately	Click in the section you want to format, and then apply formatting.	
Insert column breaks manually	On the Insert menu, click the Break command, and then select Column Break.	
View a single page of the document as it will look when printed	In Page Layout view, on the Standard toolbar, click the Zoom down arrow, and then click Whole Page.	
Modify formatting between columns	On the Format menu, click Columns. To add a line between columns, select the Line Between check box. Modify spacing and column width in the Spacing box and the Width box.	

To	Do this	Button
Position text precisely on the page	On the Insert menu, choose Text Box, and then type or paste the text.	
Insert a drop cap as the first character in a paragraph	On the Format menu, click Drop Cap. In the Drop Cap dialog box, click the style of drop cap you want.	
Enter text in Overtype mode	Double-click OVR on the status bar. *or* Press INSERT on the keyboard.	

For online information about	On the Help menu, click Contents And Index, click the Index tab, and then type
Inserting columns, column breaks, and lines between columns	**columns**
Working with sections	**section breaks**
Positioning text on the page	**positioning text and graphics**
Positioning graphics and text on the page	**positioning text and graphics**
Changing the view of a document	**viewing documents**

Review & Practice

Estimated time
35 min.

You will review and practice how to:

- Compare changes and accept or reject changes.
- Reorganize a document.
- Create merge fields in a main document and attach the document to a data source.
- Format a document into columns and arrange text on the page.
- Merge documents.

In this Review & Practice section, you have an opportunity to fine-tune the document organization and merging skills you learned in Part 3 of this book. Use what you have learned about comparing document versions, outlining documents, and merging documents to complete several special projects for the West Coast Sales marketing efforts.

Scenario

After a recent reorganization, the West Coast Sales Marketing Department and its Terra Firm division have joined forces to create an exciting product brochure. As the communications manager, you have already distributed a draft of the brochure to the team members for their review. You will compare the changed document with the original document, and then accept or reject each change. And you will reorganize the ideas in the document. Next, you will format the document into multiple columns and add interesting graphics and other special effects to improve the appearance of the final document. Finally, you will create a cover memo to accompany the completed document that you will distribute to team members for their final evaluation.

Step 1: Compare Changes

You can compare the merge document with the original.

1. Open the P3Review file, and save it with the name Terra Brochure in your SBS Word folder.

2. On the Tools menu, point to Track Changes, and then click Highlight Changes. In the Highlight Changes dialog box, select the Highlight Changes On Screen check box.

3. On the Tools menu, point to Track Changes, and then click Compare Documents. In the Compare Documents dialog box, double-click P3Original in the SBS Winword Practice folder.

For more information about	See
Comparing documents	Lesson 9

Step 2: Accept or Reject Changes

1. Use the Track Changes command on the Tools menu to accept or reject the changes.

2. Click Find.

3. Accept each of the first three revisions. Reject the next four revisions. Then accept the remaining revisions.

4. Save the document.

For more information about	See
Accepting or rejecting changes	Lesson 9

Step 3: Reorganize a Document

Because you want to rearrange "chunks" of information in the document, use the outline feature to reorganize the document more efficiently.

1. Display the document in Outline view.

2. Promote the first line of the document to Heading 1.

3. Collapse the document to display the first three heading levels.

4. Move the first heading to after the last heading, and then expand this heading to see all the subordinate text.

For more information about	See
Outlining a document	Lesson 10
Promoting headings	Lesson 10

Step 4: *Format the Document into Columns and Arrange Text*

1   Insert continuous section breaks just in front of the first heading, "Terra Firm Products" and just before the start of the last paragraph.

2   Format the second section into two columns.

3   Create a text box. Cut the testimonial text and the customer's name and city, and then paste it inside the text box.

4   Double-click the frame and specify a line width of your choice on the Colors And Lines tab. On the Wrapping tab, choose the Square style and the Both Sides option.

5   Size the framed text so it is about 2 inches on all sides, and place it in the center of the document between the two columns.

6   Display the Drawing toolbar, and draw a rectangle around the first body paragraph. Change the line style of the rectangle to dashed, 4 ½ points and fill the rectangle with a bright green color. If the color obscures the text, click the Draw button, point to Order, and then click Send Behind Text.

7   Draw a horizontal line above the last heading in the document. Format this line with the same line style as the rectangle in step 6.

8   Hide the Drawing toolbar.

9   Return to Normal view, and then save and close your document.

For more information about	See
Correcting columns	Lesson 12
Inserting section breaks	Lesson 12
Positioning text with text boxes	Lesson 12
Drawing lines and borders	Lesson 12

Step 5: *Create a Main Document and Attach a Data Source*

1   Create a new document based on a memo template. Save it as Main MemoRP3.

2   Select the Mail Merge command on the Tools menu, and create a main form letter document based on the document in the active window.

3   Attach the data source document RP3 Data from your Winword SBS Practice folder.

For more information about	See
Creating main documents and attaching a data source	Lesson 11

Step 6: *Modify the Main Document and Merge Documents*

1   Select each placeholder text heading at the start of the memo, and replace them with the appropriate merge fields.

2   On the Subject line, type **Terra Firm Brochure Meeting**

3   For the body of the memo, type:
Thank you for your contributions to the draft product brochure. Several great ideas surfaced during this process, so I felt it would be good for all of us to get together to figure out how we can incorporate as many of your ideas as we can. In addition, I would appreciate your special expertise in the area of <<*expert area*>> to help us in this effort.

Be sure to insert the <<expert area>> merge field as indicated in the text above.

4   Save your work in the main document.

5   Merge your documents to another document or directly to an attached printer. You don't need to save your merged document.

For more information about	See
Adding merge fields	Lesson 11
Merging documents	Lesson 11

Finish the Review & Practice

 If you are finished using Microsoft Word for now, on the File menu, click Exit.

Appendixes

If You Are New to Windows 95, Windows NT, or Microsoft Word 97

If you're new to Microsoft Windows 95 or Microsoft Windows NT version 4.0, and to Microsoft Word 97, this appendix will show you all the basics you need to get started. You'll get an overview of Windows 95 and Windows NT features, and you'll learn how to use online Help to answer your questions and find out more about using these operating systems. You'll also get an introduction to Microsoft Word 97.

If You Are New to Windows 95 or Windows NT

Windows 95 and Windows NT are easy-to-use computer environments that help you handle the daily work that you perform with your computer. You can use either Windows 95 or Windows NT to run Microsoft Word—the explanations in this appendix apply to both operating systems. The way you use Windows 95, Windows NT, and programs designed for these operating systems is similar. The programs have a common look, and you use the same kinds of controls to tell them what to do. In this section, you'll learn how to use the basic program controls. If you're already familiar with Windows 95 or Windows NT, skip to the "What Is Microsoft Word?" section.

Start Windows 95 or Windows NT

Starting Windows 95 or Windows NT is as easy as turning on your computer.

   1   If your computer isn't on, turn it on now.

In Windows 95, you will also be prompted for a username and password if your computer is configured for user profiles.

2 If you are using Windows NT, press CTRL+ALT+DEL to display a dialog box asking for your username and password. If you are using Windows 95, you will see this dialog box if your computer is connected to a network.

3 Type your username and password in the appropriate boxes, and then click OK.

If you don't know your username or password, contact your system administrator for assistance.

Close

4 If you see the Welcome dialog box, click the Close button.

Your screen should look similar to the following illustration.

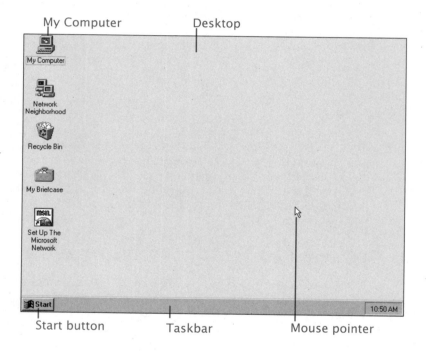

Using the Mouse

Although you can use the keyboard for most actions, many of these actions are easier to do by using a mouse. The mouse controls a pointer on the screen, as shown in the previous illustration. You move the pointer by sliding the mouse over a flat surface in the direction you want the pointer to move. If you run out of room to move the mouse, lift the mouse up, and then put it down in a more comfortable location.

You'll use five basic mouse actions throughout this book.

When you are directed to	Do this
Point to an item	Move the mouse to place the pointer on the item.
Click an item	Point to the item on your screen, and quickly press and release the left mouse button.
Use the right mouse button to click an item	Point to the item on your screen, and then quickly press and release the right mouse button. Clicking the right mouse button displays a shortcut menu from which you can choose from a list of commands that apply to that item.
Double-click an item	Point to the item, and then quickly press and release the left mouse button twice.
Drag an item	Point to an item, and then hold down the left mouse button as you move the pointer.

 IMPORTANT In this book we assume that your mouse is set up so that the left button is the primary button and the right button is the secondary button. If your mouse is configured the opposite way, for left-handed use, use the right button when we tell you to use the left, and vice versa.

Using Window Controls

All programs designed for use on computers that have Windows 95 or Windows NT installed have common controls that you use to scroll, size, move, and close a window.

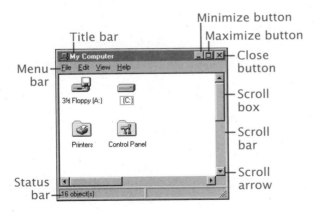

To	Do this	Button
Move, or *scroll*, vertically or horizontally through the contents of a window that extends beyond the screen	Click a scroll bar or scroll arrow, or drag the scroll box. The previous illustration identifies these controls.	
Enlarge a window to fill the screen	Click the Maximize button, or double-click the window's title bar.	🔲
Restore a window to its previous size	Click the Restore button, or double-click the window title bar. When a window is maximized, the Maximize button changes to the Restore button.	🗗
Reduce a window to a button on the taskbar	Click the Minimize button. To display a minimized window, click its button on the taskbar.	➖
Move a window	Drag the window title bar.	
Close a window	Click the Close button.	❎

Using Menus

Just like a restaurant menu, a program menu provides a list of options from which you can choose. On program menus, these options are called *commands*. To select a menu or a menu command, you click the item you want.

 NOTE You can also use the keyboard to make menu selections. Press the ALT key to activate the menu bar, and press the key that corresponds to the highlighted or underlined letter of the menu name. Then, press the key that corresponds to the highlighted or underlined letter of the command name.

Open and make selections from a menu

In the following exercise, you'll open and make selections from a menu.

1 On the Desktop, double-click the My Computer icon.

The My Computer window opens.

You can also press ALT+E to open the Edit menu.

2 In the My Computer window, click Edit on the menu bar.

The Edit menu appears. Some commands are dimmed; this means that they aren't available.

Command is not available.

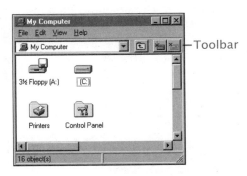

Shortcut key

Command is available.

3 Click the Edit menu name to close the menu.

The menu closes.

On a menu, a check mark indicates that multiple items in this group of commands can be selected at one time. A bullet mark indicates that only one item in this group can be selected at one time.

4 Click View on the menu bar to open the View menu.

5 On the View menu, click Toolbar.

The View menu closes, and a toolbar appears below the menu bar.

Toolbar

6 On the View menu, click List.

The items in the My Computer window now appear in a list, rather than as icons.

Large Icons

7 On the toolbar, click the Large Icons button.

Clicking a button on a toolbar is a quick way to select a command.

8 On the View menu, point to Arrange Icons.

A cascading menu appears listing additional menu choices. When a right-pointing arrow appears after a command name, it indicates that additional commands are available.

251

9 Click anywhere outside the menu to close it.

10 On the menu bar, click View, and then click Toolbar again.

The View menu closes, and the toolbar is now hidden.

11 In the upper-right corner of the My Computer window, click the Close button to close the window.

TIP If you do a lot of typing, you might want to learn the key combinations for commands you use frequently. Pressing the key combination is a quick way to perform a command by using the keyboard. If a key combination is available for a command, it will be listed to the right of the command name on the menu. For example, CTRL+C is listed on the Edit menu as the key combination for the Copy command.

Using Dialog Boxes

When you choose a command name that is followed by an ellipsis (...), a dialog box will appear so that you can provide more information about how the command should be carried out. Dialog boxes have standard features, as shown in the following illustration.

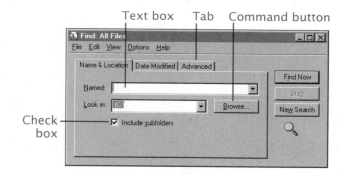

To move around in a dialog box, you click the item you want. You can also use the keyboard to select the item by holding down ALT as you press the underlined letter. Or, you can press TAB to move between items.

Display the Taskbar Properties dialog box

Some dialog boxes provide several categories of options displayed on separate tabs. You click the top of an obscured tab to make it visible.

1 On the taskbar, click the Start button.

The Start menu opens.

2   On the Start menu, point to Settings, and then click Taskbar.

3   In the Taskbar Properties dialog box, click the Start Menu Programs tab.

On this tab, you can customize the list of programs that appears on your Start menu.

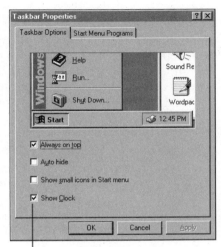

Click here. When you click a check box that is selected, you turn the option off.

4   Click the Taskbar Options tab, and then click to select the Show Small Icons In Start Menu check box

When a check box is selected, it displays a check mark.

5   Click the check box a couple of times, and watch how the display in the dialog box changes.

Clicking any check box or option button will turn the option off or on.

6   Click the Cancel button in the dialog box.

This closes the dialog box without changing any settings.

Getting Help with Windows 95 or Windows NT

When you're at work and you want to find more information about how to do a project, you might ask a co-worker or consult a reference book. To find out more about functions and features in Windows 95 or Windows NT, you can use the online Help system. For example, when you need information about how to print, the Help system is one of the most efficient ways to learn. The Windows 95 or Windows NT Help system is available from the Start menu. After the Help system opens, you can choose the type of help you want from the Help Topics dialog box.

To find instructions about broad categories, you can look on the Contents tab. Or you can search the Help index to find information about specific topics. The Help information is short and concise, so you can get the exact information you need quickly. There are also shortcut icons in many Help topics that you can use to go directly to the task you want.

Viewing Help Contents

The Contents tab is organized like a book's table of contents. As you choose top-level topics, called *chapters*, you see a list of more detailed subtopics from which to choose. Many of these chapters have Tips and Tricks sections to help you work more efficiently as well as Troubleshooting sections to help you resolve problems.

Find Help about general categories

Suppose you want to learn more about using Calculator, a program that comes with Windows 95 and Windows NT. In this exercise, you'll look up information in the online Help system.

1 Click Start. On the Start menu, click Help.

The Help Topics: Windows Help dialog box appears.

2 If necessary, click the Contents tab to make it active.

3 Double-click "Introducing Windows" or "Introducing Windows NT."

A set of subtopics appears.

4 Double-click "Using Windows Accessories."

5 Double-click "For General Use."

6 Double-click "Calculator: for making calculations."

A Help topic window opens.

7 Read the Help information, and then click the Close button to close the Help window.

Finding Help About Specific Topics

You can find specific Help topics by using the Index tab or the Find tab. The Index tab is organized like a book's index. Keywords for topics are organized alphabetically. You can either scroll through the list of keywords or type the keyword you want to find. You can then select from one or more topic choices.

With the Find tab, you can also enter a keyword. The main difference is that you get a list of all Help topics in which that keyword appears, not just the topics that begin with that word.

Find Help about specific topics by using the Help index

In this exercise, you use the Help index to learn how to change the background pattern of your Desktop.

1 Click Start, and on the Start menu, click Help.

The Help Topics dialog box appears.

2 Click the Index tab to make it active.

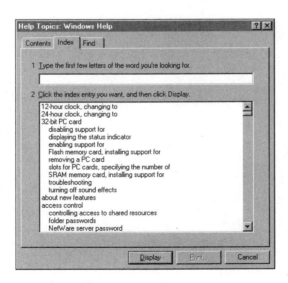

3 In the Type The First Few Letters Of The Word You're Looking For box, type **display**

A list of display-related topics appears.

4 Click the topic named "background pictures or patterns, changing," and then click Display.

The Topics Found dialog box appears.

5 Be sure that the topic named "Changing the background of your desktop" is selected, and then click Display.

6 Read the Help topic.

7 Click the shortcut icon in step 1 of the Help topic.

Shortcut

The Display Properties dialog box appears. If you want, you can immediately perform the task you are looking up in Help.

8 Click the Close button on the Display Properties dialog box.

9 Click the Close button on the Windows Help window.

NOTE You can print any Help topic, if you have a printer installed on your computer. Click the Options button in the upper-left corner of any Help topic window, click Print Topic, and then click OK. To continue searching for additional topics, you can click the Help Topics button in any open Help topic window.

Find Help about specific topics by using the Find tab

In this exercise, you use the Find tab to learn how to change your printer's settings.

1 Click Start, and then click Help to display the Help Topics dialog box.

2 Click the Find tab to make it active.

3 If you see a wizard, click Next, and then click Finish to complete and close the wizard.

The wizard creates a search index for your Help files. This might take a few minutes. The next time you use Find, you won't have to wait for the list to be created.

The Find tab appears.

4 In the text box, type **print**

All topics that have to do with printing appear in the list box at the bottom of the tab.

5 In step 3 of the Help dialog box, click the "Changing printer settings" topic, and then click Display.

The Help topic appears.

6 Read the Help topic, and then click the Close button on the Windows Help window.

Find Help in a dialog box

Almost every dialog box includes a question mark Help button in the upper-right corner of its window. When you click this button and then click any dialog box control, a Help window appears that explains what the control is and how to use it. In this exercise, you'll get help for a dialog box control.

1 Click Start, and then click Run.

The Run dialog box appears.

Help

2 Click the Help button.

The mouse pointer changes to an arrow with a question mark.

3 Click the Open text box.

A Help window appears, providing information about how to use the Open text box.

4 Click anywhere on the Desktop, or press ESC, to close the Help window.

The mouse pointer returns to its previous shape.

5 In the Run dialog box, click Cancel.

> **TIP** You can change the way the Help topics appear on your screen. Click the Options button in any Help topic window, and then point to Font to change the size of the text.

What Is Microsoft Word 97?

Microsoft Word 97 is a word processing program that you can use to create new documents and modify existing documents. Using a word processing program means that you can type the text of your document and then *edit* (make changes to) the text without having to retype the entire document. These changes can be as simple as typing over existing text or inserting new text. But you can also rearrange and reuse text, which reduces the amount of text you need to type and also reduces the number of errors you make. Other ways to reduce errors include using Word's AutoCorrect features (which correct mistakes as you type) and proofing tools that check for spelling and grammatical errors. Using preformatted templates and wizards that are available for a variety of documents, you can quickly create letters, memos, reports, newsletters, and many other kinds of documents. All you do is supply the text.

To improve the appearance of your document you can *format* it, by positioning text where you want it, applying formatting effects (such as bold and italics), and applying borders and shading to text. With the ability to insert and create graphics and unique text effects, Microsoft Word provides all the features you need to create effective and exciting documents with very little effort.

Quit Windows 95 or Windows NT

1   If you are finished using Windows 95 or Windows NT, close any open windows by clicking the Close button in each window.

2   Click Start, and then click Shut Down.

The Shut Down Windows dialog box appears.

3   Click Yes.

A message indicates that it is now safe to turn off your computer.

 WARNING   To avoid loss of data or damage to your operating system, always quit Windows 95 or Windows NT by using the Shut Down command on the Start menu before you turn your computer off.

Matching the Exercises

Microsoft Word 97 has many optional settings that can affect either the screen display or the operation of certain functions. Some exercise steps, therefore, might not produce exactly the same result on your screen as shown in the book. For example, if you cannot find the Winword SBS Practice subfolder or if your screen does not look like the illustration at a certain point in a lesson, a note in the lesson might direct you to this appendix for guidance. Or, if you did not get the outcome described in the lesson, you can use this appendix to determine whether the options you have selected are the same as the ones used in this book.

Displaying the Practice Files

You begin most of the lessons by opening one of the sample documents that came on the Microsoft Word 97 Step by Step Practice Files disk. The practice files should be stored on your hard disk, in a subfolder called Winword SBS Practice. The Winword SBS Practice subfolder is located in your system's Favorites folder. If you cannot locate the practice files you need to complete the lesson, follow these steps.

Open the Winword SBS Practice folder

Open

1 On the Standard toolbar, click the Open button.

Clicking the Open button displays the Open dialog box, where you select the name of the document to open. You must tell Microsoft Word 97 on which drive and in which folder the document is stored.

*Look In
Favorites*

2 In the File Open dialog box, click the Look In Favorites button.

3 Double-click the Winword SBS Practice subfolder to open it.

When you open the Winword SBS Practice subfolder, the names of the Microsoft Word 97 Step by Step practice files (the sample documents) appear. Click the left or right arrow in the scroll bar to see all the names.

After you open the correct folder, you are ready to open a practice file. Return to the lesson to learn which file you need to open to complete the lesson.

Returning Microsoft Word to Its Original Settings

A fast way to ensure that your results match those described in the lessons is to create a special Word shortcut on your desktop that you use only when you are working through the Step By Step lessons. By making a minor modification to this new shortcut you can reset many options to their original "out-of-the-box" state. Do not, however, use this special shortcut for doing your regular work in Microsoft Word.

1 Create a shortcut by locating the WINWORD.EXE file and dragging it to the desktop.

Use the Find command on the Start menu to help you locate this file if you are not sure where it is on your computer.

2 Use the right mouse button to click the new shortcut, and on the shortcut menu, click Properties.

3 Click the Shortcut tab.

4 Click the Target line, and press END to move to the end of the line.

5 Press SPACEBAR and type /a

6 Click OK to return to the desktop.

7 Consider giving your new shortcut a new name by clicking the Rename command on the shortcut menu and typing a new name, such as "Word Reset" or some other name to distinguish it from other shortcuts you might already have on the desktop.

8 Double-click the new shortcut to start Word from the desktop.

One fast way to confirm that you are working in Word with original settings in effect is to click the File menu and verify that no filenames appear at the bottom of the File menu.

Matching the Screen Display to the Illustrations

Microsoft Word makes it easy for you to set up the program window to suit your working style and preferences. If you share your computer with others, previous users might have changed the screen setup. You can easily change it back so that the screen matches the illustrations in the lessons. Use the following methods for controlling the screen display.

If you change the screen display as part of a lesson and leave Microsoft Word, the next time you open Microsoft Word, the screen looks the way you left it in the previous session.

Display or hide toolbars

If toolbars are missing at the top of the screen, previous users might have hidden them to make more room for text. You can easily display the toolbars that contain the buttons you need in the lessons.

You can also hide specialized toolbars that you no longer need so that you can see more text on the screen. However, most of the lessons require that the Standard and Formatting toolbars appear.

1 On the View menu, choose Toolbars.

2 In the Toolbars dialog box, click to insert a check in the check boxes for the toolbars you want to see; click to clear the check boxes for the toolbars you want to hide.

Display the ruler

If the ruler is missing from the top of the screen, previous users might have hidden it to make more room for text. Although the ruler is not required in all lessons, it is usually displayed in the illustrations. To display the ruler, do the following.

 On the View menu, choose Ruler.

If the vertical scroll bar does not appear

If you do not see the vertical scroll bar, a previous user might have hidden the scroll bar to make more room for text. You can easily display it again.

1 Click the Tools menu, and then choose Options.

2 Click the View tab to display the view options in the dialog box.

3 In the Window area, click the Vertical Scroll Bar check box. A check mark appears in the check box to indicate that it is selected.

4 Click OK.

If the Word program window does not fill the screen

A previous user might have made the Microsoft Word program window smaller to allow quick access to another program. You can enlarge the document window by doing the following.

Maximize

➤ Click the Maximize button in the upper-right corner of the Microsoft Word title bar.

If the right edge of the Microsoft Word window is hidden so that you cannot see the Maximize button, point to "Microsoft Word" in the title bar at the top of the screen, and then drag the title bar to the left until you see the Maximize button.

If the document does not fill the space that Microsoft Word allows

The last time Microsoft Word was used, the user might have displayed the document in a smaller size to get an overview of a document. To see your document at the normal size, use the Zoom button on the Standard toolbar.

Zoom

➤ Click the Zoom down arrow, and select 100%.

If you see the top edge of the page on the screen

The last person to use Microsoft Word might have worked in Page Layout view, which displays one page of text on the screen. Return to Normal view for the lesson.

Normal View

➤ Click the Normal View button to the far left of the horizontal scroll bar.
   or
   On the View menu, select Normal.

If spaces appear before periods when moving text

A previous user might have preferred not to use the Smart Cut And Paste feature. Because all the lessons after Lesson 1 assume that this feature is active, you can turn this feature back on.

1 From the Tools menu, choose Options.
2 Click the Edit tab to display the Edit options in the dialog box.
3 Click the Use Smart Cut And Paste check box.
4 Click OK.

If you see words in brackets

If you see {TIME...} or {SYMBOL..} or {DATE...} in the document, you are looking at the codes that instruct Microsoft Word to insert a certain type of information. You can hide the codes and view the information that Microsoft Word inserts to replace the codes without changing the document in any way.

1   From the Tools menu, choose Options.
2   Click the View tab to display the view options in the dialog box.
3   Click the Field Codes check box to clear it.
4   Click OK.

If you see "¶" in the document

You are viewing the paragraph marks that indicate the end of paragraphs. You might also be viewing other nonprinting symbols that mark spaces or locations where the TAB key was pressed. These symbols do not appear in the document when it is printed. Many users work with the symbols on all the time. If you prefer to hide the nonprinting symbols, you can do so without affecting the document in any way. Some of the instructions in the lessons require you to locate a specific paragraph mark in the document. In this case, be sure to click the Show/Hide ¶ button on the Standard toolbar to display paragraph marks and other nonprinting symbols.

Show/Hide ¶

➤   To hide the symbols, click the Show/Hide ¶ button on the Standard toolbar.

Changing Other Options

If you are not getting the results described in the lessons, follow the instructions in this section to verify that the options set in your program are the same as the ones used in this book.

Review each of the following dialog boxes to compare settings for those options that users change most often and are most likely to account for different results. You can view these dialog boxes by choosing the Options command from the Tools menu. Then you click the tab corresponding to the options you want to see.

View Options

Click the View tab to change options that affect the appearance of the document window. Here are the View settings used in this book. The first illustration displays the settings to use when a document is in Normal view. The second illustration displays the settings to use when a document is in Page Layout view.

Normal View options

Page Layout View options

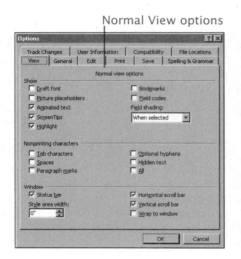 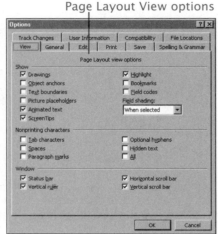

General Options

Click the General tab to change options that affect the operation of Microsoft Word in general. Here are the General settings used in this book.

Edit Options

Click the Edit tab to change options that affect how editing operations are performed. Here are the Edit settings used in this book.

Print Options

Click the Print tab to change options that affect how printing operations are performed. Here are the Print settings used in this book.

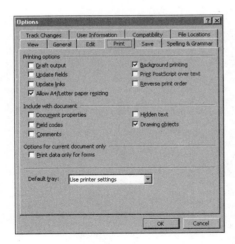

Save Options

Click the Save tab to change options that affect how your documents are saved to disk. Here are the Save settings used in this book.

Spelling & Grammar Options

Click the Spelling & Grammar tab to change options that affect how the spelling and grammar features work. Here are the Spelling & Grammar settings used in this book.

AutoFormat, AutoCorrect, and AutoText Options

To review AutoFormat, AutoCorrect, or AutoText options, you can click any of these commands on their respective menus. In any of the dialog boxes, click the Options button to display the AutoCorrect dialog box. Click the appropriate tab to review the specific options that affect how the AutoFormat, AutoCorrect, and AutoText features work.

AutoFormat

AutoCorrect

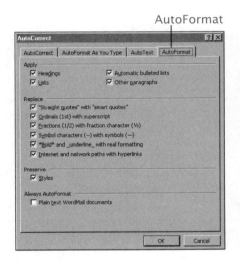
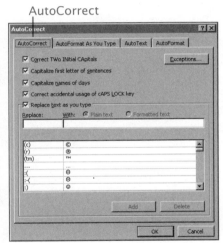

AutoFormat As You Type

AutoText

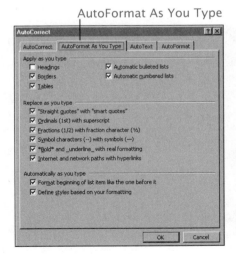
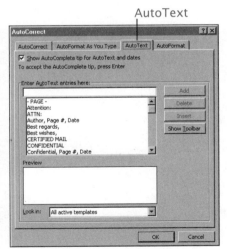

active command   A command that appears in dark letters in a menu.

active document   The document in which you are working. The title bar on the active document is highlighted.

active window   In a multiple-window environment, the window that is currently selected and whose contents will be affected by all mouse actions, commands, and text entries.

alignment   The horizontal position of text within the width of a column or between tab stops. Text can be left-aligned, right-aligned, centered, or justified.

annotation   A comment or explanatory note in a Help topic. An annotated Help topic is identified by a paper clip icon.

application   *See* program.

arrow keys   The UP ARROW, DOWN ARROW, LEFT ARROW, and RIGHT ARROW keys used to move the insertion point or to select from a menu or a list of options.

ascending   A method of ordering a group of items from lowest to highest, such as from A to Z. *See also* sort.

bitmap   A collection of bits that make up a dot pattern or graphic image. Bitmaps with a BMP extension are the default file type for the Paint accessory.

body text   Text not formatted in a heading style.

bookmark   [1]A command used to mark a Help topic so that you can retrieve and view it at a later time. [2]Selected text, graphics, or a location tagged with a reference name or tagged so that you can move quickly to the selection.

boot up   To start a computer.

border   A line that goes around text or tables. You can assign a variety of widths and styles to a border.

bullet   A mark, usually a round or square dot, often used to add emphasis or to distinguish between items in a list.

button   [1]On a toolbar, a small, square area that you can click to perform an action. Buttons on the toolbar are used to perform the same action as a menu command, such as clicking Copy on the Edit menu. Toolbar buttons usually are identified by a graphic. [2]An option in a dialog box, for example, Cancel or OK. [3]The Minimize, Maximize, and Restore control elements used to change the size and position of a window.

callout   A label that annotates or identifies a graphic, picture, or feature in a document.

cascade   A command that arranges windows so that they are overlapped with the active window in front.

cascading menu   A menu that branches off or cascades from another menu. A command name followed by an arrow indicates that a submenu appears when the command is chosen.

category   A heading that precedes a group of related documents.

cell   The basic unit of a table. The intersection of a row and a column forms one cell. You type text, numbers, or formulas into cells.

changed line   A vertical bar next to a line that contains a revision.

character   An individual letter, number, or symbol corresponding to a key or key combination. Each character can be formatted individually.

character attributes   A named set of character settings that can be applied to selected characters in a paragraph, usually to emphasize specific words and phrases. Character attributes include effects such as bold, italic, and small caps.

character formatting   The format settings such as fonts, case, attributes, or size. Character formatting affects only words or selected text.

character style   A named set of character format settings that can be applied to selected text.

check box   A dialog box option that is not mutually exclusive. Clicking a check box inserts or removes a check mark or an X.

click   To press the primary mouse button once.

Clipboard   A temporary holding area in computer memory that stores the last set of information that was cut or copied (such as text or graphics). You transfer data from the Clipboard by using the Paste command. Information remains on the Clipboard until you cut or copy another piece of information.

close   To end a program.

collapse   To reduce the number of rows displayed in a view by showing only categories or by eliminating responses.

column   A vertical section of a worksheet or a table.

column break   The line that identifies the end of a column and the beginning of another column.

command   An instruction issued by a user that causes an action to be carried out by the program.

comment   Feature you can use to add comments to a document. Comment flags appear in the document when you point to them with the mouse.

context-sensitive help   A type of online help used to identify any screen element in a window or to provide relevant information about the current operation.

control   A type of field used to enter responses to questions or to provide information.

copy   To duplicate information from one location to another, within a file, to another file, or to a file in another program. Copied information is stored on the Clipboard until you cut or copy another piece of information.

crop   To cut away parts of a graphic.

cursor   *See* insertion point.

cut   To remove selected information from a document so you can paste it to another location within the file, to another file, or to a file in another program. The cut information is stored on the Clipboard until you cut or copy another piece of information.

data   A set of information used by a computer or program.

data source   The file that contains the variable information for a merge document.

default   A predefined setting that is built into a program and is used when you do not specify an alternative setting. For example, a document might have a default setting of 1-inch page margins unless you specify another value for the margin settings.

delete   To remove information such as a file or text. The user can choose the Delete command, press the DELETE key, or press the BACKSPACE key.

demote   In Outline view, an action that changes a heading to body text or a higher heading level to a lower heading level.

descending   A method of ordering a group of items from highest to lowest, such as from Z to A. *See also* sort .

Desktop   The entire Windows 95 or Windows NT screen that represents your work area. Icons, windows, and the taskbar appear on the Desktop.

destination   A document or program receiving information that was generated in another program. *See also* source.

dialog box   A box that displays additional options when a command is chosen from a menu.

dimmed   The grayed appearance of a command or option that is unavailable.

disk   A round, flat piece of flexible plastic (floppy disk) or inflexible metal (hard disk) that stores data. The disk is coated with a magnetic material on which digital information can be recorded. To protect this material, disks are enclosed in plastic or metal casings.

disk drive   A hardware mechanism that reads information from and writes information to a hard disk, floppy disk, CD-ROM, or network drive.

document   Any independent unit of information, such as a text file, worksheet, or graphic object, that is created with a program. A document is saved with a unique filename by which it can be retrieved.

double-click   To press the primary mouse button twice rapidly. Double-clicking an object performs the default action.

drag   A mouse technique for directly moving, copying, or selecting a set of information.

drag-and-drop   *See* drag.

edit   To add, delete, or change information, such as text or graphics.

electronic mail   Notes, messages, or files sent between different computers using telecommunication or network services. Also referred to as e-mail.

e-mail   *See* electronic mail.

endnote   An explanatory comment reference inserted at the end of a section or document.

expand   [1]To display all subordinate entries in an outline or in a folder. [2]To display a list of all documents in a view.

export   The process of converting and saving a file to be used in another program. *See also* import.

extension   *See* file extension.

field   An area in a table or form in which you can enter or view specific information about an individual task or resource. Built-in fields can display information provided by the program or the computer. There are different types of fields, such as text fields, test fields, or check box fields.

field characters   The braces that enclose or surround a field code.

field code   A field name and instructions enclosed or surrounded by field characters.

field name   [1]A unique name that identifies the field contents, for example, CITY or STATE. [2]A word inserted at the beginning of a field that describes the action of the field.

file   Any independent unit of information, such as a text document, a worksheet, or a graphic object, that is created using a program. A file is saved with a unique filename by which it can be retrieved.

file extension A period and up to three characters at the end of a filename. The extension can help identify the kind of information a file contains. For example, the extensions CMD and BAT indicate that the file contains a batch program. The file extension is an optional addition to the filename.

filename A name used to identify a file. Depending on the file system, a filename can be 1 to 256 characters long, including spaces and punctuation marks, with an optional extension of 1 to 3 characters.

floating palette A palette that can be resized and repositioned anywhere in a window. *See also* palette.

floating toolbar A toolbar that can be resized and repositioned anywhere in a window, has a title bar, stays on top of the other windows, and is not fixed in position. *See also* toolbar.

folder A container in which documents, program files, and other folders are stored on your computer disks. Formerly referred to as a directory.

font A family of type styles, such as Times New Roman or Arial. Effects, such as bold or italic, and various point sizes can be applied to a font. *See also* point.

footer The text or graphics printed at the bottom of every page in a document.

footnote An explanatory comment reference inserted at the bottom of the page on which the reference mark is located or at the end of the document.

form A structured document used to collect and/or distribute information.

format [1]The way text appears on a page. The four types of formats are character, paragraph, section, and document. Styles can be applied to any of these formats. [2]To prepare a disk to record or retrieve data. Formatting a disk usually erases any information the disk previously contained.

frame [1]A box that you insert around text or a graphic, so you can position and format the framed object. [2] Division on a Web page in which other Web pages can be viewed.

gridlines The horizontal and vertical lines that appear in a table that identify the structure of table. You can see the gridlines if you hide the table borders.

handles Small black squares located in the lower-right corner of selected cells or around selected graphic objects, chart items, or text.

hanging indent A paragraph indent in which the first line is flush with the left margin and subsequent lines are indented.

hard page break A marker in a document that forces the succeeding text to start on a new page.

header The text or graphics printed at the top of every page in a document.

Help system   A form of online assistance where you can get instructions, definitions, and context-sensitive help.

HTML (HyperText Markup Language)   A set of rules used to format World Wide Web pages. HTML includes methods of specifying text characteristics (bold, italic, etc.), graphic placement, links, and so on. A Web browser, such as Internet Explorer, must be used to properly view an HTML document.

hyperlink   An object, such as a graphic or colored or underlined text, that represents a link to another location in the same file or in a different file, and that, when clicked, brings up a different Web page. Hyperlinks are one of the key elements of HTML documents.

I-beam   *See* insertion point.

icon   A small graphic that represents an object, such as a program, a disk drive, or a document.

import   To convert a file that was created in another program. *See also* export.

inactive command   A command in a menu that appears in dimmed letters. An inactive command cannot be selected, usually because the function is inappropriate to the current mode.

indent   The distance between the left or right edge of a block of text and the page margin. A paragraph can have a left, right, and first-line indent. Indents can also be measured relative to columns in a section, table cells, and the boundaries of positioned objects.

indent marker   Ruler marker that controls where the lines of a paragraph begin and end. The four indent markers are the first-line indent marker, the hanging indent marker, the left indent marker, and the right indent marker.

insertion point   The blinking vertical bar that marks the location where text is entered in a document, a cell, or a dialog box. Also referred to as a cursor or insertion point.

install   To prepare equipment or software for use for the first time.

Internet   A worldwide "network of networks," made up of thousands of computer networks and millions of commercial, education, government, and personal computers, all connected to each other. Also referred to as the Net.

intranet   A self-contained network that uses the same communications protocols and file formats as the Internet. An intranet can, but doesn't have to, be connected to the Internet. Many businesses use intranets for their internal communications. *See also* Internet.

jump   [1]An underlined word or phrase in Help that displays a definition of the word or phrase when clicked. [2]A method for presenting information where text is linked together so that the user can browse through related topics, regardless of the presented order of topics.

kerning   The space between a pair of letters.

landscape   The horizontal orientation of a page. *See also* portrait.

layout grid   The nonprinting guidelines that define where elements should appear on the page.

leading   The space between lines of text. The term *leading* comes from early type-setting, when thin bars of lead were set between lines of type to adjust the spacing.

link   [1]*See* hyperlink. [2]To copy an object, such as a graphic or text, from one file or program to another so that there is a dependent relationship between the object and its source file. Also refers to the connection between a source file and a destination file. Whenever the original information in the source file changes, the information in the linked object is automatically updated.

list   A selection of choices in a dialog box.

main document   The document containing standardized text or graphics that is merged with a data file to produce merged documents. A main document contains placeholder text to represent information that varies in each document.

margin   The absolute boundary of text and graphics on a page.

margin guides   The guides that define the margins of a page. You set margin guides when you create a publication.

marquee   A moving dotted line that surrounds your selection.

master document   A holder for subdocuments displayed in an outline structure. A master document is usually a long document divided into smaller documents.

maximize   To expand a window to occupy the full screen. *See also* minimize; restore.

menu   A list of commands or options available in a program.

menu bar   The horizontal bar that contains the names of the available menus.

merge   To combine items, such as lists, without changing the basic structure of any item.

merge field   The placeholder text in the main document that marks the location at which data is inserted when the main document is merged with the data source. In a data source, merge fields contain the data that is merged into the main document.

merged document   Material (often a form letter) in which customized information is combined with repetitive or boilerplate text.

minimize   To contract a window to an icon. This can be reversed by double-clicking the icon, or by using the Restore command or the Maximize command from the Control menu. *See also* maximize; restore.

modem   A hardware device that converts digital computer information into audio signals that can be sent through telephone lines. These signals are received and converted back to digital signals by the receiving modem.

monitor   A visual peripheral device that contains a screen.

move   To transfer information from one location to another—within a file, to another file, or to a file in another program.

network   A group of computers and associated devices that are connected with communication links.

nonprinting characters   The characters such as tab characters, paragraph marks, spaces, and breaks that do not appear in a printed document. Nonprinting characters can be displayed to aid in formatting.

object   A table, chart, graphic, equation, or other form of information you create and edit. An object can be inserted, pasted, or copied into any file.

Office Assistant   A feature that you use to help you work in Microsoft Word. The Office Assistant offers tips, demonstrations, quick access to Help information, and wizards.

OLE   A Microsoft programming standard that allows a user or a program to communicate with other programs, usually for the purpose of exchanging information. Dragging, linking, and embedding are examples of OLE features. *See also* link.

online   Connected to a network or connected to your Internet service provider's server.

operator   A symbol used for simple math calculations. For example, the operators for addition and subtraction are the plus sign (+) and the minus sign (-).

Organizer   A feature used to copy styles, AutoText entries, and toolbars between documents and templates.

page break   A break that determines the end of a page and the beginning of the following page. Documents contain automatic page breaks (also referred to as soft page breaks) based on the margins. Manual page breaks (also referred to as hard page breaks) are inserted to break a page at a specific location.

palette   A box containing choices for color and other special effects you use when designing a form, a report, or other object. *See also* floating palette.

paragraph style   A named set of paragraph settings that controls the overall appearance of a document and can be applied to entire paragraphs. Formatting attributes include font, point size, tab stops, frames, borders, line spacing, and alignment.

password   A unique series of characters that you type to gain entry into a restricted network system, messaging system, or protected file or folder.

paste   To insert cut or copied text into a document from the Clipboard.

path   The location of a file within a computer file system. The path indicates the filename preceded by the disk drive, folder, and subfolders in which the file is stored. If the file is on another computer on a network, the path also includes the computer name.

point   A typographical unit of measurement, often used to indicate character height, line thickness, and the amount of space between lines of text. There are 72 points to an inch. Abbreviated "pt." *See also* font

portrait   The vertical orientation of a page. *See also* landscape.

program   Computer software, such as a word processor, spreadsheet, presentation designer, or relational database, designed to perform a specific type of work.

promote   An action that changes body text to a heading or a lower heading level to a higher heading level.

prompt   A set of characters or words on the screen that indicate the computer requires additional information to proceed.

pull quote   Text located in a text box, surrounded by the other text in the document. Often includes testimonials, announcements, or quotations related to the surrounding text. *See also* sidebar.

query   A database object that represents the group of records you want to view. A query is a request for a particular collection of data.

Recycle Bin   An object on the Desktop used to hold deleted objects. You can restore objects from the Recycle Bin until you empty the Recycle Bin.

reference   A cell address used in a formula.

reference mark   A number or character indicating that additional information is located in a footnote or endnote. By default, reference marks for footnotes are Arabic numerals and reference marks for endnotes are roman numerals.

report   A formatted collection of information that is organized to provide project data related to a specific area of concern.

restore   [1]To expand a minimized application by double-clicking it or to return a window to its previous size. [2]To recover information previously deleted.

rich text format (RTF)   A text formatting standard that makes it possible to transfer formatted documents between programs or transmit formatted documents over telecommunications links.

row   [1]A horizontal section of a worksheet. Rows are usually identified by numbers. [2]The data in all the cells in a single row of a list. A row is called a record when the list is used as a database.

rule   A line or border. *See also* border.

ruler   A graphical bar used for measurement that's displayed in a document window. You can use the ruler to indent paragraphs, set tab stops, adjust page margins, and change column widths in a table.

save   To transfer data from temporary memory to a floppy disk or a hard disk.

scroll   To move vertically or horizontally in a window so you can view objects that are not currently visible.

section   A part of a document separated from the rest of the document with a section break. You can use sections to change the page setup, headers and footers, and column formatting in different parts of the same document.

section break   A line that identifies the end of a section and the beginning of the following section. Section breaks are used to format different parts of a document, for example, columns or headers and footers.

selection bar   An invisible area at the left edge of the document window used to select text quickly with the pointer.

separator   A 2-inch horizontal line that identifies footnotes or endnotes and separates them from document text.

shortcut icon   An object that acts as a pointer to a document, folder, or program.

shortcut menu   A menu of commands that opens when you use the right mouse button to click. The commands listed in the menu vary depending on what element you click.

sidebar   Text located in a text box, positioned to the side of existing text. Often includes background stories, profiles, or other text related to the surrounding text. *See also* pull quote.

soft page break   A marker inserted automatically in a document to indicate where a full page ends and a new page begins. The locations of soft page breaks are automatically adjusted when material is added to or deleted from a document.

sort   To automatically reorder text or numbers in ascending or descending order, alphabetically, numerically, or by date.

source   [1]In a Web page, the text page that displays all HTML tags. In Internet Explorer, the source for the displayed Web page can be seen by choosing Source from the View menu. [2] The document or program in which the file was originally created. *See also* destination.

status bar   The bar at the bottom of the screen that displays information about the currently selected command, the active dialog box, the standard keys on the keyboard, or the current state of the program and the keyboard.

style   [1]A named collection of text formatting choices, such as font, size, leading, spacing, and alignment, that can be applied to change the appearance of text. Body Text, Headline, and Subhead are examples of styles that are often used. Styles are stored in a document or template. [2]A variation in the appearance of a character, for example, italic, bold, shadow, outlined, or normal.

style area   The vertical area on the left edge of a document in which the style name of each paragraph appears.

subdocument   A separate document that is part of a master document, usually assembled with other documents.

subfolder   A folder that is located within another folder. All folders are subfolders of the root folder.

subscript   A letter or digit written below the adjacent characters.

superscript   A letter or digit written above the adjacent characters.

table   One or more rows of cells commonly used to display numbers and other items for quick reference and analysis. Items in a table are organized into rows (records) and columns (fields).

taskbar   The bar located at the bottom of the default Windows 95 or Windows NT Desktop. The taskbar includes the Start button as well as buttons for any programs and documents that are open.

template   A special kind of document that provides basic tools and text for shaping a final document. Templates can contain text, styles, glossary items, macros, and menu and key assignments.

tile   A command that sizes open windows equally and positions them edge to edge.

title bar   The bar at the top of a window that displays the name of the document or program that appears in that window.

toolbar   A bar below the menu bar of Windows-based programs that displays a set of buttons used to carry out common menu commands. Toolbar buttons can change, depending on which window or view is currently selected. Toolbars can be moved or docked at any edge of a program window. *See also* floating toolbar.

ScreenTip A brief description that appears when the pointer is positioned over an object.

upload To transfer a file from your computer via a modem or a network.

virus A program that attaches itself to another program in computer memory or on a disk, and immediately spreads from one program to another or remains dormant until a specified event occurs. Viruses can damage data, cause computers to crash, and display offending or bothersome messages.

Web *See* World Wide Web.

Web address The path to an item such as an object, a document, or a Web page. An address can be a URL (address to an Internet site), a path and filename, or a path (address to a file on a local area network). *See also* path.

Web browser Software that interprets and displays documents formatted for the World Wide Web, such as HTML documents, graphics, or multimedia files.

Web page A document on the Web, formatted in HTML. Web pages usually contain links that you can use to jump from one page to another or from one location to another. *See also* link.

Web site A collection of Web pages at the same location.

wildcard Special character used in place of any other characters. An asterisk (*) takes the place of one or more characters; a question mark (?) takes the place of one character.

window A separate rectangular part of the screen identified by a border. A window represents an open object and displays information. Multiple windows can be open at the same time.

Windows Explorer A program that displays a hierarchical list of folders and a list of files in each folder.

wizard A tool that guides you through a complex task by asking you questions and then performing the task based on your responses.

WordArt A feature used to create unique and creative effects with text. Using WordArt, you can display text at angles, and in a variety of patterns and shapes.

word wrap An automatic function that continues a text entry to the next line.

World Wide Web The collection of available information on the Internet that is connected by links so that you can jump from one document to another. Also referred to as the Web, WWW, and W3.

Index

Index

Index

The
Step by Step
Practice Files Disk

The enclosed 3.5-inch disk contains timesaving, ready-to-use practice files that complement the lessons in this book. To use the practice files, you'll need Word 97 and either the Windows 95 operating system or version 3.51 Service Pack 5 or later of the Windows NT operating system.

Almost all of the *Step by Step* lessons use practice files from the disk. Before you begin the *Step by Step* lessons, read the "Installing and Using the Practice Files" section of the book. There you'll find a description of each practice file and easy instructions telling how to install the files on your computer's hard disk.

Please take a few moments to read the license agreement on the previous page before using the enclosed disk.